WOMEN DREAMING

Brenda Mallon is thirty-eight and married with three children. Apart from two years spent working in Iran, she has lived and worked in Manchester all her life. She often wonders why: she yearns for the sybaritic life but is bound to her work with people. She is a professional counsellor and runs courses in assertiveness, inter-personal skills and management training for a variety of public and private organizations. She has been re-searching and preparing this book for the past six years.

D0237976

Brenda Mallon

WOMEN DREAMING

Fontana/Collins

First published by Fontana Paperbacks 1987

Set in Linotron Plantin

Made and printed in Great Britain by
William Collins Sons & Co. Ltd, Glasgow

To Karl and Styx

Contents

Acknowledgements   9

1 In the Beginning Were Dreams   11
2 Fear and Flying   25
3 Meanings in the Menstrual Cycle   50
4 Pregnant With Meaning   63
5 Sex and Sexuality   80
6 Family and Friends   107
7 The World of Work   130
8 Why So Anxious?   146
9 Trials, Troubles and Tribulations   173
10 Violence Most Foul   200
11 Psychic Phenomena and Dreams   223
12 The Use of Dreams in Therapy   250
13 All This and So Much Left Unsaid   277

Questionnaire   301
Bibliography   302
Index   305
Index of authors   315

Acknowledgements

I am deeply indebted to the hundreds of women who took the time to fill in questionnaires and to the hundreds who talked to me about their dreams; without them this book could never have been written. I hope *Women Dreaming* will stand as a token of my grateful thanks for their honesty, trust and creativity. My clients, students and dream group friends gave good-humoured support as well as many insights into dreaming.

I couldn't have done the research nor written the book without the basic practical support of my family. So for keeping the kids out of my hair for enough time for me to write a little each day I thank Karl, Styx, and my mother and father, May and Joe Mallon. It was my mother in fact who unknowingly passed on the Celtic appreciation of dreams and to her go my first and final thanks for introducing me to the vast treasures that dreams reveal.

Mic Cheetham was the first person to see the embryonic book. Her enthusiasm and belief in me were especially important, as was Helen Fraser's, my editor at Fontana.

In order to ensure the anonymity of all those who have talked to me about their dreams, identities have been changed throughout the book.

Brenda Mallon
Manchester 1986

1

In the Beginning Were Dreams . . .

I feel waves of sadness as I recall a recurring dream that I had as a round-faced, blue-eyed, beplaited girl. I dreamt about a great ladder stretching to the sky and I watched as my father ascended it, disappearing into the clouds. I was terrified he would never return. In my dream I sobbed as I stood on the backdoor step gazing into the sky while neighbours too stood around muttering about the strange goings-on. The fire brigade were called to search for my father and they too climbed skyward, vanishing behind the same fluffy clouds. The sun continued to shine. People shook their heads. No one spoke to me. I was alone . . . There was a leap in the dream and three days had passed. Suddenly my father came back again. Everything was restored to normal. There were no questions, no explanations.

At the time I had no idea what the dream was about, but it upset me and I dreaded its return. Return it did, again and again. I cannot recall when it stopped but I feel sorry for the little girl who did not tell her dream to anyone else.

Looking at the dream now, I understand that I was experiencing a typical female childhood fear: a fear that wells up in the dark night but is hidden from daily discourse. Typically, it is connected with our families. My deepest fear, at seven, was that my dad would 'go to heaven' – every Catholic girl's euphemistic term for death. It had been literally translated in my dreams. In retrospect the fear was that he might leave me. I could not contemplate that he would go for any reason other than to be with God who lived beyond the clouds, though I realize now that I was aware of much more, at a deeper, unconscious level, than I recognized then.

My dream showed in dramatic form my awareness of relationships in the world of adults. What was hinted at made me afraid, but I was powerless to change anything; I could only stand by and look on as events took their course. In the end all would be resolved and my father would not disappear, as the dream showed, but the dreams of my childhood show the pain. Today, thirty years on, I embrace the bereft little girl who was so outwardly secure but inwardly afraid; I acknowledge her as part of myself and feel more complete for doing so.

I recall other dreams that were recounted to me. My mother used to tell me about hers, though I don't remember telling her any of mine. I think I found withdrawal safer, and guarded my privacy with all possible zeal. I knew intuitively that dreams could reveal the secrets of my soul so I hid them. However, she told me one which has stayed with me ever since. I was about fourteen at the time and getting ready to go to school. I'd had my customary breakfast of tea and toast and was about to leave when she came downstairs. This in itself was unusual so early in the morning, so anticipation was already in the air when she announced, 'Marion is going to have a baby.' I was usually the first to see the post, so I knew there hadn't been any recent letters from the States, where my sister Marion lived . . . but perhaps I could have missed it. She continued, 'I had a dream', speaking with such certainty, such confidence that now I warm to her self-assuredness. At the time, though, in my adolescent revolt, I showed only grudging interest in what she had to say.

'I had this dream. There was a lovely, wee nest with a baby bird in it. That's Marion. You mark my words, she's having a baby.' Mother was sure. And of course, shortly afterwards, we heard from Marion that she was indeed pregnant with her second child. My mother's interest in her own dreams and her belief in their importance had led her to a knowledge of what the different symbols in her dreams meant. Birds in nests meant babies and in this case it was my sister to whom she attached the message.

So it feels as if I had the notion that dreams were important from a very early age. Nothing was ever said outright; there was just 'the feeling'. I should explain that 'the feeling', for want of a better term, was the implicit understanding that we in our family had about different things. For instance, no one ever said that we shouldn't talk about sex, but none of us did; no one ever told us that women were strong, but we offspring had 'the feeling' that they were very strong; no one ever said that singing and drinking until four in the morning was great, but we knew that it was; and, similarly, we knew that dreams were revealing.

My early good fortune was suppressed by many years of academic preoccupation, during which I ignored my own feelings about dreams while learning of good educational practice, good psychological practice and accepted therapeutic practice. Only in the latter were dreams and their importance acknowledged. Now, with hindsight, I shudder when I think of the long hours I spent counselling adults and children, trying to get to grips with issues when dreams could have enabled us to reach the heart of the matter much more quickly and directly. It is because of this knowledge that I wanted to write this book. Dreams are far too important to be left to the professional analysts or the soothsaying charlatans – we must reclaim them and use them to help ourselves.

The first time I tried using dreams in counselling was a gamble on my part. It was in a very formal, conservative educational setting, where even women wearing trousers were considered revolutionary. I knew I risked the censure of my colleagues, who might scorn the idea of dreams being useful, so I was slightly apprehensive.

I was the visiting counsellor/troubleshooter/kid-catcher at a local school: if a child gave trouble, he came to me. I wanted to duck sometimes. There was a lot of 'Sort him out if you can. Counselling! Needs a bloody good thrashing if you ask me. Things haven't been the same since they stopped hanging!' Where did dreams stand in the face of such authoritarian views? Wherever it was, it was not in the 'accepted, accredited' quarter – but then neither was Sally's behaviour.

Sally was neither disruptive nor aggressive; she had never given much trouble. For many members of staff it appeared she'd simply been absent – nothing of special importance in a school where absenteeism among staff and pupils alike was high. But there was something wrong, as the head of the pastoral care indicated:

'Brenda, will you see this girl? I'm really worried about her. I've been trying to get through to her but it's impossible. I've asked her if she'll see you and I've told her that if she does it will be confidential. She has said she's willing to meet you.'

Sally: fifteen, overweight, dark straight hair in a full fringe covering her eyes while the rest conceals another two fifths of her face. She glances at me as I am introduced to her and mutters something indecipherable. She sits opposite me in an armchair. In my head I go through the facts I have.

Sally had attempted suicide two weeks previously. She overdosed on a cocktail of tablets gathered from around the house – a not uncommon happening in adolescents. Sally's attempt did not end in her death but in a rush to hospital, a stomach pump, and minimal sympathy amid the questioning. Why did she do it? No one knew and that was partly why I was there. Essentially, though, it was because she was very depressed at school. She was withdrawn, isolated, tearful and uncommunicative. Her school work had deteriorated markedly but that was of minor importance compared to her poor psychological health.

'Sally, I've talked to Mrs Higham, and she said you'd be willing to talk to me. I believe you have been having a difficult time.'

'Yes.'

'How have you been feeling lately?' She looks very pale and vulnerable.

'Oh, I'm all right.'

'Can I help in any way?' My concern must register in my voice.

'No one can help. I don't know how anyone can help.'

'Well, tell me about yourself at the moment. Are you eating all right? How are you sleeping?' Somehow, I want to break through this wall, a wall symbolized by her hair dropping like a curtain over her eyes. I cannot make eye contact with her. Sally is keeping me out.

Then she looks at me directly – just briefly, but we have made contact. 'I have awful nightmares. I'm scared to sleep. They are terrible.'

'Tell me the worst one.' One insecure part of me looks over my shoulder anxiously, thinking, They won't like this; while the other part says, Don't worry about them – stick with the girl and your own intuition. 'Tell me about your dreams, Sally, I think that will help.'

'All the time. All the time I dream about my dad. Every night it comes and it won't go away. It's so awful.' Tears begin to fall as I push her to tell me the dream. 'All it is . . . All it is . . . He's just sitting in this chair. A rocking chair. He's rocking backwards and forwards, backwards and forwards, saying, "Why? Why?" Nothing else, just "Why?".' The tears flow faster from her veiled eyes. 'But

14

there's something else: blood is pouring from his wrists. He's slit his wrists.'

By this time, Sally's pain is as visible as the tears which drop onto her clasped hands. She holds the plump fingers together as if that will allow her to control the world which is in turmoil around her and to dispel the haunting image of her father who accuses her as he dies.

It gradually emerged that some months earlier, Sally had been asked by her mother to intercept a letter expected from an aunt who lived in Buxton. Her mother had said that she was planning a surprise for her dad and, if there was a letter from Aunt Rose, Sally should hide it from her father and give it to her mother secretly. One morning the Buxton postmarked letter arrived and Sally hid it, revealing it only after her father left for work. On reading the letter, her mother told her that they were all leaving.

She helped her mother to get the younger children ready, packed some belongings and all together they set off on a train journey which ended the marriage. Sally's enquiries and protestations were futile in the face of her mother's determination. Weeks later they returned to Manchester after a stunned father had agreed to vacate the matrimonial home. He telephoned a few times to talk to Sally; he left messages asking to see her, unable to comprehend her complete rejection of him – he had always had a good relationship with his eldest daughter.

Tears flooded afresh down this child-woman's face as she explained that she could not see him because it was all her fault. His accusatory 'Why?' in the dream blamed her. If she had not intercepted the letter and given it to her mother, then the family might still be together. She would not have caused the split and she would still be able to see her father. As it was, she refused any contact with him, though her younger siblings saw him and relayed his messages to her. She neither saw him nor told anyone of her terrifying dreams. Eventually it was all too much to bear and the only way out was to take her own life. She saw herself as responsible for the 'death' of her father, so distressingly depicted in her dream.

By the end of that first session Sally was able to look straight at me. I could appreciate her need to hide the raw pain that was locked in her eyes. We talked, or rather she talked and I listened, and she began to voice the idea that maybe, just maybe, it was not all her fault. After four sessions, she had met her father and, though nervous, had got on well with him. There was still a hint of surprise when she said, 'You know, he said it wasn't my fault.' Her tentative steps at rebuilding their relationship were going well.

She continued to improve, though I did not see her for counselling again after that session. She said that she was feeling strong now and didn't think she needed to see me again. She had had her hair cut and was looking the world straight in the eye. She never had that dream of her father in the rocking chair after our first session, and when I saw her two years later, her dreams and her life were much sweeter.

My first attempt at using dreams in counselling had been very encouraging.

I have been struggling to understand why dreams exert such a pull over me. Why is it that I and so many other women respond at a gut level to our dreams? Why are they so important? Men do not talk about them in the same way; they are far more objective and distanced from them. But, for women, they colour our days, affect our moods and puzzle and intrigue us. Could it be that we are tuning in to a source of power that is less well developed in men and consequently largely dismissed by them? Maybe if we start to respond positively to what our dreams tell us, if we learn to use them and if we learn from each other, we can discover what that power is all about: that power to be honest with ourselves and to be strong enough to be complete. Dreams help us to become whole, and that is what women want.

It has taken me a long time to arrive at this point. For years I have studied my own dreams, recording them, thinking about them, trying to decipher them. I was always certain they were telling me something. I talked to other people about their dreams, but not in any great depth until after I had completed a course dissertation on 'The development of self-awareness through dreamwork'.

For six months I wrote down my dreams every morning, or even in the middle of the night, and during the day I would spend some time thinking about what they meant. That period was a watershed for me. Sitting here writing, I feel my heart race with excitement as I recall the thrill as I used to uncover meanings in my dreams. It was like being given some magnificent and unexpected present. Later in the book, I'll share some of those dreams with you, but suffice it to say that what I learnt from them led me to make major changes in my life, for which I am profoundly thankful. My dreams put me directly in touch with myself. There were no intermediaries to fudge issues. There were no interpreters to alter the meaning of the message. Dreams gave me a chance to deal with unfinished business, unsolved puzzles and painful memories. They showed me a way of understanding my life, so that I was free to live it.

It did not happen all at once. The key was that first dissertation, which so thrilled me that I became evangelical. I began asking everyone about their dreams; I told people they should write dreams down and use them – 'They will change your life', was the cry. I must have been a real bore! I was like someone who had fallen in love and kept talking about the beloved all the time. The captured listener attempts to change the subject, but three sentences later you're back to describing the colour of his eyes, or the shape of her mouth, or the amazing intellect.

After a period of listening to other people's dreams, patterns began to appear which I could not find discussed in any learned books. Deep down I was not surprised to learn that no one had ever done a study of women's dreams based on what women themselves believed, felt and thought. The bit between my teeth, I devised a questionnaire, advertized in magazines and newspapers, wrote articles in local newsletters, spoke on radio and appeared on local TV, and in each case the message was the same: Tell me about your dreams. This book is the result of that appeal. It is my repayment.

As well as the women who wrote and talked to me about their dreams, many other women have come to me for counselling and therapy, recounting amazingly clear dreams to help the therapeutic process along. This is not a new idea: therapists under different names – shamans or wise women or witch doctors – have always attached importance to dreams. Though Freud gave dreams a new emphasis in his *Interpretation of Dreams*, they have in fact been used in diagnosis and treatment of physical as well as psychological illnesses since 2000 BC.

There is, however, one difference now, and that is that more people question the omnipotent 'expert'. We are no longer prepared to follow blindly what is told to us, whether in the field of health or relationships. We now ask and seek understanding; and I believe this applies to dreams as much as to anything else. In the past, dreams have been told to an 'expert', who then supplied the meaning which was accepted by the dreamer. I am sure that the person who really and truly knows what the dream is saying is you, the dreamer. You have the key. I can help you turn it but at the end of the day it is your secret box and your key.

Gabriella found that she was willing to turn the key and was astonished by what she discovered.

Gabriella, a French journalist working in England, came to see me because she was having difficulties in her marriage. Alain, her husband, had had four affairs during their twenty-year marriage and Gabriella had been informed by a friend that he was conducting yet another. Now, remorseful and desperate for forgiveness, he wanted my client to accept him once again; while she, for the first time, was seriously questioning whether to leave him or insist he leave.

The previous infidelities had taken place in Paris, New York and Rome; but, whatever the venue, Alain, when discovered, had managed to persuade Gabriella that it was really all her fault. She was no good in bed, he said, and she was a bad wife. As her mother had done, he criticized her constantly. The only time he was nice to her, she realized on reflection, was when he was in the midst of an affair or just after he had been found out. Now she wanted to explore how she felt and to come to a decision for herself, rather than being swayed by his forceful personality. She had been a naïve and dependent virgin when they married and for a long time believed him when he said that only men had pleasure from lovemaking. Only men had orgasms, he told her, and she accepted this until a sensitive GP realized that she needed clarification, not medication. Gabriella wanted to find her way through this maze, but was very anxious about her ability to do so.

She told me one of her dreams:

'I am driving in a car and stop for petrol. I ask for directions to my home but people do not answer. Then a young lady asks me for a lift to her home. Even though it was in the opposite direction I agree to take her, and she gets into the car with another girl, who looks like my daughter. They are in the back and, as we approach some crossroads, the first girl tells me to turn left, which I do, but immediately afterwards I know this is the wrong way, so I reverse. Back at the crossroads I take another road.

'I arrive at a village square where a lorry is on fire and there are people inside. I can see a child inside. Flames leap from the vehicle but no one goes near because they all fear an explosion. They say the child cannot be saved.

'I go up to the lorry while everyone still looks on but does nothing. I reach the cab and try to rescue the child but realize I am looking at a puppet. Then I see a boy hiding deep within and help him out. I pass him to the people, who have come closer. I tell them to take care of him. Then I look back to the inferno and see a little black girl. She has shiny, curly hair. I reach inside to bring her out. Some people come to help us away from the danger. I feel very tranquil as I carry her to safety. The lorry is suddenly completely engulfed and I am unscathed.'

Gabriella did not link the dream to anything she had ever experienced in her life. She had never been in a fire, nor did she recognize the six-year-old girl whom she had saved. I asked her what she had been like at that age.

She told me that, at six, she had started school; it had been awful because 'My mother always told me what to do, what to like, what to think. She gave me no mental independence. I just followed other people around.' She was so afraid that her mother could see everything that she did not play with the other children – in case she was doing something wrong and her mother hit her. Gabriella had been told that she was stupid, really stupid, and had been prevented from expressing any form of opinion. Her mother forced her to over-eat so that by the age of ten she was grossly overweight and subject to her mother's abuse about her ugly, misshapen body. But even by the age of six her life had been a series of traumatic events initiated by a disturbed mother; the only exception was the time when Gabriella and her brother Claude were sent to stay with Tante Maria.

Their mother had gone off to stay with their father, who was working abroad on a mining contract. Their aunt delighted in the company of the two children. Gabriella played and swam and had such a glorious time that the memory of it fills her with tremendous joy – it was the only happy experience in her childhood. She went on, 'That summer, you know, I was black. I played in the sun all the time.' Gabriella looked stunned, changed. She said, 'That was me. That little black girl in the dream was me. I saved her. No one else would do anything, no one else was brave, but I knew I had to do it. I saved myself.'

Gabriella had come face to face with her own power. From the dream she understood that she had the strength to face the struggles in her life. Symbolically these were dramatically represented as fierce heat, possible explosion and imminent danger so fearful that no one else dare approach. In acting assertively and courageously she saved herself. For the first time in her life she understood her great resilience in surviving ordeals that would have broken a more vulnerable spirit. Having come to her own interpretation of the dream, Gabriella would never be the same again.

This book is about how dreams have set women free. It is about how we as girls and women are taught to deny our own power; how we are socialized into denying self-determination. It is also about transitional women, women like me who were taught neither how to encompass the liberating developments of the 1960s and 1970s without feeling guilty, nor how to cope with the present backlash which could again force us into devalued, powerless roles. It is about the trapped, fearful child within who, in her terror, refuses to let us become a whole woman. It is about my journey and the journeys of other women.

I found out how women felt about dreams by gathering responses to the specially devised questionnaire which you can find at the end of the book; by interviews, when working with women in dream workshops; and by using dreams in therapy. You will notice in the book differences in the amount of detail given, according to whether or not I have seen the dreamer face to face, but whatever the method the material is very telling.

Women have talked about childhood dreams, pregnancy, sexuality, hopes and fears, loves and hates, beginnings and endings and spirituality. These women speak for me and I believe they will speak for you, too. On the journey you may come across terms that you have never met before; the following brief glossary is meant as a simple guide – read it now or come back to it later when it is more relevant to you.

Computer theory of dreams

Introduced by Christopher Evans, who died in 1979, this approach uses the analogy of the computer to explain what happens when we dream. When we are 'off line' during sleep – that is, when we are ticking over with only our major bodily functions running – the day's information is classified and stored. Irrelevant, outdated information is 'updated'. If dreaming is consistently disturbed, such sorting cannot take place and we become confused, irrational and prone to bizarre behaviour – the system breaks down. We can do without our sleep but not without our dreams. If we have endured a traumatic event, then rapid eye movement (REM) sleep (q.v., page 24) will focus on finding some way of clarifying it in order to file it.

The computer theory sees dreams as the interface between the outside world and the unexplored regions of the mind. It goes a long way towards explaining the differences in the types of dreams we have, and is not merely a mechanistic view of dreams and dreaming.

Dream drawing

This simple process involves recalling a dream, then drawing a picture of it. You may prefer to depict the most intense part of the dream or to draw each significant part in comic-strip form. Whatever the format, include as much detail as possible. Once the image is complete, you can use various methods described later in the book to explore its meaning.

Dream diary

Keep a notebook or a tape recorder by your bed so that when you wake from a dream you are able to record it. Most of you will find writing more convenient and you should prepare for the dream by writing down the date before sleeping and then report the dream in as much detail as you can as soon as you wake. Don't worry about neatness, don't censor the material, and don't think you'll remember it later because it is such a brilliant dream – lots of dreams get lost that way! Get into the habit of keeping a dream diary and you'll find your rate of dreaming and recall will increase dramatically. Later, fill in any further details and see what you associate with the dream. Does it relate to anything happening in your waking life? How do you feel about it? Were you active or passive in the dream? Who were important figures? Who do the dream characters remind you of? Why should they appear now? What would you like to change? How does it fit in with other dreams, does it show development and progress? What is the message of the dream?

When you have been recording your dreams for some time you will find certain patterns occurring and will be able to build up your own unique dictionary of dream symbols. You will also learn which dreams warrant special attention, for instance warning dreams or diagnostic dreams. This will enable you to react appropriately to your own dream messages.

Freud, Sigmund

Known as the father of psychoanalysis, Freud regarded *The Interpretation of Dreams* as his most important contribution to the understanding of human behaviour, and indeed every therapeutic approach to dreams devised since owes him a debt. He saw dreams as the products of our unconscious minds and he believed that behind the 'manifest' or obvious dream story there lay a hidden or 'latent' message. The message had to be deciphered by psychoanalytic methods such as 'free association' and interpretation. Traditional Freudian thinking is strongly male-oriented, which means that it may lead women's dreams to be interpreted in a distorted way.

Gestalt therapy

The Gestalt school of therapy was founded by Fritz Perls, who aimed to bring dreams to life by asking the dreamer to recount his or her dream in the present tense as if it were happening at that moment and then to identify with and speak as each component of the dream. For example, if you have a dream in which a tree figures, you speak as the tree: 'I am a tall tree. I'm gnarled and old and I've seen a lot of changes. My roots go deep but people don't see that. They take me for granted . . .' By acting out each part of the dream imagery, repressed areas of your personality can be rediscovered and faced, which in turn leads to greater self-awareness.

The main purpose of dreams, Perls thought, was to resolve unfinished situations, thus releasing energy for more positive activities. Gestalt techniques are extremely powerful and rely on personal re-experiencing of the dream and its impact rather than on interpretation by an 'expert'.

Incubation of dreams

This is a process that was widely used by the ancient Greeks and others to encourage healing, problem-solving dreams. Special temples provided a place where priests and priestesses would assist the dreamer to prepare for sleep by observing certain rituals and would be there to interpret the dream on waking. The dreamer hoped to receive a communication from the relevant god/goddess, of whom a specific question would be asked. You can usually 'incubate' your own dreams, without help, if you follow some of the methods described in this book.

Jung, Carl Gustav

Jung developed and modified Freud's work on dreams, enriching in particular our understanding of symbolism. He saw dreams as carriers of essential messages from the instinctive to the rational parts of the human mind and emphasized the importance of *dream series*. Each part of a dream is seen as representing an aspect of the dreamer's unconscious qualities. Jung is responsible for introducing such terms as *archetypes*, *animus* and *anima*, *shadow* and *the collective unconscious*.

Lucid dreaming

This is when the dreamer knows that he or she is dreaming while the dream is in progress. The most usual form of this is when you have a frightening dream and you tell yourself, 'I must wake up,' or, 'It's only a dream so I can change it.' Highly developed lucid dreamers can decide in the dream what they want to do and manipulate the dream to that end. The Senoi tribe educate their children in lucid dreaming.

Psychic dreams

Telepathy, astral projection, prophetic dreams and warning dreams are examples of psychic activity during sleep. Communication with those already dead, on 'the other side', come into this category.

Rapid eye movement (REM) sleep

This is also known as 'dream sleep' or 'paradoxical sleep'. In the 1950s it was discovered that rapid eye movement is the outward indication of dreaming. There is a recurring 90-minute pattern of non-REM sleep and REM sleep, and on average we spend two and a half hours dreaming each night, though this varies with age: babies spend most of their time in dream sleep, processing new information, whereas elderly people spend very little time in REM sleep.

Right brain

The right hemisphere of the brain specializes in creativity, the affective or feeling aspects of our personality, imaginative thinking, fantasy and dreaming. Recent research into right-brain activity shows how important it is to develop this side as much as the logical, analytical left brain, which is emphasized in traditional educational systems. By working on your dreams you increase right brain creativity.

2

Fear and Flying: Dreams Recalled From Childhood

I had never spent so much time on my knees; the rosary was followed by the incantations: 'May St Theresa bless our souls; may St Jude, the patron saint of lost causes, look down and bless us; may . . .' On and on the litany went. I hadn't known that there were so many saints. This was one of the changes I would have to get used to now I had passed the eleven-plus.

My primary school, St Aloysius – small and grimy and filled with small, frequently grimy children, sons and daughters of Irish immigrants like myself with names such as Bernadette O'Keefe, Liam Shaunessy and Deirdre Kelly – had given way to the restrictive disciplined order of St Joseph's. No gleeful cavortings in the corridors here, but silent lines of green-garbed girls, wearing thick, green, scratchy knickers – our uniforms as strict and constraining as the nuns who taught us.

I felt as if I was straitjacketed: afraid of doing wrong in this strange environment where everyone else knew the rules, or seemed to; where everyone else spoke with posh accents, or at any rate didn't talk like me; where obedience was the most prized virtue. I felt the outsider: there were no friends from the old primary school to share the transition. For the few others who had passed the exam, the question had immediately arisen: 'Are they going to let you go?' Uniforms for the grammar school cost a lot of money, especially since they had to be bought from Henry Barrie's, the best and most expensive place in Manchester; if you wore C & A's, you stood out like a pauper at a wedding feast. There were two other major considerations: would such an education be wasted on a girl, who was, after all, only going to get married; and would going to St Joseph's or St Bede's bring about a split in the family? A frequent lament was: 'You'll only get above yourself if you go there. They aren't like us.'

My parents were not interested in such concerns, or at least did not mention them at that stage. They were pleased that I had passed but were as unaware as I of the implications of an academic education. No one in our family had gone that way before.

Nobody realized how difficult it was for me to fit in until about six or seven months into that first year at St Joe's. Night after night I walked in my sleep, going into my parents' room, oblivious to my mother's entreaties to tell her what was wrong. When I asked her about this recently, she said, 'It was the school that got you down. It was all the religion. You were used to going to mass but there was so much more there. I know myself the nuns can be hard. We took you into our bed when you were so upset and lost in your sleepwalking, but you were still unhappy.'

The sleepwalking began at about the time I was having recurring dreams about going into a large factory which housed machines in the shape of giant cotton reels. Once I entered, they grew larger and larger, as I, totally alone, grew smaller and smaller. There was never any resolution. I was equally powerless in another dream in which I again entered a room, only to find that a table with a chair behind it receded further and further from me. The more I tried to move towards it the more the room elongated and enlarged as I became tinier, more inconspicuous and terrified. In each of these dreams I was totally unable to affect my surroundings.

Those dreams reflected my feelings about school: alone and vulnerable, I was overwhelmed by an impersonal world that was blind to my attempts to make contact. At the time, however, I didn't know that; I was just frightened of the dreams and wished they would stop.

Sister Agnes proved to be the last straw. After a bout of tonsilitis, I returned to school and domestic science – that is, the class in which you spent three quarters of an hour on your knees praying for the salvation of your blackened soul and three quarters of an hour cooking. When, knees numbed, the time came to write down a recipe, I could not find my exercise book. Positive that I had handed it in at the end of the last lesson before I was away ill, I told Sister Agnes, who would have none of it. She called me every bad name that it is possible for a bride of Christ to use, which is quite a few, and insisted I had left it at home or thrown it away or destroyed it. However, not one to be unreasonable, she added in melting murmurs that, if I was so sure I had left it in the classroom, I could come to the room to look for it every morning break, lunchtime and afternoon break until I found it.

After two weeks, the exercise book was still missing. I was pointed out as the 'bad girl' who argued with her betters, who dared to disagree with those in authority. I was so daunted by sister Agnes's acid sarcasm and pure vengeance that I lived in dread of her thereafter. Never again while I was at that school did I do or say anything that would distinguish me from an abject worm, though my unconscious fought to air my pain in dreams.

My puzzled parents, seeing me so troubled in sleep and growing quieter day by day, decided that such unhappiness was not to be tolerated. My mother made an appointment to see the headmaster of the nearest high school, who agreed to admit me 'even though [I was] a Catholic' at the beginning of the second year, just a couple of months away. My mother told him, as she told the nuns, that the move was because she wanted me nearer home – a hundred yards down the road as opposed to two miles on the bus.

It made no difference when, during my last week at St Joe's, the missing exercise book turned up. We were spending our domestic science lesson scrubbing everything that offered itself up for scrubbing, while contemplating how we could scrub away the sins of the soul by prayer and good deeds, when Clare Donellan unearthed the missing book from behind a cupboard. Sister Agnes did not falter for an instant. She fixed me with her frozen eyes and smiled slightly as she said, 'Well, Brenda, I wonder how it got there? You didn't put it there, did you?' It is strange how you can feel so wrong when you know you are right. The moment of my vindication became an occasion for another of her viperish attacks.

In a roundabout way my dreams led to my being transferred to another school, but I now know that the powerlessness I experienced has been shared by many other women. It is particularly the theme of separation from security which recurs in the poignant dreams recalled from childhood. While mine were concerned with separation from safe places, others' are about separation from family.

Family

Jan's vivid dreams began at the age of four and recurred until she was seven. In them she was sitting on the floor of an empty room while all her family left. In tears she would watch as one by one they departed. Still affected by the mood of those dreams as an adult, she found them disturbing to recall. Instead of remembering security at such an early age she experienced the sickening fear that she would be left behind, unable to reach those whom she loved.

This imagery of separation, and fear of what was happening in the family, is a major theme of dreams women have in childhood. In Sandra's dream the trigger of a daytime event, the reading of a story, set off feelings and insights about her own life:

'I remember that my first childhood dream was a nightmare. It followed my father's reading the first chapter of *Alice in Wonderland* at bedtime one night when I was five years old. Though enthralled by it, I dreamt that I was trapped in a deep, black, underground cavern. Its walls were closing round me as I screamed for release. And beyond it there was a small passageway where my mother and grandmother, both beautifully "dressed up", were standing impersonally staring at me in my distress.

'The PS to this nightmare – from which I awoke screaming and was rescued by my father coming in and comforting me – is that I had for a long time had a "thing" about deep, black holes. I believed there was a black hole somewhere in the world down which one could fatally fall.'

Sandra used to question her mother if they saw a manhole cover raised, but the replies never really satisfied her young mind. She was utterly convinced that there was a rapacious black hole somewhere in the world. In a sense there was, but it was not a physical one that could be avoided. For Sandra it appeared some years later:

'Somehow I see this dream as prophetic, for seven years later, after a two-year decline into alcoholism and despair and confusion in our family life, my mother committed suicide. My grandmother was knocked much further than sideways by everything and my father changed utterly. I did find myself at the bottom of a, if not the, black hole: alone and in absolute despair. My mother was dead; my grandmother, because of her own grief and physical distance, was unable to do more than look on; and, this time, my father did not come to "rescue" me.'

Sandra remembered that, at the time she had the dream, she and her sister were surrounded by love and were very happy. There was no apparent reason for the dream other than the bedtime story, but as with so many dreams it did touch an underlying fear. Like everyone else, Sandra was afraid of some unknown, dark place which symbolized the 'terror', that which we cannot define but which we know is there. Jung called it 'the shadow'.

In a comparative example concerning separation, Linda had to make superhuman efforts in her attempts to 'reach' her family; whatever had happened in her young life left her feeling that they were trapped in a living death:

'I am buried in a cemetery, as all my family are, and I try to crawl out of my grave to reach them. I never do, as I wake up screaming.'

Some event had rendered Linda so low that she felt she was being buried alive, alone in her pitiable separation. The dreams she reports having as an adult continue this theme of isolated anxiety begun in childhood.

The bond we make with our family, in particular with our parents, is, for better or worse, probably the most intense and most significant that we ever make. Small wonder that our dreams show us trying to keep contact with those who should love and protect us. All too often the power that parents have over children is abused – as witnessed by agonizing press reports of children blinded, mutilated or murdered. These are the worst cases, of deliberately inflicted cruelty, but the dreams of Sandra and Linda reveal how profoundly vulnerable even 'ordinary' children may feel in relation to their parents.

Children are 'done to'. They are physically smaller and weaker than the adults on whom they rely; they are emotionally and financially dependent, and subject to the directions of those in authority over them. The success of their progress and comfort depends on their parents. Sometimes the child is caught between warring factions, as was Lisa. She often dreamt of 'a huge dark space with black and white chequered tiles on the floor. Three figures, robed and faceless, stood on top of the stairs and threw me from one to the other, across the dark space between.'

Lisa had no control over her life as she was tossed around by these anonymous figures who at any moment might fling her to her death. The setting is a key feature, as is common in dreams. Could the black and white chequered tiles be a games board, the sort we use in draughts or chess? Is Lisa merely a pawn in someone else's game? No one asks what she wants or what she feels; she is totally controlled by others. These figures probably represent members of her family. Often figures in dreams are not clearly defined because we could not cope with the bald truth, so they are 'mysterious', hooded or shadowy; real identity is only hinted at. The stronger we are emotionally, the more directly we are able to communicate.

Tina found growing up more difficult than most other children. Her parents had for years been keeping up the pretence of 'a good marriage'. Their troubles, though hidden from the outside world, did not remain hidden from their daughter. She, in turn, tried to conceal her worries from them, but they found an outlet in her dreams, which always ended in one of two ways:

'I walked into the sea and quite painlessly drowned. My family or myself were quite powerless to do anything about it. This happened about 90 per cent of the time. The other times I went on a rocket to the stars and then woke up.'

Tina dealt with her difficulties by escaping through death or through fantasy trips into space. Like Alice, a thirteen-year-old whom I saw after a self-poisoning episode, she felt that, if she diverted attention from her parents' bad marriage, they would stay together. She also felt guilty and thought it was her fault that they did not get along any more. In her dreams the fact that she felt powerless 90 per cent of the time shows through. Working on the dream, even now, would enable Tina to see more clearly her part in this family drama, so she could disclaim responsibility for other people's failed relationships.

Mothers and daughters

From all that has been written in the last few years about the mother-daughter relationship, we can no longer be in doubt about the central importance of that first bond which can suffocate us as it succours us, which enraptures and terrifies us at the same time. I would refer you in particular to such excellent books as Nancy Friday's *My Mother, Myself* and Eichenbaum and Orbach's *Inside Out, Outside In*.

I remember my sister Rona sending me a card after my daughter Crystal was born in which she said that I would find raising a girl a very different experience from raising a boy. I am beginning to appreciate what she means. With a male the physical differences are there right from the start, but with a daughter . . . I wonder if she will go through the same things as I. And I find myself being especially protective yet wanting her to be strong, because my life has taught me that as a woman I must be strong, otherwise assumptions will be made about me based on what I am supposed to be rather than on what I actually am. It's more difficult for me to be the mother of my daughter than to be a mother to my sons. Sometimes I wonder if I can protect Crystal yet allow her to grow and blossom at the same time. She is too young to talk about these things and her dreams give me no clues, but I hope with all my heart that she never has a dream like this one of Aileen:

'I once dreamt that my mother was screaming for me and coming upstairs with a leather belt to beat me. I could hear her screaming and her footsteps on the stairs getting closer and closer. I was terrified.'

The dread is plain. The dream shows a damaged mother-daughter relationship, characterized by intimidation and physical abuse. When Aileen spoke of her dream, she still grieved for a lost mother, a mother she never really had. At the time she had the dream she was afraid even to mention it to her mother, in case she got hit anyway. Her dreams, like her feelings, were not acceptable to a woman warped by her own experience of life. The situation was very different for Naomi, who dreamt frequently that an evil man captured her:

'My mother cried helplessly. He would cover my torso with a large cushion and cut off my arms and legs, one by one, with an axe. I would feel nothing, just sadness that I was making my mother cry so much. I would awake as the axe fell on my neck.'

Her mother is powerless to stop this attack. Naomi is unprotected; she has become numb; she cannot feel her own pain but she can feel guilt. She feels guilty about something which is beyond her control.

She feels responsible for her mother and suppresses her own feelings. Silently she accepts her position. Naomi, however, did know that her mother cared for her; the tears tell us that. Such signs are more encouraging than indifference in dreams. Naomi was going through a growing period, painful though it was, in which she learnt that her mother could not protect her from the world.

Ruth's childhood dreams revealed acknowledgement of reversed responsibility. She used to dream that her mother was bathing her, when, suddenly, 'she began to wail and moan. The noise increased and I repeatedly shook her to try to stop her moaning.' Try as she might, Ruth could not ease the terrible pain and grief her mother expressed. She ended up being responsible for her mother; she became the care-taker.

Girls such as Naomi and Ruth are given too much emotional responsibility for others at too early an age. In the absence of fundamental change, the same inhibiting patterns will continue to keep women prisoners. By constantly making too onerous demands of such girls, we damage personal autonomy. Without experiencing freedom and self-direction in childhood, we cannot be free, self-directed adults. The wheel turns full circle and we teach our daughters to be the same. The teaching need not be conscious: they learn from what they see.

Fathers and daughters

In many families the father is still held to be the most powerful member of the unit. He is the one who lays down the values and standards, particularly in such patriarchal groups as Moslems and Mormons. Both religions regard the male as being head of the family and thus in control of their daughters' lives; and, interestingly, both support male polygamy. Happily, in most other Western religious and secular practices women are no longer seen as chattels, be they daughters or wives, but the Victorian assumption that men can and should tell women what to do persists. The problem is that power corrupts and absolute power corrupts absolutely, as child victims of incest know. Gail's dream reflects a deeper acknowledgement of certain characteristics of her father which she could not face up to as a child:

'When I was little I would seem to wake up in my bedroom, see my father enter very benevolently and approach my bedside. I was feeling secure and eager to display affection. But as his face approached mine, it would distort horribly and become evil and leering.'

As a child she recognized the conflict within and the limitations of her father, and part of her feared that Jekyll and Hyde nature. This is not unusual.

A friend of mine, Nina, has been fostering a seven-year-old girl who was taken into the care of the local authority when it was discovered that she had been sexually abused by her father. Helen's nights are filled with horrifying dreams. Nina, warm and strong, is giving the waiflike child the space to come to terms with her hurt. Anyone who has worked with emotionally damaged children knows that hurt and suffering are shown in many other ways besides agonizing dreams; bedwetting is typical. Every night Helen wets the bed but Nina no longer lifts her in the small hours to forestall the soaking sheets. Helen's screams of 'No. No. Please don't touch me. I'll tell. I'll tell. *Don't* . . .' were so traumatic for child and woman that wet sheets seem a small price.

Too often no one talks to children about their dreams, yet the majority recalled from childhood are about fear and in particular fear about the family. What happened to the rest of us to make us so terrified that our parents would leave us, or our mothers would beat us? We know that far, far more children are subject to physical and emotional abuse at the hands of their immediate family than are ever reported in the press. If we talked about dreams the tensions could at least be expressed.

Michele Elliott, who has written a much-needed practical guide to talking with children about sexual assault, noted the increasing concern about sexual abuse of children.[1] It is estimated that one in ten adults were sexually abused as children, though many would put this figure much higher. The majority (75 per cent) of this abuse is committed by someone the child knows: a neighbour, friend, even a father, brother, or uncle. Ninety per cent of reported offenders are men, usually married, and they come from every class and social group.

Children are easily coerced by adult authority; their fear of being punished or being in some way blamed leaves us with the disturbing statistics from America that child molesters average seventy-three victims before they are caught. Michele Elliott's book tells us how we can make children more powerful. This applies especially to girls, since they are assaulted far more frequently than boys. By explaining that their bodies are their own and that no one should touch them in a way that makes them confused or uncomfortable, adults can give children power. If that happens, perhaps some of the spectres which prowl in dreams will disappear.

Girls learn to feel guilty early in life and it often shows up in dreams. Fran had a dream which she related at an assertiveness workshop. Shy and timid, she wanted to become more independent from her father without upsetting him:

'One vivid dream [in childhood] was of my dad leaving me to find another daughter because he thought I wasn't suitable, and replacing himself with a substitute father.'

Fran obviously did not feel that her father was heartless, since he managed to find a replacement to take care of her, but she felt guilty because she was not a good enough daughter. In her dream she was 'not suitable', somehow she did not come up to scratch.

Her mother had died when she was a baby, leaving her in the care of her grieving father. He struggled to work and rear her, aided by neighbours and his own mother. Fran, now twenty-one, is subject to embarrassing blushing fits and is still living at home with her over-protective dad. She has always felt that it was, and is, her responsibility to make her father contented. She will not do anything that he might disapprove of, although she sometimes feels he is suffocating her. Maybe it is nothing to do with him; the guilt feeling may come from others who say, 'Isn't your dad good, sacrificing his life for you? Not many men would do that, you know.' Plenty of women do so of course, but then that's their real purpose in life, isn't it?

Her early childhood dream made the point that Fran should be a good daughter or she would be dropped because of unsuitability. Now that she is an adult, she feels she will never be suitable for any man, though she is a good girl in the traditional sense of going to church, being a virgin, being quiet and helpful and in no way drawing attention to herself. The guilty girl has grown into the traditional powerless woman. And she still harbours the belief first learnt in childhood that sex is 'bad'. She blushes furiously when there is any mention of sex, but now at last she is learning to view herself as a woman who has her own life to lead, rather than a good girl whose first task is to be approved of by others.

Sex can be confusing when you are growing up. I know it was for me. My mother never told me the facts of life: the task was given to my newly married sisters, or else they took it on themselves. I can remember going to see Rona at her rented flat above a sort of a farmhouse in Runcorn. The setting seemed important because it was an unusual one for me; I thought I was in the heart of the country. Marion had come from Warrington for the afternoon and I was to stay for a few days. It was a real treat and I was taken completely unawares when Rona asked me if I knew what periods were. Oh my God! Panic. I knew a bit from the kids at school but equally I knew that I shouldn't know anything. It was dirty. What should I do?

Heart thumping, avoiding their gaze, I moved to the window and looked down onto a dog sniffing in the yard below. 'Of course I know, the girls at school told me.' Surprisingly, no one fainted. Persuaded to share what knowledge I had, I continued, 'What happens is that, when you're "on", you wee blood instead of the other, that's all.' Whew! That took some doing. I still recollect that feeling of intensity as I locked my eyes onto the scene in the yard below, as if my whole life depended on it. I can't recall what happened next; I presume they corrected my uninformed ideas.

In my mind anything to do with 'that' – menstruation, sex, men – was taboo. And I believed that you could get pregnant by kissing! Being a virgin, whatever it was, meant being pure and holy, like Our Lady, so glorious in her ice-blue robes. A model for all young girls to follow, since she was never touched by evil or impurity. For other girls, such as Heather, a different knowledge surfaced in their dreams:

'As a teenager I dreamt of my father driving a stake through my heart as I lay in a coffin as a vampire.'

Heather was puzzled by her own developing sexuality. She might have been a horror-movie addict but, even so, casting herself in the role of vampire is significant. Typically, vampire stories involve the tasting of delicious virgin's blood: the blood from the symbolic breaking of the hymen? The vampire can only be killed when a stake is driven through the heart. But what is Heather doing as a vampire?

And what is her father up to, killing his own daughter? Could the dream be informing her of lustful cravings stirring below the surface, desires which so far have been repressed? Does she need her father to save her from herself? Or would her father be so shocked at his 'vamp' daughter that he would kill her rather than have her sexuality acknowledged? Is her father/rescuer also her destroyer? Only Heather has the answer.

Not all dreams featuring fathers are negative, although the majority I collected were. Some, like Dot's, show the protective dad who is as dependent on the mother as the daughter is:

'I had a recurring dream that my mum would not come back from work one day. My dad used to say she had gone on a trip and would be back. In the dream I saw myself grow up. When I was grown up I found out that mum had left my dad and us. All of a sudden there would be a knock on the door. I would open it and there would be my mum, not changed one bit from when she left. Without talking, I would suddenly wake up.'

Such dreams again reveal childhood insecurities. They tell us that the child needs to be constantly reassured that she is loved and cared for. To grow strong and caring we need a secure base, otherwise we can so easily be trapped by a fear of losing others, or of being rejected, that it contaminates all our adult relationships.

Siblings

Being the youngest of five, I never had responsibility for looking after younger siblings, though my brother Brian, who was five years my senior, occasionally had to take care of me. One task he had when I was at St Aloysius' primary school was to escort me as far as the traffic lights and see me safely across the road. He dealt with this unacceptable intrusion into his life with the best grace he could muster. He walked on with his friends while I trailed an acceptable five or six yards behind. I was allowed to catch up at the traffic lights to ensure he fulfilled his fraternal duties and, to give him some credit, I never did get run over.

Margaret's sister did not get run over either in 'real life', but she did in Margaret's dream:

'There was a broken person, my younger sister, who had been

knocked down by a number 10 bus and was broken into thousands of pieces. A friend told me to get some sellotape and we stuck her back together. She had no head, though. I was scared to death my mother would come and tell me off. Then the dream would repeat itself.'

While the trigger for this recurrent dream was having to care for her sister – an adult responsibility on a child's shoulders – the person who was under threat or destroyed in this dream was the dreamer herself. In her dream she was faced with an impossible task; what is shattered cannot be made whole, and all the time she was terrified of her mother's reaction. It was as if Margaret could not get her own head together again. She could not pick up the pieces and, renewed, go forward. Instead, she was repeatedly faced with an insoluble problem. Though she had help, in the form of her friend, the two girls were not up to coping with the severity of the situation. They did not have the emotional maturity to sort it out, but then why should they have had?

Now an adult, pale and childlike, Margaret has her own baby to take care of. As a young single parent she finds the isolation difficult. Once again her own needs are pushed into the background as she repeats the pattern of caring for others, taught so well to girls growing up.

Just as my brother hated to be associated with me when he was an adolescent, so I disliked him. One image engraved in my mind is of me sitting on the step of the outside toilet, sweeping brush grasped in clenched hand, ready to inflict mortal wounds on the big brother I had chased inside. I can't remember the cause of the outrage but I do recall that my anger was in full flood that day. Only the arrival of my mother saved him. Somehow she calmed me, though I suppose the length of time spent on the step also had a cooling effect. Such are the furies of childhood and mine, rare as they were, had waking expression. In that sense I was fortunate; I don't recall feeling aggression towards my brothers and sisters in my dreams. For many women such emotional honesty is not allowed.

Sibling rivalry happens between all brothers and sisters, though the first child often has the most difficulty. From being the centre of attention, cosy in her position in the family, the first child is ousted with the arrival of a new baby. Suddenly here is someone else, not here for an hour or two, or even a few days, but here to stay. And the child has no say in the matter. Imagine if your loving partner turned up one day with another woman and said, 'You are such a fantastic woman and I love you so much that I decided to get another one just like you! Here she is and she is going to stay with us.' No wonder there is rivalry. And with rivalry there is fear that we will be the loser. Such threat causes hostility.

At the age of six, Jill felt murderous hostility towards her new sister and she vividly recalls the dream that vented those feelings:

'My sister was about eighteen months old. She was sitting in a high chair . . . I go into the garage and get a can of paraffin, return and pour it over her. She does not seem alarmed so I strike a match and set a light to her and she goes up in flames. I am horror stricken and remorseful and wake up screaming, recognizing the wickedness of the act.'

Consumed by her own jealousy, Jill wanted to destroy her sister, but at the same time she was afraid of the passionate feelings that engulfed and threatened to ruin her. Sibling rivalry is miserable for everyone involved.

The importance of grandmother

Both my grandmothers died long before I was born. Mary Ann Short, my maternal grandmother, died at the age of fifty-two, having been a widow for twenty-odd years. My paternal grandmother, Elizabeth Mallon, died in her twenties; while out gathering black-berries, she slipped and haemorrhaged, losing the baby she was carrying and leaving behind three sons all under five.

I regret that I never had the special relationship, the love and sharing, spoken of by so many women in my survey. Warm re-assurance shows in Becky's recurring dream, as does the pain of her loss following her grandmother's death:

'I used to bring her to me. She would sit and stroke my hair and say comforting things. Much later I really believed she had haunted me; now I don't know. I wasn't scared.'

Becky's wish-fulfilment dreams allowed her grandmother to return and comfort her. The same happened to Rose, a clerical officer in the civil service; six years after the death she still has the same dream:

'I dream about my grandma, who is dead. I know in the dream that she is dead but I am so happy because I am able to see her again. It is as though she has come back to visit me. When I dream of her I usually wake up sobbing, with tears streaming down my face. I was very close to her.'

The dream also tells us that Rose has not yet fully distanced herself from the love that was such a boon. In her present loneliness her dreams return her to past safety but only to wake up to an unresolved problem: she has not 'let go' of her grandmother. Her dream tells her that she needs to complete the unfinished business of grieving. She needs to come to terms with the death so that it becomes a memory of past sadness instead of present emotional pain.

Most people learn of human mortality for the first time when a grandparent dies. Significantly, those women who recall dreams of grandparents find that, in them, the grandparent, grandmother especially, comes to say goodbye, or is depicted as leaving. Such dreams usually help us to come to terms with the loss. Shortly after her grandmother's death, Mary had vivid dreams:

'When I was about nine, I was in a large whitewashed stone house on a moor and my grandmother was walking down the garden path. The scene was uttely desolate, with hills stretching way into the distance, and there was nothing except this one empty house.'

Typically, houses represent women, a view we shall discuss in more detail later, and here the house is as empty as the granddaughter feels. At this point so shortly after her bereavement, her dream takes her through the process of grief, helping her to accept separation. The grandmother goes off along her path leaving the house, Mary, empty and alone.

Other childhood dreams

Cover yourself up, someone might see

We must have had trouble with our vests as children since we spent an awful lot of time pulling them down in order to make ourselves 'decent'. I remember dreams in which I was out in the street, mortified to discover that I was wearing only a vest. I was so ashamed and embarrassed. For me the dream was about trying to uphold ideas about female modesty which were taught at home and at school. Nice girls kept themselves covered, did not flaunt their bodies and were, in every way possible, demure and ladylike. Our neighbourhood might have been rough but that was no reason not to behave like a lady!

'My 'vest' dreams came when I was beginning to develop breasts and becoming aware that my body was changing. Like Nancy's, they were typically set in public places:

'I had a series of dreams where I went to school wearing only a vest. I would only discover that I was half naked when other children or teachers approached me. I always tried to hide myself but never could.'

Such anxiety points to the vulnerability we felt as girls. In my survey not one person recalled a dream from childhood in which she was deliberately showing off her body in a healthy, proud way. Instead, we apologetically cower and pull down our vests to conceal whatever it is that might give offence.

Karen's 'vest dream' was the only one of its kind that I came across while researching this book. At the age of five she dreamt that she was walking around the house in only a vest, but there was an unusual development: 'I looked down and found I had a prick.' She was not worried about wearing no more than a vest, only surprised to find she had a penis. Was this an early awareness of masculine aspects of her personality? It could be that the dream related to Karen's lesbianism; without talking to her at greater length, I can only surmise.

Fear

Childhood dreams reek of fear. This is not new. In the 1920s, C. W. Kimmins, chief inspector of London schools, made a study of children's dreams. His voluminous report, drawn from the experience of both boys and girls, unearthed masses of fearful images. Fear about unknown animals, ghosts, houses on fire, scenes from recently read books, and so on. Children, of course, continue to dream about such things, except that we now have characters from television programmes to stir our imaginations as well. Kimmins found, as I did, that school figures rarely. I heard of only two dreams from childhood that were about school. In the first, the dreamer had a recurring dream of having her hand chopped off just before sitting the infamous eleven-plus; the second, again at exam time, involved carrying piles of heavy books up a hill but getting nowhere – an accurate reflection of that seemingly futile struggle that comes at revision time. 'Taking exams' dreams recur at times of stress in adult life.

Violet's dreams reveal generalized fear:

'There were dreams about dying. About screaming but no one hearing me. Running but not getting anywhere, and falling. I also remember being able to fly, soaring away from the ground, to escape from someone.'

No one helps, no one hears her screams. She is immobilized. She is not only unable to progress, she falls. Her only safe exit is to fly from reality into fantasy. Violet's dreams are typical of the widespread fears of childhood so often overlooked by adults. The misguided view that children have it easy, that they have no worries, is perpetuated by those who do not want to recognize the problems of dependency and powerlessness.

Susan's childhood dreams demonstrate utter helplessness:

'I remember a couple in which I was attacked and murdered and I read about it in the newspaper with my picture on the front page and the story making headline news. It was quite frightening.'

Such scenes occur in waking fantasies of both adults and children, particularly when the people concerned feel undervalued and unappreciated. In Susan's dream her life is taken by an anonymous person and she has no power to save herself. She achieves passing importance by making headline news, but at what cost? There are parallels here with victims of anorexia nervosa; recent research shows that it is an illness which springs from issues of power and control.[2] In most cases it strikes females who feel they must exercise control over one area of their own lives since being autonomous in any other area seems impossible. In her dream, Susan was no more than an observer of her own life.

Fears become more manageable as personal power increases. If a growing girl learns that she has the right to a say in how she lives her life, and is caringly encouraged to use that right, she will come to express her own power creatively. For Veronica, now in her forties, the caring, strong base which should have been her foundation from which to grow disappeared:

'It was the very first dream I had, when I was four or five, and it is still as vivid today as it was then, especially since it turned out to be prophetic . . . It was very simple. I was standing at one end of a gigantic chessboard, and far away across the board stood the figures of my mother, father and elder sister. They gradually sank below the level of the board and vanished from my sight. I wept and called to them, but I was rooted to the spot and had to watch helplessly as, without a word, they disappeared.'

Four months later, her mother was taken seriously ill and had to be hospitalized for several months. Veronica, confused and vulnerable, was sent away to her grandfather's house in Halifax. Her elder sister had just started a job and could not afford to give it up. Her father, struggling to keep his house and family on a meagre income, could not take time off from his job; there were too many other hungry men desperate for work who would jump at the chance of taking it. So the little girl found all safety disappearing.

At the time of the dream, Veronica had no idea that any of this would happen – though, in looking at the dream now, she feels that it symbolically depicted the 'moves of fate' which separated her from her family. As in the case of Lisa (see page 29) the chessboard is used to indicate a game over which the dreamer has no control; she cannot affect the rules or the moves, and is a piece to be acted upon by others. Veronica watches as her family sink without trace. She cannot reach them, they cannot help her, she is stranded at the other end of the 'board', an onlooker. She is 'rooted to the spot', which typically means that the dreamer feels powerless to alter what is happening. The causes of such freezing of personal power vary enormously, from fear of the consequences to a depression which has obliterated all forms of energy. In Veronica's dream, her powerlessness would appear to be a realistic understanding of the amount of influence a child can have at times of emotional upheaval and economic privation.

While Veronica believes that the dream was prophetic, I feel that she is not giving herself enough credit. She is not admitting her own skills. This dream shows a very sensitive, intelligent little girl who knew that something was happening, even though no one ever said anything directly. She had picked up that her mother was not well and, from other conversations and observations, she could have imagined that, if anything happened to her mum, it would have dire consequences for herself. I'm not saying that she was consciously thinking this, but that at a subconscious level she was aware of the threatening possibilities. Her dream tells us that some part of her psyche was exploring the idea of being separated from all that was secure and familiar. Painful though the experience might have been, it constituted a helpful form of preparation and rehearsal.

Taking off: flying and adventure

If children cannot take autonomous action as their parents or other custodians can, then it is not surprising that flying should figure so prominently in dreams remembered from childhood. Even in groups where women have trouble remembering any dreams at all, when another woman says, 'I used to dream I could fly', the forgetful ones usually pipe up: 'I had those. Oh, I remember now, I used to . . .'

Flying provides a means of escape in dreams, just as flights of fantasy through day-dreaming, soap operas, novels and the like do in adult life. Women do not recall as many dreams of flying as girls do, maybe because in childhood their subconscious is not so heavily influenced by the gravity of reality.

Anita's dreams were about flying downstairs, in her case to escape an invisible pursuer. For others there was a complete metamorphosis, as Dee recalled:

'I had the ability to change into a butterfly and fly off to safety whenever I felt threatened.'

She could spread her wings and take off. Quite a power to have, but it takes danger to provide enough impetus to use such power. Why don't we use it for pure joy and exhilaration rather than waiting for the fear to press us?

Dreams in which the dreamer is able to fly indicate greater self-generated personal power than those where flying might take place but does not, as in Eve's case:

'I dreamt I was climbing up some steep, narrow steps with a precipice on each side. Lovely blue sky and sun shining. Just as I reached the last few steps, a dimly seen figure ran towards me and threw me into the abyss. Then I awoke but I was not frightened by the dream, only disappointed because I had not reached the top of the stairs.'

Eve did not feel outraged at being attacked. She did not seek escape. She did not soar. On waking she passively registered her disappointment, but did not allow herself feelings of anger and grief. She had internalized the message that little girls do not show rage or fight back, or indeed show any strong emotions at all. The start of the dream indicates this narrowness: she was on a tight, confined path which allowed no flexibility, and she had no protective barriers to save her from a possible fall. If she had been given more encouraging messages about herself, she might have felt more powerful. She might have flown.

Animals

Crystal, my daughter aged two and a half, has just started to talk about her dreams. She wakes up in the middle of the night and tells me that 'billy goat' was in her room or that there was a red dog on her bed. These imaginings are related to bedtime stories but other animal dreams recalled from childhood have no discernible roots in stories. They may have connections with waking events, though, as in Renée's case:

'I dreamt of a lamb which danced against the night sky. The lamb was made of its own shit. I knew that, but it looked like thousands of tiny coloured dots. It was very pretty.'

Renée, like most children before they are taught otherwise, was proud of what her body produced. There were no qualms in the dream about social niceties and taboos concerning shit, but pleasure at her first experience of creation. An innocent lamb is moulded from a substance from which others might recoil. Renée is now a successful painter. She was not pressured into denying her earliest feelings about creativity and so it was allowed to blossom.

Animals occur very frequently in children's dreams. The child may be chased or attacked by wild beasts. Following Jung's basic premise that dreams are not necessarily deceptive, the simplest interpretation is that such dreams reveal fears of the beasts concerned.

Hilary's experience is typical of one group of children's dreams in which the child is frightened but adults either ignore or dismiss those fears:

'I had a recurring dream that a large dog was licking my face. He was licking very hard with a tongue like sandpaper and I knew he was stripping all the skin off my face and my face was disappearing. But, when I called out to the many adults who were standing around, they told me not to be silly, he was just being friendly.'

Adults help children to define the world and to understand what life is about. However, Hilary's dream shows us the contradictions: what she is told and what she feels are very different. The adults deny her feelings; they tell her 'the dog is being friendly', but she feels she is being stripped, made faceless by this 'friendliness'. Such contradictions carry over into adulthood, particularly in dealings with experts, who are of course symbolic parent figures – they are all-powerful and all-knowing. The situation that immediately springs to mind is a doctor saying, 'There's nothing wrong with you,' when you feel dreadful; it may even make you feel worse than before because now you are likely to be labelled neurotic as well! There is the difference between what the 'expert' says and what we feel, and far too many women deny their own experience and accept what they are told. Too often we do not give ourselves permission to listen to or express the inner feelings. The price can be high; you can be made 'faceless' and lose your identity through such acquiescence, as Hilary's dream shows.

Many animal dreams are about developing sexual awareness. I have been struck by the number of dreams recalled from adolescence which were about wolves: wolves surrounding the house in which the girl is trapped or wolves lying in wait to attack. The film *Company of Wolves* is based on this idea, which has very old roots, as Bruno Bettelheim's brilliant book *The Uses of Enchantment* shows. We are dealing with an image, the wolf, which has for centuries been linked with sexuality. How do girls develop this fear? Possibly through fairytales such as *Little Red Riding Hood* or through language like 'wolf whistle' and 'wolf in sheep's clothing'. This theme is dealt with more fully in Chapter 5.

Before we leave the subject of animals and sexuality, you might like to consider whether this dream is about a child's unconscious knowledge of the sex act:

'When I was a child I lived in India in a bungalow which had a long path. My mum's and dad's bedroom had five windows. I had the dream when I was about six . . . It started with my mum saying she wasn't well and that I would have to call the doctor. I phoned the doctor and while we were waiting for him my mother was rolling around on the bed in pain. As the doctor, dressed in a black and white striped shirt and trousers, came up the path, he seemed to be changing into a fox. I told my mum that the doctor had arrived and she got out of bed. She went to the first window and the doctor/fox, who had a sharp, pointed umbrella, stood outside it. He stuck the umbrella into my mum and she had a large visible hole in her. He did this through the other windows so she had five large holes in her. Then he went back down the path slowly changing into our own doctor.'

What is it about this dream that makes me link it to sex? Is it the striped suit that makes me think of pyjamas? There is a mysterious quality about the dream; things are not what they seem to be. The doctor becomes the sly fox; the healer becomes the attacker; and the child looks on, doing and saying nothing. The Freudian view would be that a long, pointed object represents a penis, and the pushing in and out of the umbrella could be seen as the movements during intercourse. Many women who went to see Freud in Vienna talked about witnessing that most intimate of acts between parents, but he felt the need to put such experiences down to fantasies and hysteria. I wonder if this girl had seen her parents making love and her dream represented an attempt to make sense of it? Or had she merely been reading a fairytale about a fox?

Other dreams of this type are more concerned with the 'animal nature' that children are taught to repress, but as they occur also in adulthood I will leave that subject until later in the book. Suffice it to say that children dream of worms with top hats and walking sticks; personable, talkative ducks; dragons who tell the dreamer that parents have moved away while they were at school; outraged ostriches; and thousands more variations of animal antics. What do these dreams tell us about growing up a girl?

Childhood feelings of powerlessness carry over into womanhood. The early anxiety themes of being chased, for instance, create in women the same feelings of dread and cold fear in the pit of the stomach as they do in children. These will be discussed in detail in Chapter 8, but it is important to remember that the feelings of powerlessness that permeate women's dream lives begin in childhood.

Much of the emphasis in education is still on compliance rather than the development of the self; conformity at the expense of individuality. This suits the school system and is almost universally encouraged but, as Ann Dally points out in *Why Women Fail*, those girls who rebel against the system are most probably the healthier ones, even if the teachers don't like it! 'It is not surprising,' she writes, 'that many rebellious children turn into strong, surviving people and many school conformists become inadequate, self-destructive adults.'

Everywhere, we are still surrounded by images of women as passive and subservient; not the 'doers' but the 'done to'. A friend of mine whose dreams are featured elsewhere in the book, under a different name of course, completed a master's degree with a thesis entitled 'A Sociological Analysis of the Images of Females in Award Winning Children's Books in the 1970s'. What she discovered was fascinating but not surprising. Her summary was as follows:[3]

> We can conclude that not only do females appear far less frequently than males in children's books but, when they do, they are portrayed in a stereotyped role, usually that of wife and mother if adult, and as passive, inactive and I think I can say boring! Boys seem to have all the fun in children's books.

Children's literature plays an important role in maintaining women in a passive position. Literature is not separate from the rest of society but a product of it and an influential factor in the way images of women are built. The images affect men and women alike and, of course, are not restricted to literature; they are there in advertising, on TV and radio and in the newspapers. A great deal of excellent research has been done in this area, so for anyone who is still not sure just how negatively women are viewed or how strongly we are conditioned to be passive and powerless, let me refer you to Judith Bardwick's *Psychology of Women* as a starting point.

Few of the dreams recalled by women from childhood show the dreamers in a positive situation in which they are doing something they want to do. Most of the time the reverse is the case: girls are being hurt, are fearful of people and external events, feel unable to influence the outcome of a situation, and are less than assertive. Girls are still taught to please, to be deferential, to behave in an acceptable, usually highly restricted, way. We have a long way to go if girls are to learn something more than how to be compliant and malleable servicers of others. Growing girls continue to adopt the role of dependency which ill fits women of today. As transitional women who want to share influence in the world, we must teach our daughters how to be independent and interdependent; rather than how to please others at the expense of achieving their own fulfilment.

How to help children with their dreams

Children are much more likely to recall dreams if an interest is shown in them. Ask children about their dreams, listen actively – by that I mean show involvement; don't just sit there glassy-eyed, grunting at regular intervals to give some semblance of interest. Listen to the dream adventures, for they provide a healthy means of self-expression and communication.

One famous 'dream' tribe in Malaysia used dreams as a cornerstone of their culture. The Senoi encouraged children to recount their dreams, to deal with the fears expressed, to talk about any material which came in dream form. No dream was ever considered to be stupid or irrelevant. On the contrary, children were expected to try to understand their dream characters and symbols in order that they might fully benefit from nocturnal messages. If a tiger came in a dream and the child ran away, then during waking hours the young person would be helped to act out scenes in which he or she confronted the tiger and either overcame it or made friends with it. If a child was particularly fearful, then there was pressure to find a dream assistant, in the form of a person or animal, to come to the rescue. It was expected that the child could be powerful in dreams; attaining such power was seen as proof that personal strength was developing.

Using Senoi principles, we can influence dreams by actively requesting particular items or events to help us face difficulties. Girls can do this in order that they may begin to take their personal authority more seriously. When awake, they too can act out stories as a way of working through the dream so that its message is more completely understood. As Patricia Garfield, a dream recorder and writer of many years standing, reports in *Creative Dreaming*,[4] by the time adolescence arrives the Senoi child no longer has nightmares. Indeed, he is regarded as immature until his dream characters co-operate with him and assist him in socially useful ways. When his dreams are positive, he is considered a man.

Devote time to talking to children about their dreams. Ask them about their reactions but don't give your interpretations. Children are highly impressionable and need encouragement to talk, but they don't usually benefit from amateur analysis. If the dream is scary, ask how it could be more favourably concluded. Act out that conclusion or help the child to conceive of a successful ending. Encourage assertive, self-proving behaviour in both dreams and waking life.

Engendering self-confidence is one of the best ways to help girls to assert control over their own lives. The dreams of childhood seem to be a very good place to start this vital process of empowerment.

Notes

1. Michele Elliott, *Preventing Child Sexual Assault*, Bedford Square Press, 1985.
2. Marilyn Lawrence, *The Anorexic Experience*, The Women's Press, 1984.
3. Polly McEneaney, *A Sociological Analysis of the Images of Females in Award Winning Children's Books in the 1970s*, M.Ed. thesis, Manchester University, 1984.
4. Patricia Garfield, *Creative Dreaming*, Futura, 1976.

3

Meanings in the Menstrual Cycle

Have you noticed that you feel sexier at certain times of the month? Or that on particular days you feel more lively, energetic and creative? Such fluctuations are reflected in your dreams.

Dreams are different according to where you are in your menstrual cycle and they mirror not only your moods but your level of creativity. In this chapter we look at what this relationship reveals and how you can use it. If you have not noticed it yourself, then record your dreams over a period of months, putting a marker next to the dream record which shows where you are in your cycle. I usually put P for when I am actually menstruating, O for around the time of ovulation and PM for premenstrual times. Other women, as you will discover, also include details of the phases of the moon, because they have found strong links between their menstrual cycle and the lunar cycle. If you keep a record, you will probably find a pattern in your dreams of which you were previously unaware.

Premenstrual dreams

Just prior to menstruation, many women have violent bloody dreams. Linda, for instance, dreams about blood flowing:

'Last night I dreamt I was walking around the town. My chest wall was exposed as if I had been blasted. There were no ribs, just a gaping hole. I could see my heart and lungs and the skin flaps. It was all very bloody, but there was no pain at all. I was trying to cover it up with bits of gauze and thought I'd go to my mum's. She would suture it for me.'

Linda was due to start her period the next day, and for her it was a typical premenstrual dream. Note how, although the blood flows, there is no pain. Linda does not have period pains.

Jenny and Clare both suffer from premenstrual tension and their

50

turbulent emotions at this time are mirrored in their dreams. Clare finds herself aggressively wielding sharp knives or other weapons, whereas Jenny experiences very vivid dreams involving bloodshed and stabbings. This fits in with the findings of Serois-Berliss and de Koninck, who saw a correspondence between a significant increase in menstrual stress and an increase in dream anxiety and hostility.[1]

Just before the onset of a period women's bodies prepare to expel the lining of the womb. For some women, pains, cramps, lethargy and feelings of great irritability go hand in hand with that premenstrual stage. The aggression that may be generated by these symptoms is evident in the dreams of Jenny and Clare, as are the possibilities of sharp pain, like the stabbing pain that knives can inflict.

While I have no physical discomfort premenstrually, I do experience mood changes. I'm irritable, easily upset, take everything personally and would be much better off just cosseting myself since I'm a liability to myself and everyone else at that time. That isn't to say that I can't cope or get on with everyday living, but I have learnt that I need to take more care of myself to ease the premenstrual tiredness and emotional vulnerability. It's much healthier than playing the martyr, which is a role I used to adopt.

Premenstrual tension is worse for women who are deprived of rapid eye movement (REM) sleep, that is dream sleep (see page 24). Ernest Hartmann, in *The Biology of Dreaming*, suggests that changes in the menstrual cycle indicate a need for more REM sleep late in the cycle before menstruation. In fact, he points out the similarity between premenstrual tension and dream deprivation.[2]

Research has shown that what felt like the right thing for me to do, in that premenstrual time, such as going to bed earlier and deliberately slowing down, can be beneficial. How much more could we each learn from ourselves if only we listened to the inner voice and responded to self-imparted messages? We can learn from our senses, our intuition, our dreams and our reveries. Giving ourselves permission to do so is the hardest part, so trapped are we by the propaganda that such behaviour is unproductive, selfish or, worse still, self-indulgent.

Self-indulgence can work though. Penelope Shuttle was plagued with severe menstrual depression and physical pain but the treatments prescribed by doctors did not improve matters. Eventually after years of searching she found that she had the answer herself; through dream analysis linked to her menstrual cycle, she was able to conquer the disabling aspects of menstruation and turn them to positive, creative attributes. This is documented in *The Wise Wound*, written with her partner Peter Redgrove, which is one of the most thorough books available on menstruation, myths and realities.[3]

When Zoë dreams of soiled pants and blood, she knows her period will start within forty-eight hours. Such dreams, even though they are usually short, can be so vivid that we wake up and check the sheets to see if we've started! Susan gave an example:

'I have a recurring dream at that time in which I'm noticeably heavy and bleeding through my clothes. Most probably this is a fear-related dream because it did once happen to me.'

Susan still feels uncomfortable about that past incident and her dream shows that she has not forgotten the embarrassment. If she is troubled by it, she can do a number of things to resolve the dream so it does not recur. I will discuss these methods in more detail in Chapter 12. For the moment, she could talk through the dream; actively try to recall in detail that waking event and describe it to a supportive friend, or write it down. Next she could compare the way she was at that time with how she is now; then she was more inexperienced, less confident, less knowledgeable about her body and its workings and, obviously, younger. She could consider whether realistically it is likely to be repeated and what she would do if it was. By facing the fear head on, in the Senoi way (see page 262), she can free herself from it. Her other dreams are about falling or being in embarrassing situations, such as peeing in a glass-walled, very public toilet; doing or saying something in company which makes her look ridiculous; and being imposed upon by someone who thinks they know best so that she cannot do what she wants. These dreams convey the message loud and clear that she needs to improve her self-confidence and self-esteem.

Many women find that they have nightmares before the onset of their periods or that the quality of their dreams is distinct in some way. Fiona, a shop manageress in her mid-twenties, finds that her premenstrual dreams are very vivid:

'I remember them more, maybe because I sleep badly then. I notice more colours, and they are often sexier. This is probably because I get all tensed up sexually but avoid intercourse with my husband as I feel I don't want to five in to him too much, and if he doesn't find a good way of getting round me, he's out.'

Although Fiona is more sexually aroused at this time, she tells us that she uses sex to manipulate her husband. She doesn't say what is wrong between them, but he has to 'get round' her, he has to persuade her to have sex. She doesn't tell him that she wants more attention from him at other times but plays a game so that he has to be careful otherwise she'll punish him by denying sex – he'll be 'out' unless he watches his step! In her attempts to frustrate her husband's desires, she certainly denies her own. She falls into the trap of using her sexual power in a negative way which benefits neither of them.

Thérèse Benedek, a psychologist who researched the subject of menstruation and pregnancy, suggested as early as 1939 that the sexual content of women's dreams is related to the hormonal changes in the menstrual cycle.[4] She explained that the psyche and the body are not divisible. The menstrual phases are accompanied by predictable changes in mood, including increased libido. While Fiona fights against her natural inclinations other dreamers are not so reticent.

Carol has been involved with Jeff for five years and describes their relationship as steady and secure, yet she is flooded by disturbing dreams of sex, particularly during her period. Initially she is making love with Jeff but then the lens takes in a wider scene:

'Suddenly a gang of bikers, big scruffy hard men, burst into the house wrecking everything, then they take me and my sister to rape. The gang ritual usually involves some ultimate in violence, some form of atrocity, but I always find that my rapist, the leader, comes to really like me. He is gentle and kindly and doesn't go through with the task but escapes with me.'

Though she feels stronger when she comes through unscathed in this and other dreams, Carol is still troubled by them. They continue the myth, internalized by many women, that 'romantic', handsome rapists can be changed by a 'good' woman. Her more subtle, 'Freudian phallic' dreams, as she describes them, which also appear during this stage of the cycle, are more disquieting and not nearly so romantically adventurous or sexually titillating:

'I dream of poisonous worms and snakes turning into males,

chasing me and finally 'spitting' venom either in my mouth or on my skin. It is deadly.'

I can understand Carol's surprise at these dreams when she declares that she enjoys sex and has no inhibitions. The dreams indicate some dislikes and fears; I wonder how she feels about oral sex? I stress *how she feels*, not what she thinks; there can be a tyranny in what is fashionably acceptable, in sexual practices as well as everything else. Such pressure prevents many of us expressing our own preferences, so it is important to concentrate on feelings rather than rationalizations. Does she like it? Or does she feel that semen is 'venom', which is what the dream indicates? She has no desire to have children – in fact, she says, 'I thoroughly dislike them. I harbour no maternal feelings at all.' Maybe that is why the 'venom' is so deadly to her. Her dreams tell us that she is not completely happy sexually and she could gain a lot if she worked at understanding their meaning.

Menstruation

In *Creative Dreaming*, Patricia Garfield noted distinct changes in dreams according to where she was in her cycle, but she found that dreams during the menses were difficult to recall. My own observations show them to be more vivid at this time. Van der Castle also reports no decrease in dreaming, and points out that during the menstrual period a more active role towards males is often adopted.[5]

Diane can confirm the active role towards males. Leading a demanding life as mother and part-time proof-reader, she finds that her menstrual dreams involve seeking out men to seduce. The most erotic dreams occur while she is having her period and she thinks this is because she feels least worried about contraception then. As an ex-pill user she is still finding the search for an acceptable alternative a daunting task and welcomes the freedom that comes with menstruation.

Tina's dreams are more vivid just before ovulation and during her period, a pattern echoed by many other women in my survey. Mainly, the dreams at both stages emphasize sexuality and erotic liaisons. Tina says:

'As I am on the pill, perhaps my natural hormonal activity will be somewhat subdued by the artificial hormone ingestion of the pill daily. However, I do feel distinctly more sexy just after "ovulation", in the middle of the month/pill packet, and especially during my period. I experience the sexual dreams around this time.'

Sheldrake and Cormack confirm that changes in the levels of oestrogen and progesterone in the body influence dreams.[6] Havelock Ellis noted this double peak in the 'menstrual wave of sexual desire' just as these dreamers discovered: one during or around menstruation, and the second in the middle of the cycle.[7]

Jean, mother of a sixteen-year-old, has got her sleeping and waking life working in unison. Jean regularly has her 'ultimate sexual atmosphere' dream during her period: satin sheets, fur covers and a big bed, doing 'daring things that I might not have the nerve to do in real life', but more and more the eroticism of her menstrual dreams spurs her on to similar waking adventures.

Dreams can guide each of us to discover our own sexual pattern and highlight times when sexual appetite is at its height. They can help us to match our sexual activities, personal desire and need, rather than following the social rules which decree when sexual intercourse is permitted or proscribed.

Many women are still influenced by taboos about menstruation, including the one that sex during a period is dirty, shameful or unpleasant. If you decide that it is any of those things, then that is your choice and your responsibility, but if you have never tested those views you are the victim of prejudice. It was not so very long ago that menstruating milkmaids were banned from the milking parlour in case they turned the milk sour! Looking further back in history, Pliny (*circa* AD 23–79) damned menstruating women. In his famous *Natural History*, he wrote:

> On the approach of a woman in this state, new wine will become sour, seeds which are touched by her become sterile, grass withers away, garden plants are parched up and the fruit will fall from the tree beneath which she sits.

Men failed to understand how women could bleed and not die. The menstrual taboo came into operation to shame women and ensure the maintenance of a strongly negative self-image. How could women feel good about being women when such a natural female function was so reviled? Abstinence from sex during menstruation confirms the belief that there is something wrong with the menstruating woman, and many cultures still insist that menstruating women keep themselves apart from the rest of the tribe. Who holds the power there?

Ovulation

After recording her dreams for many years, Kate has identified a definite pattern. Dreams at ovulation, for example, concern holding or looking at small, delicate objects, especially jewellery. For her, as for many others in my survey, 'small, delicate objects' are symbols of eggs released at ovulation, their gem-like fragility echoing the nature of the human egg on its journey from fallopian tube to uterus. A typical 'ovulation' dream from Kate's dream diary shows the rich symbolism involved:

'I dreamt of cut-glass jewels; tiny, multicoloured cubes in my hand. One had a hole down the middle like a bead but it had broken in half so that there was a little furrow where the hole had been . . . I took off some green alabaster scarab earrings only to find that one of them had cracked into four pieces though it remained in the setting.'

Fertilized eggs divide first into two, then into four, and so on. It is as if Kate's dream continues that natural development in symbolic form. The voyage the egg takes in the hidden channels of her body is symbolically enacted:

'This dream was all about journeys. I had been on several different trains and then spent a lot of time walking down tunnels and across rough land . . . I came to this rough track with a farm worker's cottage at the end of it where a man and a woman were standing. The woman was pregnant again but she knew that this time she was going to give birth to a fish. As we watched, she delivered the long, smooth, greeny-coloured fish, which later changed into one of those sea-green ornamental dolphins. It was covered with big bobbly scales and had a curly tail and big lips. It was beautiful, translucent and glasslike . . . Some time later I noticed in passing that the whole thing had fallen to the floor and smashed into tiny glass fragments. It did not seem important though.'

The final part of the dream indicates the disintegration of the unfertilized egg; Kate takes little notice of that since it is part of the natural order. She is in tune with her body and its rhythms.

It is quite unusual for someone to be so cognizant of this union of psyche and body that Benedek identified (see page 53) but Kate shows that with methodical recording of dreams you can develop a highly sensitive degree of self-knowledge. Benedek also found that dreams of precious gems, round, fragile objects and delicate items were common during ovulation. There are dreams of babies, of course, which need special interpretation! But here is another example. June had this dream the day after she ovulated:

'I am going on a trip with my parents. We come to a youth hostel/hotel of some kind and when I go into my room there are bunk beds. There is a twelve-year-old boy in the bottom bunk. He has been left behind while his party have gone off . . . I also find a purse rather like a small make-up bag I have, and in it I find some semi-precious stones and a gold fish swimming around, although there is virtually no water in it. I want to get some more water for the fish as he seems lucky to have survived so far and should be all right if I act quickly.'

June would like to have another child, and so she can if she acts quickly and takes care of 'the little fish'. Fish in dreams are frequently linked to conception and pregnancy. The twelve-year-old boy represents June's son. He had been moaning to her recently that, unless she got a move on, he would be twelve before she had a baby brother for him. Nothing in the dream is wasted. We find the characteristic journeying typical of this stage of menstrual dreaming, the semi-precious stones symbolizing the egg, and the fish. Just a hint of warning, though, that the life-giving water might be running low. June's son, the result of a previous conception, will be 'left behind', just as the boy in the dream has been 'left behind'. He is very firmly part of this picture, just as he is in waking life. He plays a central role in his mother's life and his inclusion gives clarity to the dream narrative.

Such a dream is very useful. It tells June that she needs to make moves now to get herself completely fit for childbearing if that is what she wants; and she has some serious thinking to do about whether or not to have another child.

The Menopause

Amy, aged forty-three, has begun to notice that after many years of sparse dreaming, her dreams are becoming more insistent. They are easier to recall: indeed, they seem to demand recall though at times she fights against it. Not too happy with the changes that are happening to her body, she is loath to talk to others about 'the change' and this reluctance surfaces during sleep.

Amy dreams of dead people and about being in dissecting rooms filled with bodies on slabs. As she walks around, she is terrified that she might accidentally touch one, for in some way this will taint her. She has no waking experience of such places and no one close to her is ill or has died recently. So do these dreams reflect her psyche coming to terms with ageing and accepting that parts of herself are ending, particularly her fertility? Again, the dream setting is important: a room where minute, detailed examination takes place, where students learn about how people are made and what constitutes physical reality. It's a place of life and death and Amy needs somehow to 'learn' about this even though she is scared. What dissection does Amy have to do in order to understand herself better?

Like many women at this stage in life, she is depressed, suffering from the 'empty nest' syndrome. Her children have grown up, left home and lead lives which do not involve her. She was always 'just a housewife', devoting her skills to child-rearing and homemaking, and now there seems little point to her existence. Pauline Bart, a psychologist who has written about depression in middle-aged women, found that such feelings sprang from lack of self-esteem rather than from hormonal changes of the menopause; as she says, 'There's no bar mitzvah for menopause.'[8]

Ann Mankowitz echoes this view and shows how such feelings are revealed in dreams. In *Change of Life: A Study in Dreams of the Menopause*, she shows how they relfect the way the menopause is unsympathetically treated in our society; it carries none of the significance of other 'rites of passage' such as marriage or childbirth, no one marks it in any way. This may well be because it is seen as the end of a woman's creative, reproductive cycle. Most women have spent more than thirty years, apart from pregnancies or ill health, living with a monthly cycle which confirms their potential to create new life. The creative force is there even though the woman may not bear children. When the cycle stops, that power is taken away and we need time to come to terms with its loss.

As long as women continue to be defined largely by the functions of the uterus, the menopause will be a difficult time for us. I cannot think of any advertisements, television or radio programmes or popular literature that deals with issues raised by the menopause in a helpful way. Like incest, it is still a taboo area.

The women's movement has not so far placed much focus on the menopause but it will receive more attention as the women at the forefront of developments two decades ago themselves become menopausal. There are early signs of this in America, where a group known as OWL has emerged. The Older Women's Liberation movement is concerned with the issues which western society customarily shuns. Ageing women, other than smiling grandmas, do not fit the consumer image of females as fresh, clear-skinned beings with no hint of decay. Women getting old, lined, infirm, needing to be cared for: these are not acceptable images for most media men. The reality is that other women – nurses, daughters or other 'carers' – take on the ultimate responsibility that 'the change' signals.

The lunar cycle

The incidence of violent crimes, whether committed by men or women, fluctuates in accordance with the lunar cycle,[9] and the effects of the moon are felt in many other ways: it influences the reproductive cycles of all living creatures; it controls the tides . . . But, not unexpectedly, our materialistic, rushed lifestyles give us little chance to tune into the subtle variations of mood which may be affected by the moon. The influences show up in dreams, though.

Dreams have been 'the light at the end of the tunnel' for Olive at times when the going has been really rough, and in her faithful work on dreams she has learnt many things:

'I have a very active dream life just before menstruation and this is further reinforced when there is a full moon. Recently the eclipse of the new moon seemed to initiate a lot of powerful dreams, including a regression dream which took me back to an incident when I was twelve months old. The situation had been extremely painful, resulting in a lot of blocked anger and hurt. I am still working through this.'

Olive knows from past experience that such dreams help her to change negatives into positives, so she is empowered by her dreams. When I asked her what she had gained from working with dreams, her enthusiasm flowed:

'Well, I've not so much changed as learnt to accept and integrate parts of myself which I had long ago rejected. I feel a more rounded person, on an exciting journey, a thrilling adventure, finding out about me. There have been bad times but, having said that, dreams represent the possibility for acceptance and change and greater self-awareness. They help us get in touch with our own humanity and our own spirituality.'

She feels that she has also had help from her dreams which left her feeling grateful but slightly perturbed:

'I dreamt that I was almost led into a motor accident twice on a particular stretch of road. One half of the road had lost its surface and the other half was temporarily out of action because of a burst water main. About a month later this did happen to a particular stretch of road and I did indeed almost collide with another car.'

The dream prepared her for an unexpected event which could have had disastrous consequences. She is far from alone in having this type of precognitive warning in dreams as you will see in Chapter 11.

'At the new moon,' confided Pat, 'and at the first quarter stage I dream constantly. I wake up in the morning feeling as though I've been living a separate existence and that I have not slept at all.' Had she been influenced by her reading or was it a coincidence? Her experience fits in closely with one of the many myths associated with lunar cycles, particularly the myth about the goddess Diana. The new crescent moon is held to represent the bow of Diana, a maiden and a warrior. The powerful huntress asserts her individuality and independence by travelling the night skies. Her opposite, the full moon, is seen as the ripe, mature, fertile woman. The waning moon is, variously, the old hag, the crone, the seer or the wise woman, or the witch of old who lived in the moon. She holds the key to mysteries and power. Though centuries old, these images of women remain with us, just as they have done in many diverse cultures.

Among American Indians, the moon is called 'the first woman' and is said to 'sicken' or to be menstruating in the waning period of her cycle. The twenty-eight-day menstrual cycle and the lunar cycle are so similar that the link between the two is universal in early religious symbolism and in mythology. Moon cults are menstrual cults; they acknowledge the power of the female cycle. In fact, the words 'moon' and 'menses' derive from the same Latin root.

Nor Hall, a Jungian analyst, beautifully describes connections with the moon in our own culture when she writes about the 'sabbath', the day traditionally associated with religious observance and rest from work.[10] She says that the word originally came from '*sabbutu*' which means heart rest. It was known as the day of the goddess Ishtar's menstruation, which coincided in Babylonia with the full moon, and originally the sabbath was observed only once a month, just like periods.

As we saw earlier, few women are fully aware of the effects of the moon on their cycle. However, Tom Robbins, in his book *Still Life with Woodpecker*, drew a heroine, trapped and existing without any artificial light, living in total unison with the cycle of the moon:[11]

By May she was menstruating regularly at the new moon, just as the ancients did, and in July she observed that she had begun to ovulate when the moon was full, as will any healthy woman whose nights are not polluted by synthetic lighting. She could always tell when she was about to ovulate because her vaginal mucus would become wetter and more abundant than usual, and more smooth and slippery too. Her glands were greasing the tracks, as it were, for the Sperm Express. Of course, testing for ovulation can be hazardous, since a primed vagina, in its enthusiasm, can mistake an exploratory finger for a serviceable phallus and try to draw it in. Her resistance was admirable, however, if not quite heroic, and the mucus tests proved that she had begun, inadvertently but successfully, to practise lunaception.

You can see how women's cycles are moon cycles. If you want to prove it to yourself, then record your dreams. Maybe, like Julie, you'll find that your dreams are 'disturbing and restless when there is a full moon'. She thought it sounded crazy to say so but many women share her experience, and our everyday language reflects this link. How do you think lunatics came to be so labelled?

Notes

1. Michelle Serois-Berliss and Joseph de Koninck, 'Menstrual Stress and Dreams: Adaptation or Interference', *Psychiatric Journal of the University of Ottawa*, Vol. 7 (2), pages 77-86, 1982.
2. E. H. Hartmann, *The Biology of Dreaming*, Charles Thomas, Boston, 1967.
3. P. Shuttle and P. Redgrove, *The Wise Wound*, Penguin, 1980.
4. Thérèse Benedek and Boris Rubinstein, 'The correlations between ovarian activity and psychodynamic processes' in *Psychosomatic Medicine*, Vol. I, No. 2, April 1939, pages 245-70.
5. Robert Van der Castle, *The Psychology of Dreaming*, General Learning Corporation, New York, 1971.
6. Peter Sheldrake and Margaret Cormack, 'Dream Recall and the Menstrual Cycle', *Journal of Psychosomatic Research*, Vol. 18, pages 347-50, 1974.
7. Havelock Ellis, *Studies in the Psychology of Sex*, Random House, New York, 1942.
8. Pauline Bart. See Chapter 6 of *Women in Sexist Society* quoted in Bardwick, op. cit.
9. M. B. Parlee, 'The Premenstrual Syndrome', *Psychological Bulletin*, 80, pages 454-65, 1973.
10. Nor Hall, *The Moon and the Vigin*, The Women's Press, 1980.
11. Tom Robbins, *Still Life With Woodpecker. A Sort of Love Story*, Corgi, 1980.

4

Pregnant With Meaning

The intensity of the dream shook me. As I awoke to another ordinary day, I felt as if I was reeling, and I just could not get the dream out of my mind. Why had it been so disturbing? My dreams were usually so easy-going, but this one left me feeling as if I'd been hit by a sledgehammer.

This harbinger of doom had begun with my looking into a baby's eyes. As I looked, the pale blue irises seemed to shatter into a thousand tiny pieces of glass. The scene suddenly changed. At night, in the back garden of my house, I faced a man in a trenchcoat. Coldly, malevolently, he swung a rope to which was attached a chunk of metal. He threw it at me but missed. I knew he was trying to kill me . . . I called to Orly, my dog, to help. Surely she would see off this murderous intruder? But then he set a ferocious alsatian on me. I was stunned. Why was the dog attacking me? Why was this stranger determined to injure me? Again I screamed for help, imploring the sleeping inhabitants of my house to come and save me. I woke up in a cold sweat.

All the next day the dream kept coming back to me. Somehow, though, I did not want to do proper 'dream work' on it. I put it off. Maybe it was because I was so busy with work and my six-month-old daughter. Also, I was just a little bit anxious that the baby at the beginning of the dream might be Crystal. So I managed to push it to the back of my mind.

Three days later, the trenchcoated assailant returned. The first thing I recall is two black dogs jumping through the air towards me. I was utterly helpless. As they lunged at me, I saw that the nearest one had a syringe strapped to his paw. I gasped in horror as I understood it was going to enter me . . . Next, I was sitting talking in a very remote place. I couldn't see the other person, I only knew there was someone else there. I was told, 'When a person goes into the water, into the sea, you can see how near death they are by how much of their body is submerged.' . . . Then I was with a friend asking her for a safety pin because my stomach had swollen and the buttons on my skirt had popped . . . Finally, I was in a station waiting-room which was like a refugee/homeless person transfer point. I wanted to put some music on but the record was scratched and impossible to play. The dream ended.

This time I woke up afraid and terribly sad. Pain, death, defeat and hopelessness had been overpoweringly communicated in the dream. I considered what the swollen stomach might mean. I didn't have to wait long for enlightenment. Three days later my regular-as-clockwork period failed to arrive. I was pregnant.

In my two previous pregnancies, I had had beautifully intense dreams about storks – corny but true – and about lovely sweets changing from suger-almond delicacy to stronger, more robust objects. Those dreams reflected the successful conception and birth of two wonderfully healthy babies. But the 'black dog' dreams, as I came to call them, heralded a devastating miscarriage. Later in this chapter, when we've considered more favourable pregnancy dreams, I'll return to the painful subject of miscarriage.

Conception dreams

Women are naturally concerned with the whole business of conception, birth and rearing of children; even if we do not experience powerful reproductive urges, we are socialized into considering seriously the importance of childbearing. Obviously these issues come into our dreams,[1] and one of the characteristics of dreams right from the start of pregnancy is that they are so luminous.

For some women, crisp, clear dreams of fertility are the first intimation that conception has taken place, occurring before symptoms such as morning sickness, tender breasts or a missed period are noticed. They may be wish-fulfilment or anxiety dreams but their quality is recognizably different from other dreams. Women who had had 'conception' dreams had no doubts about their meaning. In *The Analysis of Dreams*,[2] Medard Boss describes such an experience:

. . . the young woman who saw her body as a field through which a plough was cutting a furrow had, a few days previously and for the first time, unreservedly surrendered to the love of a man. She experienced this event itself as a 'natural event'. She had become pregnant without being aware of it at the time of the dream. These two events had so intensely attuned her whole existence that it seemed to overflow her human body and corresponded to Mother Earth herself, to a field ripe for sowing.

While Paula's situation lacked such subservient trappings, she too had a significant dream before she knew that she was pregnant. Working hard as a deputy headteacher of an inner-city comprehensive school in Leeds, she nevertheless found time to consider her dreams, particularly this one. As she said later, it signalled the beginning of a pregnancy that was very difficult:

'I had a really exhausting dream. I was sitting in a room and by the power of my thought I was moving this strange object through the air. It was like a clear plastic bag, the sort you buy pre-packed olives in, only it contained a beautiful stone egg. I knew in the dream that I had to concentrate completely and utterly if this "bag" was to get to the other side safely. I did it but it was incredibly hard.'

Later Paula realized that she had been about twelve days pregnant when she had the dream, and she 'knew' it was about having a baby. She did have a problematic pregnancy; threatened miscarriage, high blood pressure, forced to give up work and spend a large part of each day in bed; generally it was a worrying time. She had a son just before the expected date of confinement but often felt it was sheer willpower that had kept her and her much-wanted baby going, just as her dream had indicated.

Dreams during pregnancy

Most women find that their dreams during pregnancy are very clear. Initially the dreams mainly relate to the woman, her own body and the changes it is undergoing. Then, after the first movements of the baby are felt, they focus more on the foetus. During the final period of pregnancy, dreams seemed to be inner rehearsals for what is to come. Rosie's dream diary documents such changes:

'My dreams were often on the subject of birth and babies. In one very vivid dream I was in labour. Everything was pleasant and painless at this point. I was in a corridor close to an adjoining office with a large door and an open window. The open doorway revealed a panoramic view of the office interior. There was a desk, filing cabinets and a large, cold marble slab of table. Chris, my husband, was ordered away by a sort of doctor and I was put on the table/slab and slashed with a knife. There was a lot of blood and I remember telling Chris that this wasn't how I wanted it to be. I remember getting a baby also.'

She continues:

'Although this sounds like a nightmare, it wasn't really. I felt disgruntled about Chris going away but acceptance that such things would have to be done before the baby was born.'

In the later stages of pregnancy:

'I dreamt about seeing the baby that was coming . . . my child appeared as a tiny, delicate, skinny, black-haired mite, fragile and extraordinarily beautiful. He was so lovely in this dream that I felt it to be one of the happiest dreams I have ever experienced. My real baby was exactly like him.'

Rosie felt that her dreams helped her towards having a 'perfect birth' – a short labour and no complications, even though he was her first child. Her earlier dreams show an understanding that birth might not be a trouble-free experience but she accepts that and goes on to produce a healthy son.

During the nine months of growth and preparation, most mothers-to-be consider the possibility of having a deformed or damaged baby. I certainly did, and I discovered much later that I was not alone, yet too often it is considered neurotic or irrational to voice those fears. However, they may be revealed in dreams, as Sharon tells:

'When I was pregnant I dreamt of giving birth to a headless, armless, legless monster. It was so vivid that I phoned my sister to tell her about it. Every time I'm pregnant I fear delivering a child who is less than perfectly formed – surely every woman does.'

No wonder the first question after giving birth is usually 'Is it all right?' This apprehensiveness may be based on the knowledge that real dangers have been experienced during pregnancy, as in Sheena's dream described below, or may be a foggy fear which comes and goes and which has no identifiable source.

'I go into a grim hospital in a side street. My baby has been born but I have not been allowed to see it. I am a schoolgirl again, wearing my old school uniform . . . Inside the hospital I meet a nurse, her arms piled high with babies like plastic dolls. I ask about my baby and am told it has all the handicaps feared for it, and worse. I ask what sex it is and am told it is too badly deformed to tell. I feel great guilt and despair.'

You can see the clear expression of worry in this dream. The setting is unpleasant, off the main thoroughfare in a dingy back street, exactly the sort of place where bad things are supposed to happen. The child she has borne has been taken off her and she is reduced to the powerless schoolgirl role. Despite being thirty-two years old at the time, Sheena does not feel grown up enough for the huge and radical change of becoming a mother. The school uniform identifies those who have not had a 'rite of passage' into so-called maturity.

Sheena had contracted german measles early in her pregnancy, though not so early that a handicapped baby would be inevitable nor late enough to be certain it would be unharmed. She had to choose between having a termination and continuing with the pregnancy. She made the choice to continue, and for the first time in her life defied 'the almighty medical profession', who were dismayed at her decision.

In the nurse with her arms 'piled high with babies', Sheena sees a casual, almost careless attitude to these small bundles of humanity, as if they are inanimate, lifelike 'plastic'. But plastic cannot feel emotions and Sheena sees the nurse as treating these 'babies' as if they too could not feel anything. The dream tells us that she felt her possibly damaged child within was viewed by the medical staff who had advocated an abortion as just another one to add to the pile. Sheena is left with the feeling that she has been a disobedient girl who has gone against the advice of her betters and has been wrong. There is certainly a feeling of 'I told you so, you naughty girl' in the last part of the dream.

Sheena's dream mirrored her feelings and allowed the expression of her fears and anxieties but it was not in any way precognitive. She had a perfectly formed, unharmed daughter, though she did have a period of depression after the birth, probably as a reaction to the stressful experiences encountered during her pregnancy.

Abigail had a distressing dream while carrying her third child:

'I was in a room with people I knew and liked. I was happy to introduce my new baby here. As my sister lifted the baby from the cot – a slow-motion action – it became apparent to everyone, and especially to me, that my baby was grotesquely deformed. I noticed that he had an enormous, swollen, caved-in head, like a punctured football, floppy and hanging about. Everyone looked sorry for me but I felt only slight disappointment and still loved the baby. I then recall cuddling and comforting the baby.'

She too had a healthy, well-formed baby boy. Generally such dreams provide an outlet for understandable fears that we have during pregnancy and help us to accept the possibility that we might give birth to a handicapped child. In Abigail's case, her dream also tells her that she has the love and warmth to sustain a good relationship with her 'grotesquely deformed' dream baby. It is no accident that in the dream room she is surrounded by people she knows and likes, indicating that there is support for her in a painful situation.

Even women with a great deal of knowledge or experience of pregnancy, women 'who should know better', have disturbing dreams prior to the birth of their children. Arifa, an Indian graduate, found herself pregnant soon after she came to England with her husband. Delighted at the prospect of having a child, she found that her dreams became full of natal images:

'I had this dream many times, very little changed . . . At times my husband is on call, while at others he is in the background. I go to the toilet with an intense urge to urinate, only it's blood that comes out. Once the toilet was an Indian-style one where you have to squat down. I can see the blood flowing out and I try to call out but I can't seem to speak. I watch fascinated. I seem to be waiting for the baby to come out too. I scream inside my head, but no sound comes out . . . I used to have this dream and wake up in the middle of the night. For a while I was scared to go to the loo at night even though I have been a family-planning worker and know that abortions don't happen by going to the toilet.'

Shortly after those dreams, Arifa, feeling more confident in her new lifestyle and having made some new friends, had a very reassuring experience:

'This is still one of my favourite dreams. I am back in India at my grandmother's house. My grand-aunt who'd died was there, my present family was there and we were waiting for Meher Baba to come to see us. (Meher Baba is our spiritual master. He died in 1969, but my family was very close to him. We believe he was the incarnation of the spiritual leader of all religions.) When he entered the house, he came up to me, placed his hand on my stomach and I felt the baby rise up to get closer to his hand. There were a lot of people around, but it seemed that the time between him and me was special. After a while he moved on and I went to sit with my grandmother and uncle, who are my favourite people at home. I felt very warm and protected and safe. It was an incredibly lifelike dream. I could feel the people around me, smell the food cooking in the kitchen, even hear the sounds of the traffic outside, as well as my dogs barking. There was a lot of sunshine. I can't remember if my husband was there; he wasn't so important in the dream.'

Labour

Dreams about labour may actually help the process of giving birth. Research by Carolyn Winget and Frederic Kapp revealed that the content of dreams during pregnancy is related to the length of labour.[3] The more anxious the dream content, the more likely the dreamer to have a quick, satisfactory first labour. They conclude that anxious dreams served to prepare the women they studied for the stresses of childbirth, while those women who had long labours were too fearful to allow even symbolic representation to come through in their dreams. Interestingly, the latter also gave much briefer dream reports than their counterparts who had a more positive experience of birth. By dealing with difficulties in the dreams, it appears, the first group were more capable of dealing with them in waking life.

'When I was pregnant I often dreamt that I was in labour. I would be rushed to hospital, where I would give birth. Increasingly in the recurring dream, I found that I was in the dark and had to be woken up to be told I had had the baby. I asked if I could see my baby but I wasn't allowed to although I was assured that the baby was all right . . . The dream was very significant for, when I did have my baby, I had a caesarean and didn't see my daughter for many hours because her condition was poor and she was kept in an incubator.'

This dreamer was indeed 'in the dark', in that she was anaesthetized and was unconscious while the child was born and could not see her daughter for some time.

Sometimes the accuracy of the mundane details that occur in a dream is quite startling. Karen, a woman in her late twenties living on a council estate in Birmingham, had a dream four weeks before her baby was due:

'I dreamt that there were five midwives round me telling me to push and things like that. I shouted out "It's a girl" just as she came out, before they had time to tell me. It was so real that when I woke up I thought I'd had the baby.'

Her labour turned out to be just like this. There were five women around her delivery bed, a midwife accompanied by two trainees and two female students, all urging her towards a successful birth. She did shout the sex of her daughter before anyone else had a chance to do so.

Karen's dream dealt directly with her delivery, the number of people present and the usual encouragements to push that help in that last hurdle when the baby's head is born, so it was not very extraordinary. You could say it was a coincidence that the two, the dream and the actual delivery, were so alike. However, Tricia's dream is less easily explained:

'The last time I was pregnant I wanted to have a boy, as I already had a girl. I dreamt I had given birth to a girl and because I was so disappointed they swapped it for a boy.'

At first this seems like a wish-fulfilment dream and that is how Tricia saw it, but the events which followed caused her to recall her 'changeling' dream. When her baby was born he weighed only two pounds and, as Tricia later said, 'they didn't notice his vital parts'. When told she had given birth to a girl she felt disappointed but was too worried about the health of the newborn infant to dwell on unfulfilled wishes for a boy. Sometime later an embarrassed nurse came to her as she was sleeping and woke her with the news that she had had a boy after all! 'They had made a mistake because no one had bothered to look at his sex. I often wonder if they did a swap or if my dream was preparing me for the mistake.'

Was this dream precognitive? Or was Tricia able to tune into something that was happening to her body of which her conscious mind was unaware? This type of dream is not rare. It tells us that there is a form of 'knowledge' which we possess but we have generally not learnt to explain or control. It is, I believe, merely a matter of time before we do just that.

After the birth

'The second night after Lucy's arrival I had a vivid dream. I dreamt that I had lain my beautiful little baby on the bed, exactly as I had been accustomed to doing during the day, and then walked across to the corner of the room to wash my breasts before feeding her. As I turned back, I saw Lucy falling off the bed – a very high bed. It was in slow motion and I watched as she fell on to the cold, hard floor beneath. The complete horror of the event left me terrified. I experienced all the implications of it simultaneously . . . I felt I already loved her more than anything but was unable to prevent her from being crushed on the floor. I attempted to run towards her and scream but I was locked in complete paralysis and the dream ended . . . After this dream I was most careful to place the baby well away from the edge of the bed.'

Though this dream came only two nights after Lucy's birth, it revealed a strong emotional bond and showed the feelings of responsibility that Sue, the mother, had developed. While awake Sue must have noted that laying the baby on the bed could be dangerous. The dream reinforced the unconscious message, ensuring that the baby was protected from careless injury.

Just as Sue's dream tells us that major bonding, that emotionally vital join between mother and infant, has taken place, so Natalie's dream demonstrates that she too has formed a strong emotional connection with her new son. She had this dream a few days after the birth of her fourth child:

'I'm suddenly aware that I've lost my baby. He has been taken by an unknown "them". Why did I hand him over to them? The remorse and fear are terrible. Start searching desperately. I'm in a strange town in a strange country. There seems to be a large complex building in yellow stone, like an amusement park. I must try to find him there. They will try to prevent me. Remorse.'

In her dream Natalie has become separated; she is horrified at 'losing' him to unknown, vague figures who might harm him. The dream shows the myriad fears of those who have responsibility for newborn babies. Will I be able to protect this fragile child from the dangers of the big wide world? Natalie's subconscious tells her that her essential life-giving relationship will take her into complex areas she has not known before. She will experience a metaphorical 'strange town in a strange country'.

Such dreams show that these women have accepted their roles as nurturers and protectors of their offspring. Nalatie's feeling of 'remorse' concerns an additional issue, one still not discussed widely enough.

Shortly after childbirth, usually a few days later or within a few weeks, there can be a tremendous feeling of sadness. Feelings of anti-climax, loss and misery engulf you even as you delight in the new baby. What a puzzle; and, if you are anything like me, how foolish you feel. But you have lost, physically, the child you carried inside. You have lost that complete unison. The intimacy and ultimate protection your body afforded has gone. Your child is separated. While tiredness and hormonal changes play an important role in the sudden mood changes at this time, we need to accept the rightness of tears after birth. Natalie's dream brings forth her feelings of loss; it enables her to know her emotions.

Infants are totally dependent on the person who cares for them, usually the mother, and her dreams predictably reflect the anxieties attached to such a life and death role, as this example shows:

'I had a recurring dream in pregnancy that I had had a baby but forgot about it for several days, so that when I went back to it, it had died of neglect and starvation.'

The pressures of nature and society, which stress the importance of the nurturing mother's role are evident here. The dream forces home the message that if you, the mother, do not take care of your baby, it will die. Sometimes, though, the 'baby' may be a vulnerable part of you, the dreamer. You may not be caring for yourself properly so your dreams urge you to better self-nurturing; we will examine this more fully later in the book.

Abortion

The devastation of that miscarriage heralded by the 'black dog' dreams was something I had not anticipated. Having discovered I was pregnant again six months after the birth of our daughter, we were delighted at the prospect of completing our family after such a short gap. May as well get all the nappies over with together; they would be good company for each other; and so on.

But it wasn't to be. When I was twelve weeks pregnant, I began to bleed. No pain, only traces of blood; a little spotting. Lying in bed, I was desperately upset. I consulted my bible of women's health *Our Bodies, Ourselves*,[4] longing to find a glimmer of hope which would say I was not going to lose this baby. The book told me that about one in six pregnancies ends in miscarriage, or 'spontaneous abortion' to use the medical term; about 75 per cent of those occur in the first trimester, weeks 1 to 14. I was in that critical period and clung to the hope that the bedrest advised by the emergency doctor would avert impending disaster. In my heart of hearts, I knew it wouldn't, though. The reassurances of those closest to me held no comfort as I lay there immobile, as if perfect stillness could rescue the situation.

As the bleeding increased, placental tissue coming away six months too early, I was admitted to hospital. What should have been a visit for a scan to check the viability of the foetus in its threatened state became an operation to extract the once living contents of my womb. I don't think anyone ever said outright that the child was lost; when I was admitted and examined internally, only one doctor said, 'I'm sorry, I don't think this will be a successful pregnancy.' He seemed embarrassed to be the bearer of bad tidings but delayed the definitive statement by telling me they would wait until the next morning before operating, 'just in case'.

I remember the anguish; my child was seeping away from me as I waited, arms punctured by drip attachments. The early morning light was long in coming. It was strange seeing the solution drip through yet not feel it go into my body; that seemed to sum up the paradox I was experiencing. I felt numbed and divorced from this hateful body which had somehow killed my baby.

The early light came. Earrings in envelope, ring taped to my finger, lying on a stretcher waiting. And then the dream came back. Suddenly there was a doctor with the syringe coming towards me. The syringe of the 'black dog' coming at me and into my vein, then oblivion and loss.

I have no logical explanation for the dream. There was no reason for me to dream of syringes or danger but I had done so. Something in my psyche or physical makeup was warning me, was in tune with an impending physical breakdown. For the first time in my life my body let me down and I was thrown into shock. I had always believed in a woman's right to choose but had never considered that my body might dictate otherwise. A rude awakening. In the dream I could not comprehend why dogs would attack me: me, who was always good with dogs; me, who had never been bitten. I was assailed from a totally unexpected source in both instances. The dream was right. The trusted friend became an enemy.

I had a number of dreams in the weeks that followed, mainly about hospitals and deformed babies. Gradually they faded as I began to grieve less and to accept the loss, though I feel I may dream of that 'lost' baby again. I was much relieved when I had good dreams about plants growing in rich, brown, fertile soil. I knew the story of Danny's growth and birth was not going to be a nightmare repeated. Happily, I was right, and Danny, a big, rosy baby boy, was born after a perfectly trouble-free pregnancy.

Ann Oakley, who co-wrote *Miscarriage* with Ann McPherson and Helen Roberts, herself suffered the anguish of a 'lost' baby. The account of her own miscarriage is very moving indeed, and certainly encompassed many of those feelings which I had. A long time later she had this dream:

> It's impossible to say exactly what I dreamed about. I dreamed of a dead baby, a baby whom I never saw, whom the world kept from me, like an identity I've never been able to claim. I dreamed of a breast swollen and dripping with milk and no one there to receive this nourishment. That baby was female: and as quickly as she was given to me, she departed from me . . .

As this extract from her book *Taking It Like A Woman* reveals, her feelings of grief were not quickly resolved but the experience became part of the life which defined her. Her dream also included a male child who was born fully clothed and full of maturity. As is often the way in dreams, the scene shifted so that:

> Behind a fireplace in our sitting-room I discovered a secret compartment. A small, exquisitely equipped flat completely hidden from the world. It had a thick brown carpet and a split-level oven (not something that I have ever consciously wanted) and a small sunny greenhouse protruding from the back. There I was in it, on my own. I felt whole. I felt whole because I was alone and missed no one, mourned no one, except, in a dull ache somewhere, that daughter of mine who had died. Though in the dream she had died because of the obscure cruelty of medical staff, I knew that she had really died because I had made the wrong choice about the circumstances in which she should be born. If I had given birth to her in the right place, she would be here now, and I would know what kind of person she was. But, aside from this sadness, I sat comfortably enclosed in my secret compartment.

This dream, while dealing with the shadow that death casts, tells also of the recognition of personal strength. The dreamer is shown her 'secret room', her hidden self, and is exposed to her own completeness. Such dreams validate us even when, as in this case, there is tender sadness. Healing dreams are possible.

Philippa saw this terrifying dream as a warning:

'I dreamed that a midget was chasing me with the intent of stabbing me in the abdomen with a stiletto knife. He said that, though I kept claiming to be pregnant, I couldn't be as I was too thin . . . I awoke screaming and started to miscarry within forty-eight hours. I was eighteen weeks pregnant at the time . . . I really felt that the dream foretold the miscarriage. Looking back I was under considerable strain at that time, being four months pregnant and my first child only six months old. I didn't want the child subconsciously and I felt the dream was about that. The pregnancy was not planned and I was living in a one-room apartment with no bathroom.'

The dream was telling her that the continuation of the pregnancy was in jeopardy. She was 'too thin' and under attack from a viciously armed 'midget' who insisted she was not pregnant. She was too weak to fight off even the 'midget' and the dream threat becomes waking reality. The imagery is direct and needs little interpretation. However, unlike one researcher who saw anxious dreams as being a major factor in 'fetal wastage',[5] I would say that it was Philippa's waking situation and physical condition which was responsible for the abortion and her dreams revealed the extent of the threat.

Last year, Sally, a housing assistant in a large housing association in Swansea, found to her dismay that she was pregnant. She and Frank, her boyfriend of two years' standing, had talked about having children, in the way that couples do in a relationship which has long-term possibilities. Frank was absolutely certain that he did not want to be a father. No maybes, only a definite decision that it was not for him. Sally agreed. She was twenty-six and wanted to continue her career and, though she did not feel as strongly as Frank did, she really was not bothered either way. But she did want Frank and she knew he would leave her if she had a child. The night she should have had her period, she had this dream:

'I dreamt of a man with a knife. I was terribly afraid. There was a big, thick towel covered in blood. It was my blood. I later discovered I was pregnant and had an abortion ten weeks later.'

Sally's dream preceded her experience of an actual termination; the dread is readily identified and dramatically depicted.

Other dreams of pregnancy

Meg suffered great personal tragedy. She learnt, through a dream, that all was not well with her baby:

'My first son was stillborn. I remember very clearly, a couple of months before his birth, dreaming of a baby boy lying on top of a table but I could never reach him. I knew without a doubt that he was my baby but I would never hold him.'

Maybe, like Tricia, Meg was reacting to subliminal messages from her body. At one level she knew that there were developmental problems which caused her child to be at risk.

June, a student I taught last year, wondered if her dreams were a response to an abnormality already present in the foetus, which later caused a cot death. Her dreams during this pregnancy were quite different from the ones she had while carrying her two healthy daughters:

'The dreams began very soon after the confirmation of my pregnancy and were quite frequent, once or twice a week. Usually it was the same dream: a tiny white coffin, masses of flowers and a beautiful baby boy lying inside the open coffin . . . It always appeared to be in slow motion and to last a long time, although I can't remember anything else happening.'

Understandably, these dreams were extremely upsetting and June tried not to dwell on them. However, she also had another dreadful recurring dream. She dreamt that she was going into labour screaming that something was wrong. Again it appeared to be in slow motion and the screaming would go on and on until the dream clouded and June knew she was dying. At that point she woke up.

Even during her waking hours June felt morbid, filled with a terrible sense of foreboding, although the pregnancy was fine and she was physically feeling great. When Mark was born, he was a perfectly normal healthy boy, but she still felt that things weren't right. The dream with the white coffin continued right up until a week before June found Mark dead at four and a half months. Since then she has never had the dream again.

Three years after the death of her son, June still feels his loss very deeply. They had been hoping for a boy but their delight soon turned to a tragedy which left them distraught. Now she spends a lot of time raising money for the cot death society and wonders if she could dare try for another baby. The possibility of another cot death haunts her, so she waits. Her dreams, she felt, were warning her, preparing her for the agonizing reality of burying her son in his tiny coffin. The peculiar slow-motion quality is mentioned by other women who have had precognitive dreams. Certainly, there was an unexplained form of communication going on, be it spiritually or organically based, to which June connected. Maybe one day, obstetricians and others concerned with attending pregnant women will routinely ask about dreams and use them to investigate and improve their ante- and post-natal care.

Most women dream a lot more than usual during pregnancy. The alteration in sleeping pattern caused by physical changes is one reason, and disturbance by foetal movements in the later stages another. More important, perhaps, are the psychological causes. Dreams during pregnancy show how women learn to handle and resolve fears about pregnancy and childbirth; and their recall helps us to adapt to the stress of childbirth itself. These dreams also help in the process of accommodating all the new knowledge and experiences we have at the time.

This final example, which was sent to the *Sundance Community Dream Journal*, an American publication devoted to dreams and dreamers, shows how reassuring some dreams can be. Patricia Gerhardstein of Ohio wrote:[6]

> I was in my third month of pregnancy and began to have some bleeding. I had previously had a miscarriage and so was very concerned and afraid that a miscarriage might happen again. I talked with my doctor and he suggested that I get lots of bed rest. I went to sleep and had this dream.
>
> I see a large, large strong tree, with noticeable trunk and roots. Coming off the tree has grown a branch into a nearby wall. The tree and the wall are inseparable. From the attached branch a white cup hangs by its handle in such a way that there is no possibility for the cup to come off – it is permanently attached to the tree. The scene was filled with white light.
>
> I awoke feeling peaceful and happy, knowing that I would not have a miscarriage. At the end of the nine-month pregnancy, I delivered a healthy baby girl.

Arifa, whom we met earlier, had other dreams before her delivery. In her sixth month she dreamt that she was watching TV at home when she felt her stomach tighten:

'I know it is the baby coming. It hurts and I start to tighten up and suddenly I see the midwife standing next to me and saying, "Calm. Think of the word calm." I begin to relax. In my dream I lie down and turn off the television. I don't seem to want to watch it any more. In the corner I can see her using the phone. I can hear myself counting my breaths slowly. The next one is not painful at all. My husband is there now as well, and he's counting too. I am awfully relaxed. I keep feeling like I am about to drift off to sleep . . . When I woke up I was still counting breaths!'

I talked to Arifa shortly after she had given birth to her bonny son. Her dreams had continued their helpful pattern even after his arrival and she laughingly told me of one dream which had important consequences. 'After my baby was born,' she disclosed, 'I had a terrible two days. Because of the pethidine I had been given and the discomfort from the stitches, I seemed to be absolutely dry. The baby would suck and sleep but I didn't feel I was giving him enough. That and the well-meaning advice of my mum and husband were fast driving me to change to the bottle. The third night I dreamt that I was walking in a beautiful garden. There was an elusive perfume in the air and I was drawn to it and wandered on. I came to a beautiful clearing where a bright fountain was spraying the air with that perfume. I walked to it and dipped my hand in and drank some of the liquid. It was sweet. I knew, though I don't know how I knew, that this was milk. I kept on drinking and got really bloated and then I woke up.'

The dream filled her with new resolve and that day, strengthened by her dream, she persevered through the difficulties and began successfully to breastfeed her son.

Notes

1. See Hyman S., 'Conception and Dream Material During Psychoanalysis', *Journal of Contemporary Psychotherapy*, Vol. 10, pages 136-44, 1979.
2. Medard Boss, 'I Dreamt Last Night'. Translated from the german by Stephen Conway, 1977, Gardner Press Inc. New York.
3. Caroline Winget and Frederick Kapp, 'The Relationship of the Manifest Contents of Dreams to the Duration of Childbirth in Prima Gravidae', *Psychosomatic Medicine*, Vol. 34, No. 2, pages 313-20, July 1972.
4. Boston Women's Health Book Collective (British eds. Angela Phillips and Jill Rakusen), *Our Bodies, Ourselves*, Penguin, 1979.
5. D. B. Cheek, 'The Significance of Dreams in Initiating Premature Labour', *American Journal of Clinical Hypnosis*, 12 (1), pages 5-15, 1969.
6. *Sundance Community Dream Journal*. Details available from Sundance, PO Box 395, Virginia Beach, VA 23451, USA.

5

Sex and Sexuality

I used to be shocked by the rampant explicitness of my sexual dreams. The steamy erotic encounters left me in no doubt as to the strength of my libido, even though in waking hours it remained well under control. Like many women, I was much influenced by the idea that 'nice girls' were not lustful, if indeed they admitted to being sexually aroused at all. Waking up from these dreams, satiated yet aroused, filled me with warm desire. What good fortune and what good feelings – but I was to discover it was not an experience shared by all.

Myra, for example, is very different. Indeed, there would have been no chapter to speak of if all women felt the same as this thirty-one-year-old. She has now been married for eleven years:

'I never dream of sex, though it's not surprising since we don't bother with it. Never have, though we did, just, consummate it months after the wedding day. That was our only, unpleasant, experience of it. Anyway, since sex should be for reproduction only and we don't want offspring, why bother?'

Most women are bothered. They have a lot to say on the subject. Women in the 1980s are much more willing to acknowledge sexuality in dreams than in earlier times. Wilse B. Webb reported in her research that only 6 out of 650 dreams which were recorded under laboratory conditions contained overt sexual acts.[1] The picture altered slightly in another study, where the figure rose to 76 out of 1000 dreams from 'home' dreamers, when petting, fantasies, overtures and kissing were included as criteria. This study revealed that sexual expression in dreams is both highly prevalent and wide-ranging, much more in line with Kinsey's findings.[2]

Kinsey's highly detailed exploration of female sexuality was nothing if not thorough. He and his colleagues collected masses of information from women which destroyed a number of myths about women's feelings about sex. For instance, 65 per cent of the women who took part in that research had dreamt about overt sexual activity and 20 per cent of those dreams led to orgasm. Indeed, more than 70 per cent of women of all ages have sexual dreams at some point, with or without orgasm. Not so very long ago, women who had dreams about orgasm were described as 'neurotic', while those who did not were regarded as normal, well-adjusted women!

Still, the taboos surrounding women's sexuality persist and for many people, including women, there is a denial of that basic drive. Sameera's story, linked to her dreams, is not unusual, though the religious and cultural influences are particular to her background. How many of us dream about rape because that is the only way we can allow ourselves to engage in sexual activity?

Coming from a different culture, Sameera's parents, when confronted with the sharp contrasts between East and West, felt that the only way to ensure that their children were reared 'properly' was to be very strict. They built thicker walls to protect their children from evil influences. Far from restricting Sameera, this attitude made her, when she was very young, more determined to 'glimpse over the wall', as she put it. She recalled being severely reproached for having drawn a nude man and woman when she was eight years old, and a little later she 'was unfortunately caught' while trying to become more aware of her body.

Sameera continued in her attempts to make sense of her upbringing: 'Pressure was placed on us girls not to notice men around us . . . I was racked with guilty feelings and thought I was the 'dirtiest' girl around. However, I secretly continued to 'satisfy' my curiosity, wondering, as the years passed, what all the fuss was about. Thankfully, time and maturity have helped to dissipate those negative feelings but I shall never forget the childhood experiences – or, rather, my subconscious won't let me forget them. My dreams remind me.

'My dreams of this sort usually involve me being literally raped. I was brought up to be coy around men; even to look up into their faces was regarded as being extremely forward. Therefore, in my dreams, in order to free myself from the blame of promiscuity, the element of rape comes into play. The act itself is sometimes quite explicit, often moving me to orgasm. Always, because it is a rape situation, intercourse takes place with our clothes on.'

Sameera obviously knows herself and the influences that operate on her. She understands where the guilt stems from and appreciates that her dreams about rape reflect not a desire to be dominated by men but the values that deny women the right to open, direct sexual expression. Her dreams provide an outlet for her sexual needs without breaking any religious rules. Her situation is by no means unusual. Jews, Protestants, Catholics, Rastafarians: all have taboos about sex, particularly about women and sex. The issue, though, is more likely, deep down, to be about women and power, or how to prevent women from knowing and using their own power. If we cannot look men in the eye, how can we deal with them as equals? Similarly, if we cannot accept our sexuality, how can we meet men without feeling in some way inferior? Remember that men are not conditioned to deny their sexuality; our dreams tell us not to deny our own.

Even when our dreams are not pleasurable, they may be useful indicators of sexual attitudes. Let us consider dreams at a time when our bodies are becoming sexually mature.

Amorous adolescence

Early dreams of sexual encounters are often quite direct. A group of sixteen-year-old girls training to be nursery nurses told me of their dreams. Many were clearly sexually exciting but not completely fulfilling, as in Lily's case:

'My dreams about sex usually start off with someone I know well or vaguely. First there is kissing and then it moves to the bedroom and, once in bed, my dream blanks out to the next morning. I never know what happens.'

Her limited sexual experience prevents a depiction of the 'in bed' details but the dream tells us she does find her knowledge so far to be pleasant and she welcomes further sexual expression, but not just yet.

There is no specific figure in Lily's dream; she says the undefined 'other' could be well known to her or fairly anonymous. She does not have a steady boyfriend nor is there any one person she is especially attracted to; rather, there is a generalized feeling of sexual arousal.

Her dream allows the possibility of kissing and even entering the bedroom, but lovemaking, which traditionally happens behind the closed doors of the bedroom, is blanked out. It is censored as she sleeps.

Tracey's dream is more obviously an example of wish-fulfilment:

'Occasionally I dream that I will meet a gorgeous boy and have sex with him and will go out with him for a long time.'

For Tracey, having sex with an attractive boy does not require long-term commitment; though, if she were to go out with the boy for a 'long time', that would be a bonus. She, like many other girls, is subject to strong media pressure which says that a girl should have a 'gorgeous' boyfriend and have sex with him. According to TV, soap operas, romantic comic strips and the pulp media, everyone is 'doing it' or about to. So adolescents fall victim to the view of sex as just another consumer item. Selling using sex works! This 'sex' has nothing whatsoever to do with pure sexual enjoyment or deeply passionate sexual love; it's a consumer hype. The media lobby which pushes early sexual expression can be as damaging as the opposite lobby which regards it as dirty and evil. The dreams of adolescents reflect the conflict.

Dawn's pre-sex dream shows the importance of the peer group at this age:

'I dreamt that a girlfriend and I were in Spain and I was in bed with my boyfriend making love – the first time I've dreamt of the sex act. Two friends of ours were also in the same room in the next bed . . .'

Early exploration of sexuality quite often takes place when others, apart from the immediate partner, are present. Usually the other person is a good friend who will keep the confidences and, in a way, acts as a security against too rapid progression. If you decide to stop, it is easier if there is an ally to hand. Friends spend a great deal of time together at this age, and then along comes a 'fit' boy to create a diversion. Of course, it is much better if two boys happen to come along at the same time since it makes the continuation of both friendships much more manageable and they can go around in a foursome. Should petting begin, it is much safer when it takes place within earshot, if not within sight, of each other, as in Dawn's dream. It is easier for girls to keep their power if they have another girl to act as a back-up.

I was scared to death of what my parents would say about my having a boyfriend. It was not done in my street. And I don't think it was just because we were Catholics; 'Proddies' I knew who went to Church of England or Methodist churches likewise would have been in terrible trouble if they were found out. So we never took boys home but hung about under the lamp-post just around the corner so that, if we were called in, we couldn't actually be seen. It was all so innocent: standing on the corner, talking, giggling, looking at each other with veiled longing. The thing was, we didn't know what we were longing for! Sometimes, rarely, I would go to the pictures with a boy, but always with my friend Janet in tow. To all intents and purposes, Janet and I were going together, thus avoiding any risk of parental wrath, and we would meet the lads inside; or, if it was special, outside and then they would pay. But mum and dad were kept out of it all.

Many girls today go through the same processes of keeping parents away from their early sexuality either through fear or because there is a need for privacy and separation. Adolescence is all about separating and becoming independent. Sally's dream deals with this by conveniently removing her parents from the dream scene:

'When I was fifteen and thought I was really in love, I would dream of going to his house, and when his mum and dad went out, we would go upstairs and everything would be like on television.'

Daytime opportunities, such as parents going out, are incorporated into the dream structure, just as a friend being present was included in Dawn's dream. The dream is vague but she is left feeling good because it turned out 'just like on television'. Vicky's dream also allows her safely to express her sexual desire:

'I dream about my boyfriend and me, then when I realize what I am doing I get up and put the light on to see if he is really there. My mum and dad say I talk about him in my sleep but I just deny it.'

Vicky's fifteen years have not yet given her the confidence or inclination to talk in detail about the dream, but her blushes and embarrassed body language speak volumes. Vicky's denial in the last sentence reveals her shyness about admitting strong attraction towards her boyfriend, even though the intensity of the dreams wakens her. There is a sense of shock when she becomes aware of what she is doing.

Sexual anticipation is usually part and parcel of the idealized romantic dreams of adolescents and older women alike. Predictably there are many examples of dreams about males who are attractive according to the fashions of the time, but Lorna's dream lover took her by surprise:

'I dreamt I lost my virginity to Elvis Presley and he was going to marry me and we would never be apart. The strange thing is I don't like Elvis Presley.'

In her dream Lorna acts according to the romantic script so often given to girls: you meet your ideal man, here in the guise of Elvis Presley; he sweeps you off your feet; you give your all, i.e. your virginity; and he marries you and stays with you ever after! A Pills and Doom dream! But Elvis is not Lorna's ideal man. He may be her mother's, though, because she goes on to say that her mother really likes him. Does Lorna try to please her mother and accept imposed tastes rather than making up her own mind? The dream may be saying that, if she follows the happily-ever-after script, she will get the script right but with the wrong person.

Similarly, Mo finds herself making love with someone she does not like:

'I once dreamt that I was having sex with a boy whom I have only seen two or three times but not spoken to. I don't even think that he is nice.'

This is a common phenomenon. Many of us discover that we are romantically or sexually involved in dreams with men we would not touch in waking life. These are the opposite of the romantic idealized variety. Such unpleasant sexual liaisons start in adolescence, usually because of the message given to women that 'it-is-better-to-have-any-man-rather-than-to-have-no-one-at-all'. It is as if we are unworthy as beings in our own right, and are defined through our relationships with men.

Jan had her first taste of sexual arousal, at least the first that she remembers, in a dream. Initially she was puzzled about its origins:

'I only once remember dreaming about sex and that was when I was a teenager. I suddenly became aware that I was feeling really nice . . . I was searching to find why and then was conscious that a man was making love to me. I woke up startled and realized that I must have been aroused as I was excited.'

Maybe Jan was so excited that she had an orgasm. Kinsey discovered that 5 per cent of women experience nocturnal dreams to orgasm before they experience waking orgasm. Jan had no waking experience of sexual fulfilment to which she could compare it, but she knew she was feeling 'really nice'.

For Alison there was no such sensuous enjoyment. She was exhausted with all the effort involved:

'When I was at school we had a human biology lesson. That night I dreamt I went to bed with three lads and the next day I kept having babies. I just kept having them. As soon as I had one, another would come, and it carried on for ages. It seemed like the same baby over and over again.'

Hers was a lesson well heeded for her dream very firmly repeats that going to bed with lads results in babies. There are no 'maybe' clauses in this, so Alison gives birth again and again, just in case there were any doubts. I wonder if the emphasis in the lesson had been a bit too much on the 'plumbing' of sex at the expense of emotion?

Preludes to passion

Dreams often act as confidence boosters in all sorts of ways, not only in terms of sexuality. They allow us to experiment with activities we have not previously considered consciously.

'Usually in dreams I cannot make out the man's face, but it all seems much better than in real life. Sometimes I try to remember the little details which made it so good to put them into practice next time, but it never seems to work out the same, more's the pity.'

Aimée's wistful yearnings, characteristic of the idealizations referred to earlier, are not met in waking life, for, as she continues, in dreams:

'I get swept off my feet by a man and it ends up in a situation, not usually in bed. Exotic things I wouldn't normally do, as I would be too embarrassed, but perhaps if I tried it would be better – but then dreams are supposed to be better than real life, aren't they? This is the whole thing about dreaming, I think, yearning for things we don't get out of life.'

There is rarely a display of female power in these dreams, as Aimée reveals:

'Most of them are romantic set-pieces with loads of kissing and touching. I rarely dream about the actual act of intercourse . . . I am usually in historical dress, mostly eighteenth century – I'm always in corsets anyway. There are no variations, just straightforward sex. I always enjoy the dream and wake up feeling horny.'

Some women's dreams do go part way to fulfilling needs unmet in waking life. However, Aimée could take responsibility for herself, by using her abilities to narrow the gap between her two worlds.

Orgasmic outlets

Dreams bring feelings of sexual arousal and satiation, and feelings of sexual well-being. These may be genitally focused or be experienced in a more diffuse way. The point is dreams can provide sexual outlets at any age. In *Sexual Behaviour in the Human Female* Kinsey notes that women are frequently woken by muscular spasms akin to those of orgasm and these are accompanied by increases in vaginal secretions. 'There can be no question', he writes, 'that a female's responses in sleep are typical of those she makes when she is awake.'

Marigold, smitten by her boyfriend Larry, dreams of him constantly:

'He is in his early twenties, like me, and I've been seeing him for about five months. He has been in, early all my dreams for the last two months. Quite often we are making love, although we haven't yet in real life.'

In her dreams she can respond to her inner drives even though she has not done so in waking life. However, it may not be long before she does so because her repetitive dreams are insistent and, as she says herself, 'We haven't made love *yet*', indicating that there may be changes ahead.

Orgasmic dreams need not be highly graphic. For Carol, the details are vague but the feelings are so intense that she frequently wakes up in the middle of a wonderful orgasm. She feels relaxed about her own sexuality and is not affronted by dream images that might frighten other women. For instance:

'Two or three times my dreams have been lesbian in nature, though I am not inclined that way in waking life. Here again, the feelings are intense though the details are vague. These dreams intrigue rather than disturb me.'

Freya also wakes sometimes in mid-orgasm:

'Usually I am worshipped by some hazy hunk that I fancy but I cannot identify him. He makes me feel delicious, mainly because he is such a catch, but also because he spares no effort in giving me pleasure. I wake up mid-orgasm.'

Whatever her sexual activity in real life is like, Freya can gain sensuous satisfaction through her dreams. There does not seem to be any set pattern; the dreams occur with strangers or with familiar partners, but orgasm results. The high state of arousal on waking may mean that the sleeping partner gets an unexpected awakening, though not such a rude awakening as happened in Dee's dream. She told me:

'I dream about sex infrequently . . . five years ago was the last one. I opened a wardrobe door and found a man I knew as an acquaintance in there. In real life I wasn't aware I fancied him at all. Anyhow, I grabbed his penis, then leapt on him. It was very nice.'

For Julia, her 'live' partner figures in her dreams:

'Apart from a couple of times, it is always me having sex with my husband and the experience is absolutely wonderful. In fact I'm sure my orgasms must be for real as they are so strong in my dream, and sometimes I have woken up and ravished Colin.'

Some dreams of sex are depicted more symbolically. Yvette, the owner of a London art gallery, offers a note of caution:

'I once went to a Freudian analyst. He decided that my disaster-filled, travelling-to-important events and always-being-late dreams were a result of an inability to orgasm. You know, never being able to get 'there', never achieving the 'aim'. However, now I can orgasm my little socks off and I still have those dreams! So I searched for another meaning and have decided that, at least partially, these dreams represent an innate fear of failure.'

Good for Yvette! If the interpretation by another person does not resonate, does not feel right, then continue to work on the dream meaning yourself. It's much better to learn to value yourself and build up your own skills in self-awareness than to depend completely on another to tell you what your dreams mean. Obviously, as a therapist who uses dreams with clients, I feel others can act as a guide, but healthy scepticism is valuable.

Thelma has more sexual pleasure in dreams than in waking life:

'I do not know if I am frigid, but I have never enjoyed sex. Not with my boyfriends, nor with my husband. I have dreamt about sex a few times though, and really enjoyed it very much. I have come to the conclusion that such things can only happen in dreams. Lovemaking in my dreams is out of this world and the sensation is totally unknown to me in real life.'

It is 'out of this world' because it is outside her waking experience. Should Thelma decide to make an effort to tell her partner what pleases her, should she try out that which pleases her in her dreams, then she may find that such wondrous sensations are available to her even when she is awake!

Dreams of incest

Incestuous sexual relationships occurred in 3 per cent of the dreams reported in my study. Typically, the women who wrote about such dreams gave minimal details, thus highlighting the taboo which surrounds the subject. As the rate of incest is so high, it is surprising that more women did not recall dreams of this nature. However, I expect that many of the dreams related in Chapter 10, on violence, are disguised expressions of childhood assault.

The fear of incest is recounted by Eloise and others:

'Occasionally, I have terrifying dreams about sex with 'taboo' people – parents and children.'

'Once or twice I have dreamt about making love to a woman, including my mother and my sister.'

Dreams of incest with a father were likewise reported with minimal detail, as you can see:

'I once dreamt of having sex with my father. We were on a cloud.'

'I dream of an incestuous incident with my father.'

Shelley reports her dreams in a little more detail and hints that they reveal a hidden fear of her father:

'I have recurring dreams about my father showing interest in me sexually but only in the context that he is my father and that he knows me very intimately – too intimately perhaps . . . I also have dreams that my sister and I are close to each other sexually and we are on intimate terms with each other. I am in bed with her and another girl, my best friend.'

The sense of horror we feel at having a sexual dream involving a close relative is captured by Abbie, a twenty-year-old office worker from Shropshire. She told me that she was devastated and bewildered by a recent dream:

'In the dream I was at my parents' house and it was night-time. The moon was full. It was hot yet snow lay on the ground, and indeed it was still snowing. My ex-boyfriend was walking towards me and I felt really happy. We embraced and then made love. The horrific part was, suddenly the man in my arms was not my ex-boyfriend but my father!'

When she woke, Abbie felt sick with shame, guilt and 'everything else'. She could not understand what the dream meant but felt it had something to do with relationships within the family and her own, so far unsuccessful, search for 'Mr Right'.

Abbie told me a lot about herself. She is a twin and comes from a large family. Her mother died tragically when her twin daughters were just three years old. As Abbie grew up, she came to resemble her mother more and more closely; they were like 'peas in a pod', her Aunt Mimi used to say. Somehow, around eleven or twelve, just after she had her first period, Abbie's relationship with her father began to go wrong; not for any specific reason, it went downhill, leaving the developing girl unsure and insecure. Her stepmother was very kind to all the family but that was not enough to persuade Abbie to stay at home longer than she had to. At eighteen she went to live on her own.

Her voice quietened as she continued, 'Since then I've had six or seven relationships with men who have always been much older than I. Only one of them lasted more than six months – he was, in fact, the ex-boyfriend in the dream. He is thirty-five years old, married with two children of his own, and he is one of my bosses at work. The affair ended because I told him I could no longer take it when he'd say that he'd phone me and then didn't. Now, I'm going out with a thirty-four-year-old who is divorced with an eight-year-old daughter.'

She cares very much for Tom, but is terrified lest this relationship also fails. At the moment she feels unable to say what 'love' is, even though she is so desperately seeking it. In the past she has had periods of deep sadness because of her family or her love life and yet, she says plaintively, 'All I ever wanted was to find 'Mr Right' and be happy.'

Abbie's dream verifies that her feelings towards men are closely tied up with her feelings towards her father. No great surprise in that: there is much evidence to show that we learn to relate to males through our fathers or males who hold a significant place in our childhood years. But for Abbie that process of development was blocked. Instead of growing up secure in her father's love, and being accepted as a sexually maturing young woman and given confidence in her relationship with the first man in her life, something went amiss. At the very time when she needed a great deal of support, when she was eleven or twelve and beginning to develop adult female characteristics, he withdrew from her. Why? Was she too much like her mother? Did her nearness make him too uncomfortable? Was it all too much for him?

Whatever his reasons, the consequence for Abbie is that she seeks to 'recapture' her father in other relationships. The older men who are married or divorced, or at least 'wifeless' as her father was, attract her. The relationships, however, are unsatisfactory. In the dream the ultimate horror occurs: her dream lover becomes her father, and she recoils. She cannot bear the guilt and the shame. She has not had the opportunity to grow through those stages of love and of separation from the parent of the opposite sex which are part and parcel of the maturing process. With care, support and understanding she should be able to resolve these difficult issues and accept herself as an independent person who can make a satisfying relationship with another independent person rather than a father substitute.

One last note on Abbie: there may have been an incestuous incident in childhood which has been sufficiently blocked in the conscious mind to prevent her recalling it. Sometimes, such repressed material surfaces in dreams and can indicate the need to explore and express the emotions which have been smouldering away.

Not all women are horrified by incestuous dreams. In rare instances they are reported as being pleasant, Hilda's being one:

'With both my brothers at the same time – pleasant and very erotic.'

Kris is puzzled by her dream:

'My husband is drunk and incapable but wishes to make love to me. A pushy unknown woman is encouraging him to go ahead, but I firmly refuse "until he is sober". We are in a bedroom and our teenage son is asleep on another bed, and I know I must have intercourse with both of them eventually. I feel slightly nonplussed by this, but realize it is something which must be done. Here the dream ends.'

Does it reveal her recognition of the son's growing sexual maturity? How much is it about a recognition of the 'pushy' side of herself in contrast with the sensible, abstemious, 'wait until you are sober' nature? Maybe the sleeping, immature side of her husband is symbolized in the son, whose sleep makes him oblivious to what is going on around him. At present Kris is confused or 'nonplussed' about her sexuality and needs help in clarifying exactly what must be done.

Guilt, glorious guilt

Guilt is anything but glorious. It troubles us even while we sleep. Hester, for instance, suffers intensely if she even considers being unfaithful to her husband; and she is fearful it might happen in dreams:

'I don't dream much about sex because I have a very jealous and possessive husband, so I try not to betray him even in my dreams, which is annoying sometimes . . . When I do, it usually turns out to be him; the dream lets me see through the way it disguises him. If I do dream about sex, it's usually a letdown. You can't dream about having an orgasm, I think, if you're a woman.'

Clearly, Hester has not talked to women who have experienced the sorts of dreams described earlier in this chapter. Her dreams tell us that she can recognize her own sexuality but finds it hard to accept sexuality in any male apart from her husband. She becomes the 'martyr' sacrificing herself rather than expressing herself. She can only admit to her own sexual feelings if they occur in relation to her sanctioned marriage partner. Accepting that we might feel aroused by a dream lover, or a passing stranger for that matter, does not mean that we have to turn the dream into reality; we don't have to go out and seduce or be seduced. Instead, we can use the dream to explore issues. Does Hester feel bored with her present sexual relationship? Would she prefer Mr Anonymous but won't admit it, and so in her dreams changes 'his' face to that of her husband? When her control is successful, 'the feeling is usually lost', she says, which indicates that there is something amiss. Maybe it would not be too awful if Hester allowed herself some freedom, for, like fantasy, dreams can provide an outlet for constrained emotions.

Joanne is open in admitting that her sexual dreams cause her embarrassment. Her superego, her censorious blue pencil is in control:

'I have vague memories of these dreams. I feel guilty and embarrassed about them and want to forget them, so I make no attempt to keep them in my memory.'

It is the same for Sandra, whose all-pervading sense of guilt stops her dreaming about anything to do with sex. As soon as she is about to make love to someone in her dreams, she is stopped. She is denied satisfaction. Anna, on the other hand, does not have the same facility to switch off but is left to squirm guiltily:

'. . . This man/boy had some clothes on. We were screwing but there was no foreplay. As we were screwing I heard someone walking past the open door and it was my boyfriend. I could feel pleasure but at the same time intense shame and guilt, as well as horror at what I had done. I wanted to stop immediately yet at the same time I was turned on and liked the person. The guilt stops the enjoyment.'

The key is probably in the last sentence. I wonder why Anna feels guilty. Is it because she has mixed feelings about sex? Is she not enjoying sex because it is all to quick for her – 'no foreplay'? And then there is the man/boy image. Does this reveal views about her boyfriend?

There are many opposites in this dream: man/boy, clothed/unclothed, pleasure/guilt, an open door/an act which should be private, wanting to stop but wanting to continue. Anna is full of conflicts which interfere with the full enjoyment of her sexuality. If she heeds the dream, she will examine these conflicts and deal with them so that she can stop feeling guilty and enjoy sex.

Being 'caught' gives Bronwyn problems too:

'Most of my dreams seem to revolve around guilt; being caught in bed with someone by my mother . . . I think these stem from a rather severe upbringing.'

Bronwyn feels she will be judged and condemned for sexual behaviour by her disapproving mother. We have examined elsewhere women's driving need for approval and the difficulties of escaping from this need. Bronwyn cannot accept her own sexual feelings because she is still dogged by her mother's message that sex is somehow not acceptable. Her strict childhood enchains her and her dreams highlight her fears.

Guilty feelings about sex and sexual partners in dreams occur at any age. Myrtle, a forty-two-year-old mother of three, recalled that she had dreams in which she:

'. . . used to make love to strange men but my husband was always there in the background and I generally felt guilty about deceiving him. I have never done so in real life. Nor am I aware of any lesbian tendencies, though I have had one or two lesbian-type dreams which made me feel bad afterwards.'

So Myrtle knows from her dream that part of her would find the idea of another lover, male or female, quite erotic, though she is shocked when considering it on waking. Again, just because you dream or fantasize about something does not mean that you have to do anything practical to make it a reality. Enjoy the eroticism.

Some women's dreams run exactly contrary to the guilty ones already described. Instead of feeling bad about what is happening, the chance of being 'found out' adds to the excitement, or, as in Pru's case, the partner does not mind anyway:

'I had a dream where I went away for a weekend and spent a lot of time sleeping with people of both sexes – a sort of communal love-in. Then I went back and told my husband all about it.'

In this instance, both partners enjoyed the dream!

Sadistic sex

Masochistic or sadistic sexual dreams are rarely reported by women, though, as you will see in Chapter 8, anxiety dreams about being chased by men who inflict pain are common. In Vivien's dreams she is caught and brutalized by a gang of tramps, whereas Josie is overpowered by a loathsome thug. Does this mean that women want to be abused, debased and made the weaker vessel?

It does not. Such rape dreams are a parody of normal sexual relations. They reveal our fears about male violence and our resentments about conventional male-female relationships.

Gina, a girl I taught on an evening course, was a bright-eyed, shiny-haired seventeen-year-old. By chance, she discovered that I was working on this book and stayed behind after one of the classes. 'I'd like to talk to you about these awful dreams I have. I feel a bit embarrassed really and don't know where to start.' Putting aside the desire to get home and relax after a lousy day, I responded to an obvious appeal for help and suggested we go to a local pub. In a quiet corner, she told me of her recurring dream:

'I dream that I am stripped naked, tied to a big, wooden plank and whipped. A few men come one after another and have intercourse with me. Then I see myself in a block of ice to preserve me. I wake up crying.'

She was obviously distressed, and when I gently asked her what she thought the dream was about she initially said she did not know. Then when I enquired whether she had ever been abused, her face grew ashen. 'I try not to think about it. Oh God, I thought I'd forgotten about it.'

One lunchtime when Gina was twelve years old, a van stopped as she was returning to school. She thought the two men wanted directions but instead they bundled her into the back of the van. What followed were several hours of sadistic torture as they repeatedly beat and raped her. They had wooden shelves and planks in the back of the vehicle and for most of the terrifying ordeal she was tied down. When they eventually dumped her, bleeding and broken-boned, she staggered back to her school. She remembers little about the ambulance being called, the stay in hospital, or the months that followed, which culminated in a nightmarish court case and the conviction of her attackers.

Her recurring dream sought to re-run the event, whether to find a different ending or to give some meaning to the horror is not clear. But what was certain was that Gina had somehow to find a way of working through the trauma. She told me that her parents had not wanted to talk about it and people seemed to shun her, so not only did she suffer the dreadful attack but subsequently felt guilty because people avoided her. Now she had a caring, loving boyfriend and was at the start of what seemed an important relationship. His supportive sensitivity had enabled her to tell him the basic story but she wanted to talk in more depth. Over the next few weeks we met regularly and Gina gradually exorcized the pain and anger that was evident in her dreams. Now, three years later, she is still going out with Ken and they are getting engaged at Christmas. The dreams have stopped; she is no longer frozen 'to preserve her'. Facing the terror has set her free.

Belinda, a high-flying reporter in her mid-twenties, had a relationship with Bill, an actor, who featured in the following dream:

'He wanted me to stay. I remember looking in his mirror, then I was lying in the bed. But suddenly it was as if he were attacking me from two directions – up my anus with his prick and his tongue down my throat – thin like a snake. I was scared and ran away. I spat out some black stuff . . .'

When I talked to her at greater length, I realized that Belinda was indeed under attack; attack from an unsatisfactory relationship with a married man who was using her and causing her intense internal conflict. She was going through a crisis which was forcing her to reassess her life. For years the choices she had made, while good in career terms, had been destroying her more caring, creative side. She hated the hard, sometimes brutal, person she had become and she was desperately trying to sort herself out. At times she felt as if she was cracking wide apart; she feared for her sanity.

She spoke of another dream, a recurring one, in which she was 'climbing a wall with a man – horizontally'. This dream felt very spiritual, she said; and she thought it might be linked to the deep spiritual relationship she had with her married lover, who was having a 'rest' from her. Perhaps a simpler, more prosaic interpretation would have been more accurate: i.e. that the relationship was driving her 'up the wall' – and she was lying down and taking it.

Nancy also experiences violence in her dreams:

'This man I really like takes me to a hotel room and we shower together and have a row and a fight. He hits me and becomes

96

overpowering. We then make love.'

Nancy could ask herself if she wants to be treated violently. Pain might be a familar bad feeling which, in some perverse way, is more comfortable than allowing herself to experience new emotions. She may need the row, the fight and the force in order to let herself go. Perhaps she feels guilty if she willingly enters into sex – this way, she always has the excuse that she didn't want to.

Women who have been raped in real life often have nightmares about the attack for a long time afterwards. For instance, it was reported in the newspapers that Nicola, who was raped at knifepoint after her parents had been murdered as they slept, subsequently had agonizing dreams. The nightmares were so severe that for over a year she was unable to sleep in a room alone. Her traumatized mind repeated the ordeal in order to find a way of exorcizing it. Until she finds some way of getting over the horror of those terrifying hours, her dreams will continue to reflect her pain.

Lesbian lovers

Dreams about sexual encounters with other women are not at all uncommon, nor are they confined solely to lesbians or bisexuals. Some 10 per cent of women who took part in my survey had experienced erotic dreams in which they were with another woman, though heterosexual women often found them quite difficult to discuss. They were uncomfortable admitting that they felt sexually aroused by another woman when in waking life they were aware of sexual attraction only to men.

Dreams reveal that we can appreciate sexuality in many more ways than are prescribed by majority social norms. Why shouldn't we appreciate the sexuality of someone of the same gender? After all, we respond to her warmth, humour, intelligence and caring in other ways? If we do turn to another woman and say, 'You are really sexy' or 'You have lovely hair', people look askance. It is still taboo to be open about a whole range of sexual feelings whether they are directed towards the same or the opposite sex.

Lesbians continue to be regarded as unacceptable by the majority, as do most other minority sexual groups, and their struggles may surface in dreams, as in Honor's case:

'In my dream there was an overall feeling of love and warmth at first. Elizabeth, my lover, was there and, although I wasn't touching her, I felt that she was caressing me and that I was close to her. Everything around her was red and warm. But suddenly a huge crowd of people came between us, all very active and noisy: work colleagues, my daughter and her two friends, and my husband. All were unaware of me. Suddenly, I was naked, running, breathless and frightened; in the distance was a car I needed to get to. However hard I ran, I couldn't get any nearer and I had a terrific sense of panic. I could still see Elizabeth but now, however hard I tried to attract her attention, she only looked at everyone else . . . I was screaming her name. Then my husband was bending over me telling me he loved me and beginning to make love to me. I felt a great weight bearing down on me, everything was dark and hot. I could hear what he was saying but I could only think of her. As his body bent over me, it was her hands, her kisses and her eyes I saw. I felt I had lost her and was mourning for all the other loves I've hidden and lost.'

Such a graphic dream tells its own story. Honor, married to a kind, considerate man for twenty years, left home last year to live with a woman. At forty-four, she felt she had to acknowledge the lesbianism which she had fought for years. Her son of nineteen and daughter of twenty found it difficult to accept that their 'straight' teacher mother could possibly want to do anything as outrageous as love another woman. The dream reveals the obstacles she faced and her desperation and powerlessness. She grieves for the time she has lost and the loves that went unspoken.

Judith, a committed lesbian, has sexual dreams which are wholly about women, or groups of women, in a Rubensian landscape. This dream focuses on sensuality:

'I dream repeatedly about an actual situation. The most satisfying sexual experience I have known is recreated out of context. T. makes love to me; sometimes I wake up then, but on other occasions I then make love to her. I am acutely aware of the sensation of touching her skin. Quite often I wake up feeling very aroused and masturbate.'

The sensuous quality of the dream does not rely on genital contact but on the exquisite experience of touching her lover's skin. Rose, however, wants genital contact, and in her very erotic dreams about her friend Denise she finds that Denise 'has conveniently grown a penis'.

Louise gained a lot of insight into her own sexuality when she spent time working on her dreams. Parts were easily understood but others left her puzzled:

'The sexual dreams I do have are bizarre; being made love to by a young, punk girl; or by female, old school friends, masturbating in front of people; and so on. Generally in these sexual dreams I feel uncomfortable, embarrassed and, almost, that I don't have the right to pleasure. I am noticeably passive.'

Louise knew there were other more confrontational dreams which she chose to forget: like so many women she is grappling with guilt at being active and guilt at being happy.

Dreading the possibility of her early twenties' dreams becoming reality, Lucy, now an advertising rep for a large London agency, fought to suppress it:

'I was kissing a close female friend and we were telling each other that it was all right. At the time it disturbed me very much and I broke off our friendship, although now I have accepted the fact of lesbianism.'

Deep down, Lucy knew that the dream had particular importance for her, though at the time she was unwilling or unable to deal with it. Many women have had similar erotic dreams about female friends but are not moved to end their relationships, instead they are accepting that they are subconsciously acknowledging those friends' attractiveness. No need for panic. Lucy did panic, because she was afraid of the implications of a dream which explored her deepest sexual feelings. It had a profound effect on her. Although she denied it then, she found out later that she had been trying to repress her true sexual orientation.

Transsexuality

The Finnish Broadcasting Company's social affairs programmer decided to run an experiment in 1985 to counteract the gloom of winter. Seija Wallius-Kokkonen devoted one of her ninety-minute late-night programmes to eroticism in dreams. The response was staggering, but one dream which particularly stuck in her mind was told to her by a man who had had a sex-change operation to become a woman, and who experienced female orgasms in her dreams. This reminded me of Karen, who used to be known as Warren.

Karen came to see me prior to having a sex-change operation. She had been living as a woman for two years and enjoyed the changes that hormone treatment had brought about. Though still attending speech therapy sessions to enable her to use a less husky voice, and continuing to have regular treatment to remove facial hair built up over years of daily shaving, she physically resembled a woman. She said that she at last felt she was in her own body; her dreams were near to coming true.

Growing up in a remote part of India had left Karen very mixed up. There was no contact with other boys or girls, and it was not until attending boarding school at ten that she realized she was not like the others.

'The all-boys school was awful. Boys used to make fun of me and I remember one day we went out to do games with some of the older boys. Paul, one of the fifth formers, was walking behind me and he started sniggering. "You know, Warren," he said, "you've got a lovely bum for a boy. Are you sure you are a boy? You look like a girl to me." I was thoroughly confused. One part of me was really pleased but the other was terrified. I just ran away in terror and cried.'

Later, Warren/Karen had dreams of being dressed in women's clothes: at first in the uniform of a girl's school in the nearby town, then from late teens in fashionable women's clothes. In the dreams he was always a woman.

Over the last five years Karen's dreams have become more explicit. She dreams of penetration during intercourse, though so far her own experience has been as the one who penetrated. As a man, married for two agonizing years, the only way in which Warren could achieve an erection and make love was to imagine that he was taking the female heterosexual role. The first time he had an erection as a child, he hated it and was almost sick. 'I was just born in the wrong body,' Karen says, 'and now I'm trying to get into the real one.'

Those nocturnal wish fulfillment dreams deny the waking reality. Karen will never be able to menstruate nor bear children, but she will have a body that closely resembles that of a woman rather than the male body which she abhors.

Beware

Architect Daisy had dreams which, though amusing, contained a warning for her:

'The funniest one was like a mixture of *The Kamasutra, The Sensuous Woman* and a company's regular Monday morning staff meeting, but the participants were dressed in oriental style and ready for real orgies. Even this dream carried a message for me. The end was a flop as far as I was concerned, as I noticed that I could not join in their fun because the faces of the people reminded me of other people whom I could not touch.'

The two book titles very clearly set the sexual tone of the dream. However, Daisy withdraws because she is not enamoured of the other players in her dream drama. This is in contrast to other dreams we have discussed where women are partnered by people they find repulsive. Daisy's dream may have been a warning to her but it also tells of her personal strength in asserting her own choices.

Some dreams which carry a warning about sex may not be immediately understood by the dreamer, as in the last example Rebecca mentions. The other examples give us a clue to the nature of her personality for they indicate unfulfilled desires and failure:

'I am prone to "real life" infatuations with men who don't fancy me at all, and in dreams I am equally humiliated. When I do score I tend to wake up just before orgasm. I also dream of masturbating and usually I am seen. Recently, I dreamt that my real-life, semi-impotent boyfriend had a good erection but turned away from me to commence vigorously fucking a piece of white card with a hole in it.'

Her boyfriend, she understands, would prefer a clean, untouched, unemotional piece of inanimate card to herself, for she has real feelings and desires of her own. If he has intercourse with a piece of card specially designed for the purpose, then he has no need to consider satisfying anyone else but himself and he can remain distant from his 'lover'.

Rebecca's dream warns her to beware of this man who cannot be fully reciprocal in his relationship with her for he does not want what she has to offer.

Famous and infamous

Myth hs it that women dream about royalty or media heroes all the time. Closer to the truth is that approximately 6 per cent of women dream about the famous or infamous, and some such examples are very surprising, as Cleo describes:

'I was told by a woman that I had to seduce Hitler and then kill him. I had seduced him and was sitting on him; he was also sitting upright. He had just entered me when a woman walked behind him and handed me a pair of scissors. I stabbed him in his back. I was thinking, what an awful thing to do at a time like this. I was actually enjoying the feeling of him inside me, but I told myself he was a bad, evil man who deserved to die, and I shouldn't be enjoying it.'

Cleo has a conflict on her hands: there is someone hateful with whom she is intimately involved whom she needs to destroy, but part of her enjoys and desires the involvement. There is something going on in the background, behind his back, as shown in the scissors being handed to Cleo behind 'Hitler's' back, and she stabs him 'in the back'. She has the power to radically change things if she so wishes. That another woman hands her the death implement probably means that the dream symbolism relates to her femaleness. Cleo's strength as a woman is doubled by this accomplice; she needs additional female power if she is to accomplish her task. This does not necessarily mean another female to help her, but that there is a stronger, more determined, possibly more ruthless part of herself which is available to her should she acknowledge it. The dream tells her she can activate that power.

This dream may reflect a troublesome relationship Cleo is involved in which she recognizes as being very bad. Her dreaming mind uses an ultimate image of evil in 'Hitler'. She must be careful, though, because she finds it hard to resist the sexual pleasure despite her knowledge of the grave danger involved in such an encounter.

Wish-fulfilment occurs in dreams involving famous people, as Ruby's experience shows:

'I meet a film star I really like who takes me out for a meal. I am usually about twenty-five in my dreams, though I am sixteen in reality. And, after seeing him for a while, our relationship gets closer and closer and we end up making love. Afterwards we sleep in each other's arms and then, as he is about to wake me, I am woken up by my mum, so I never know what happens.'

Perhaps Fiona's dream is also about wish-fulfilment, but it is of a much more lusty, phallic-centred variety:

'The Grand old Duke of York, I have never seen him, was sitting in a caravan in a circus ground. He had a huge penis stretching to the other end of the caravan. I can't remember the rest but I woke up feeling excited.'

Fiona adds that she usually dreams about sex when she is feeling sexually frustrated. In this dream it looks as though she couldn't get away from it if she wanted to! Is this *The Grand Old Duke of York* who marched around all those men? Up to the top of the hill and down to the bottom; up again and down again – interesting, isn't it, how this movement is associated with the act of intercourse? Certainly Freudian interpretation would consider it so. The caravan and circus ground may be symbols of impermanence, but exciting places for all that, or precisely because of that.

Variety: the spice of life?

'I once had a dream where I had a penis – I found it horrendous, though, not at all sexy.'

Diane preferred her 'romantic setpiece' dreams which did not include intercourse, so what is this dream about? Is it fear of her own masculinity? Fear that she is turning into a man? Does she have strong negative feelings against lesbianism? What so disturbs her that she finds it 'horrendous'?

Diane's reaction to the dream is important; it is very strongly negative. She cannot bear the thought of having a penis. Other women might have found the idea odd, or amusing, or even something of an adventure, but Diane hates it. She cannot bear to acknowledge the parts of her personality traditionally defined as masculine, such as her strength, her power, her aggressiveness or her anger. Yet we are all made up of masculine and feminine attributes. Diane wants to play only her feminine role and deny the other. Her unconscious is determined to make her recognize her full potential, though, because her dream has revealed her masculinity in the most direct way possible.

Toni, a copy writer working in Edinburgh, has a bizarre dream that includes a penis:

'I very often dream of babies so small they are like dolls made out of clothes pegs. The "toy" doll becomes a penis and I squeeze sperm out of it like toothpaste, then I breastfeed it. Then it is back as a baby.'

This dream describes a cycle of sexual reproduction, though the female genitals are omitted. First there is the 'toy' baby doll, then the penis from which comes sperm. The penis is breastfed and in turn becomes a baby. Now, where is the woman's part in all this? She is the 'servicer'; she gets the sperm out of the penis by squeezing it, not through intercourse, and she feeds it with breast milk. Nowhere is her sexual pleasure of importance. The whole dream has an atmosphere of wooden matter-of-factness; there is no emotion, merely tasks to perform. She is trapped in the cycle.

Toni provided further details of her sleeping life:

'In one dream I had to make love to a very thin Filipino out of pity. I felt guilty committing adultery but very worried when he told me he had got VD and showed me a scratch which proved it. Then someone else told me he was tubercular. I did not think I could catch that but I was angry at his deception. I think this dream was set in a hotel room abroad.'

A hotel room abroad is distant and foreign, but as the setting for the dream it may tell us more about Toni: she is keeping away from the tricky sex issues which emerge via her dreams. Here again we see her engaged in an act which she is not personally interested in. She is having sex because she pities this man: there is the 'foreign' element. Then she discovers he is diseased; he can infect her because she makes herself open and vulnerable. Again she is in the servicer role; she is as uncaring about her own well-being as the 'takers' are. At the end of the dream she is angry at the man's deception, but we are not left with the feeling that she is going to do anything about it. There is a sense of passive acceptance.

Toni could choose to learn from these dreams not only sexually but in ways which would affect her everyday contact with people. She could learn to be less of a doormat.

Dreams of sex with animals are fairly rare and generally unpleasant. In Bonnie's dream she is sexually debased. Part of the scenario includes her partner turning into a grotesque pig or to dust in the middle of an embrace. Louisa's 'wolf' dream is similarly about defilement:

'I was in my friend's house, who lives with her boyfriend, and I was on my own. Their bed was in the living-room, as they had recently moved in. I was sitting on the edge of the bed when suddenly there was this great sand-coloured wolf on top of me, having sex with me. Then when it had finished it looked up at me. I stood up and then I walked to the window. It was as though he was commanding me and I knew exactly what he wanted of me.

'The wolf was looking up at me all the time with black slit-like irises. He told me to look out of the window, so I did, and there was a man hanging on a rope by the neck. His eyes were the palest blue and were staring into nothingness. He had frost all over his body but there was no snow outside. I calmly put the curtain back and looked down at the wolf again. But as I looked into his eyes I was transfixed and I shall never forget the feeling of great evil power in those eyes. I just couldn't look away. I could see utter immense glee, as though he was saying he had killed that man and I belonged to him.

'Then we were on the bed again and it was having sex with me again. My friend and her boyfriend came though the door. I pushed the wolf off me but they acted completely normal as if they couldn't see what happened and as if they couldn't see the wolf.'

Louisa's dream still holds her in its grip. She continued:

'There was only one person I told, but not in as great detail as that, and he told me that he read somewhere that (please don't think I'm stupid because I've read it myself and it was a true story) a demon can come to a person and have intercourse with them. This demon is called Incubus and it can come in the form of a dog or man. This dream has frightened me and I'd just like another explanation.'

I had suggested in an article she'd read that people should keep a dream diary but after writing down a few dreams Louisa found that she could not dream any more. She said:

'It was as though my brain was refusing to let me dream, as though saying, "I will not let you dream unless you stop writing them down. What if somebody found them?" So I stopped.'

This stunningly vivid dream is interesting for a number of reasons. It carries imagery that conjures up archetypes. We see a sexually rapacious wolf like the one that eats grandmother and waits in bed for Little Red Riding Hood, glimpses of T. S. Eliot's *Waste Land*, the 'Hanged Man' of the Tarot pack, the invasive Incubus who sexually dominates helpless women, and the 'slit-like irises' of devilish rams. All are concerned with sex and power. Louisa is utterly out of contact with her own power, and the fear that results is plain to see.

She cannot avoid 'the wolf' in her dream, and her friends cannot or will not help. In waking life she fears she may be possessed; in other words, that her personal autonomy has been taken away. Just as in the dream she acts under the direction of the wolf, so in waking life she is very influenced by the opinions of others and the need for approval. She is even fearful of what people would say if they knew of her dreams. Her dream alone shows her coming face to face with that animal sexuality which is part of all of us. She has no champions to help her on that early journey of exploration and so is extremely anxious.

It is very important for women to accept their own sexuality. It is an integral part of our make-up and a powerful life force. If we recognize it and work with it instead of rejecting it or forcing ourselves into contorted positions which conform to an image of what we as women 'should' feel, we will discover much more satisfying sexual relationships.

We can use dreams to get in touch with our sexuality. They can compensate for the lack of a sexual partner – for instance, if a lover is away. They can identify conflict which is repressed during waking hours. They can stimulate and arouse and, as Kinsey found, they can show us sexual activities we have not experienced in waking life, suggesting that dreams have a prospective or rehearsal function.

Dreams about sex are a normal part of healthy self-expression and they offer so much self-knowledge that it is foolish to ignore them.

Notes

1. Wilse B. Webb, *Sleep: The Gentle Giant*, Prentice Hall, New Jersey, 1975.
2. A. Kinsey, *et al*, *Sexual Behaviour in the Human Female*, W. B. Saunders, 1953.

6

Family and Friends

Family

My mother once said to me, as I leant on the kitchen table and wondered about continuing at school if I passed my 'O' levels, 'Don't get too clever, Brenda. It's all very well, but men don't like smart women.' It was up to me whether I got a job or went on at school. As I said earlier, I was the first one in our family to go down the academic examination route, and I had more information about such things as universities than my parents did. I knew where examination success could lead and was really thinking aloud as I pondered the possibilities. Her dampening reply was meant as a warning about men's expectations of women. Deferring women and dominating men were the order of the day.

In the event, I did continue with my education, but not without major disturbances along the way. Since those teenage days I have checked with other women to see if they too were expected to 'hide their talent'. A great many were, and it is hard to balance love towards a caring parent with the anger that we were not encouraged to shine. Hiding my light under a bushel never brought satisfaction; I either felt stupid because everyone would assume I was, or patronized because it was thought that I, as a girl, should not bother with 'those things', whatever they were; or I felt I was missing out on the buzz.

Sarah's dreams showed how she felt about her family once the 'shoulds' and 'oughts' had been stripped away. For instance, in one dream her parents appeared as cardboard cut-out figures, and in another they were totally silent or indifferent to her. The dreams helped her to acknowledge the message coming from deep within that her parents offered no real emotional support. Painful as it was to admit, she recognized that neither as a child nor as an adult had they expressed much warmth towards her.

Letting go of the powerful dictates 'You *should* love your parents' and 'You *ought* to put them first' took Sarah long hours of psychotherapy. She understood that there had never been much love offered to her but she was convinced there was something mentally unbalanced and emotionally cold about her personality. She thought that every woman was totally devoted to her parents and, because she didn't share such devotion, she felt bad.

Sarah's unnecessary guilt was restricting her friendships. Eventually she was able to accept her own feelings towards her parents without castigating herself for not caring more. She accepted that, though we choose our friends, we don't choose our parents, and that many parent-child relationships do not conform to the idealized image. She negotiated a more realistic relationship which enabled her to accept her parents as they were and to give as much as she could without feeling dreadfully inadequate. Her recent dreams of successful ventures and colourful events show Sarah building up a new sense of power and self confidence.

May has no room for sentimental 'oughts' and 'shoulds' where her father is concerned; she regards him as the blight of her life. Her dreams mirror their waking relationship:

'In dreams he always plays the role he has chosen in real life: a remote, indifferent figure who looks at me vaguely as if trying to remember where he has seen me before.'

Christine has similar feelings:

'My dreams aren't obviously related to my family, but I know that they are. The dreams are all about being locked out or not being able to let anyone know that I have arrived. I suppose being lost and that sense of isolation have to do with leaving my first home in Canada so abruptly when I was six, when my father died. The dreams tend to probe too deep and have caused me real distress.'

As Christine realizes, her dreams are tied in with early loss which she has not dealt with. She is still 'locked out', kept from whatever will allow her to feel that she belongs. The only information she confided was that at six she lost her father, her home and her friends. She did not mention her mother, but perhaps her mother had been too deep in her own distress to recognize her little daughter's despair.

Christine needs to express her early pain of isolation; she has not mourned enough. Almost all her dreams are pervaded by unhappiness; she dreams of receiving a pony which-wrapped in glittery paper, but the gift is all wrapping; she dreams of losing children, failing to take care of them properly or inadvertently doing awful things to them; and she has solitude dreams where everyone is dead except her. Now a mature woman with children of her own, Christine continues to suffer because of her father's death and subsequent events.

The power of family relationships can be overwhelming at times and, when those relationships come to an end, perhaps through death, the effect may be staggering. Dreams help us to come to terms with death and to prepare for it.

Sheila, a woman in her mid-thirties, had a dream in which her father died. She was very upset but realized that it was forcing her to think about how she would feel if he did die. It was a rehearsal or preparatory dream. At breakfast she broached the subject of family relationships and death with her two boys of ten and twelve. She spoke about her sad dream, and they responded supportively and joined their dad in expressing how they might feel if their granddad's life were to end suddenly. It was easier to talk about it when there was no immediate likelihood of his death than it would have been at a more critical time. Sheila said it had brought the family much closer together.

In talking about dreams with her family, Sheila was following the practice of some family therapists. Cirincione used dreams in marital and family therapy to help understand what had gone wrong in particular relationships and to find a way of resolving conflicts.[1] In such treatment, dreams, which are used to identify personality strengths rather than weaknesses, are viewed as reflections of feelings and act as a guide to the emotional dynamics which affect each member of a family. None of us sees the same situation in precisely the same way because we are all different and have had different life experiences. Dreams are a useful way of exploring those differences.

The acceptance of the inevitability of death came for Lucy before the actual death of her mother:

'My mother walks into the swamp. She throws off her clothes and sinks without struggling. She is showing me that she is ready to cast off her material body in death.'

Amy, a wonderful creative weaver, had a numinous dream when she was in her early twenties. The images stayed with her and she still finds herself talking about it now and again. She described the dream:

'Through a door I see a light. I must go in. I see my mother as a baby on a table. My dad and sisters are onlookers. I go in and stand with them.'

At the time she dreamt this, Amy was moved but not over-whelmingly sad; there was resigned acceptance of an inevitable event. I asked her what she thought about the dream now. She replied that her mother used to get attention by behaving in a petulant, babyish way, and was totally egocentric, just as babies are. Also, she said that her mother's death was visually very similar to the dream. Her mother had become smaller in size and weight after a rapid illness and was a mere scrap of humanity. Her father and sister were at the hospital when Amy arrived at the deathbed, and they seemed to be in the only lit room in a darkened corridor, just as it had been in her dream.

The dream symbols represent Amy's recognition of her mother's dependence. The family are shown attending to the needs of the infant-woman; while Amy found this behaviour infuriating and disturbing when she was growing up at home, when she left, married and had children of her own, she had been able to gain some distance from which to understand and accept her mother. They established a good relationship within the parameters that Amy had to build so that she would not be engulfed by her mother's needs. Very early Amy's right brain, intuitive ability pointed out her ambivalent feelings.

It is perhaps pertinent that Amy is an original, inspired artist, for research described by Marilee Zdenek in *The Right Brain Experience*[2] shows that right-brain-dominated people have well-developed imaginations coupled with creative problem-solving abilities. They – and they are usually women – are able to make leaps of intuitive insight in ways that logically, analytically oriented left-brain thinkers are not. Obviously we need both hemispheres to be working in unison but, in western culture, emphasis is placed on the logical, linear skills of the left brain while the other side is neglected. As dreaming is a right-brain activity, it follows that if you pay more attention to your dreams you will be increasing your creative potential. Marilee gives many examples of people who have been helped to stimulate creativity and maximize unconscious potential through exercises, including working on dreams, and you may find her book useful to your own right-brain development.

Nancy's father is not dead but in her dreams he is dying and has shrunk to the size of a doll. Like Amy's dream this example is concerned with a decrease in stature. Probably Nancy no longer sees her father as the large, figure of authority he was when she was a child. Her increasing maturity, and her recognition of her father's ageing, lead her to symbolize him as a doll, just as Amy's mother was a tiny baby. Nancy's dream is helping her prepare for and accept the changing roles in their relationship. It forces her to face what may be impossible to accept when she is awake, and she is more worried about her father's health than she admits.

Many of us dream about family and friends who have died. In some instances the exact details of the death are repeated, while in others the dead person comes to communicate to the dreamer through the dream. Quite often such dreams occur around the anniversary of the death or perhaps at the deceased person's birthday. Our subconscious continues to recall the dates in the manner of a computer that has not been updated to omit that information now that it is no longer relevant. The person still is important to us emotionally and our dreams remind us of that fact.

Carrie, a word-processor operator, is still coming to terms with the death of her mother and her dreams reveals the wounding grief that persists:

'I have dreams involving my mother, who is dead. I ask her to hug me. Then, as she comes towards me, I realize that she is dead. It hits me with such great force that I scream and wake up crying.'

Carrie asks for warmth through a hug but her longing cannot be fulfilled. Dreams reveal what is in the depths of our being even though we can hoodwink ourselves during waking hours that everything is taken care of and under control. The dreamer can say that she is 'over' her mother's death, that she has come to terms with it, but the dream tells a different tale.

Ann's brother David died ten years ago, when he was only twenty-one. He had heart disease and the whole of their close family was devastated by his death. She told me:

'Last Sunday I dreamt he was staying at my house. He went out to the garden and fell. My mother and I rushed out and brought him in and I flew to call the doctor. No matter how hard I tried to contact one, I came upon blocks – nobody at the surgery, no one at the emergency number. Anyway, I sat on the stairs with my brother and all he kept saying was, 'I'm all right, Ann, don't worry.' Over and over again he said it. Then he died.'

Ann's account indicates her helplessness. She cannot communicate within the dream, which reflects the hopelessness she felt years ago in waking life. Her brother tries to reassure her and dies telling her not to worry. However, that Sunday was the anniversary of his death and Ann again grieved for his loss. She realized herself that the dream was emphasizing that she still missed him terribly.

A lonely widow of eight years, Betty misses her husband:

'I took my husband's death very badly, and it would seem he is always with me, even though it must be subconsciously. I do not think a night goes by without my dreaming of him. My dreams are very vivid and real and there are times when I can even 'feel' my husband lying in bed next to me. In many of the dreams I have conversations with him and ask him why he never comes home any more or takes me out; he always excuses himself on some ground or other.'

Betty added:

'Apart from dreaming of my husband, I also dream of my parents, who have passed on. I find the dreams leave me very drained and depressed in the mornings and it takes me a while to pull myself together. I do go to work, which is my life-saver, but I do wish I didn't dream as much as I do.'

Betty's depressed loneliness is common among women who have lived most of their life for, and through, other people. Her job is her 'life-saver'. In her part-time work as a shop assistant, she at least has some daily human contact; otherwise she would go for long stretches in isolation. Her life is empty as she dwells on past relationships. She does not seek fresh experiences but questions her husband in dreams as to why he is not taking her out. At an emotional level she will not let him die; it is her 'unfinished business'.

Some dreams about the death of a parent are more gentle. In Valerie's case, her dream, while provoking anxiety, leaves her with a feeling of comfort:

'I had a dream when my father first died in which he sat me down and explained his reasons for dying. Even now I don't understand them but for a moment, in the dream, they made sense.'

Other interesting issues are raised by Valerie's dreams, and I include details of them here, though what are termed 'psychic' dreams are dealt with in Chapter 11:

'Three years ago my father died. Though we were a close family, I was not particularly close to him. Yet since then he has appeared in many of my dreams. Sometimes, in the dreams, I am sobbing so hard I cannot speak. Sometimes we are having a meal or sitting together talking.

'I know that this is a classic case of just missing someone, but two points make me question this. The first is that, after his death, my sister dreamt that my father told her that his chest ached and his mouth hurt. She could not understand what he meant. It was only about two weeks later that I realized that, on the eve of his death, from a heart attack, the doctors and nurses, on finding his heart stopped, probably gave him resuscitation on both chest and mouth.

'The second point, which makes me wonder if dreams tell more than we dare think, is that my father, although he was a GP, firmly believed in ghosts, souls and an afterlife. He believed that people from the other side do get in touch.'

Valerie's father was far more important to her than she consciously realizes, otherwise there would not be so much distress in these dreams. She wonders if dreams can be communications from 'the other side', beyond the grave. Probably the explanation is more mundane, for through dreaming, we frequently come up with answers to questions we may not even have been conscious of asking.

Concerning Valerie's sister's dream, where her father says his chest and mouth are hurting, I wonder if someone had mentioned in passing that his mouth looked swollen? Or if her sister had registered this when she saw his corpse and was worried about it?

When we are not present at the death of a person for whom we care greatly, there is a deep-seated need to have details, to be aware of what was done by and to the dying person. This may be in order to expiate feelings of guilt that we were not there at the time or it may be to enable us to feel closer to that person. Details help us to come to terms with death; they complete some of the 'unfinished business'. Valerie and her sister needed to know whether everything possible was done to save their father, and the sister's dream dealt with that unspoken question.

Barbara, likewise, could not at first 'let go', but eventually her dreams told her she had accepted the death:

'After my mum died I still dreamt of her at home with the rest of the family. I was aware through my dreams that I had not accepted her death. I dreamt I would say to her, 'They thought you would die, didn't they, mum, but you didn't. You fooled them all.' In the dream I really believed that she had just been very ill and that she had pulled through the operation.

'One morning I awoke after I had dreamt about the family but for the first time my mother did not appear. I felt delighted. I really felt emotionally that I had passed a milestone, and finally I had come to terms with her death.'

Georgina tells of a reassuring dream experience following bereavement:

'After the death of my brother I had a variety of dreams in which there were either explosive devices attached to me or featured somewhere in the dream. This was for me an emotionally explosive time. Through a series of these dreams I came eventually to a time when I could defuse the 'bomb' and my feelings were no longer at a dangerous pitch. Another dream followed a little later in which I was carrying around my brother's corpse. This was obviously telling me that it was time to let go. My dreams then, as now, were good barometers of my mental state.'

It may be that vivid dreaming runs in families. It certainly does in Hazel's. Like her, her grandfather and father had and have very vivid dreams. Her grandfather also walked in his sleep and his dreams were so violent that in later life he and her grandmother slept apart – apparently he had once tried to strangle her in his sleep; this is not unheard of.

Conscience-pricking may occur in dreams, as Josie relates:

'I dreamt that my mother and sister had written to my grandmother pretending that the letter was from me. They did it because I hadn't written since before grandpa's funeral.'

Josie felt so guilty that she woke up and immediately wrote to her grandmother. She had been putting it off and putting it off until her subconscious would allow her to procrastinate no longer.

When relationships are falling apart, dreams reflect the change. Hannah, whose marriage was beginning to falter, dreamt that she was trapped in a small rowing boat, without any paddles, under a jetty. As the sea water rose, so the wooden slates of the jetty closed down to meet her. The only exit at the end of the pier was sealed with an iron grille. There was no way out. She told me that it was no use calling for help because there was no one to hear her cries. This, symbolically was a totally accurate representation of her waking situation.

Gina wrote of her feelings prior to separation:

'I had a recurring dream that my children were missing. I would sleepwalk to count them. My husband would wake me and show me my three boys. I had the dream for about five years.

'My divorce was sudden and two of my boys lived with their father for a year. I think those dreams were a premonition of my sons' leaving me.'

Her subconscious had been telling her for five years that such separation was likely, so her dream was more a case of repressed ideas being expressed than premonition.

Helen, a large matronly women in her late forties, was amazingly cheerful whenever she came to the counselling course I was running. As a nurse, she felt her work would be enhanced if she knew more about how to counsel those experiencing emotional difficulties. In the coffee break one evening she told me about a disturbing dream she'd had:

'I dreamt that Alan, my son, was at the grotto in Lourdes and my own mother, who died four years before he was born, was attending to him. I knew she was wanting him to go with her but I didn't know to where, and I pleaded with her to leave him to me, and said that I was the one who should look after him. I might add that he is a very self-sufficient twenty-three-year-old.'

Helen was upset by the dream but, in keeping with her usual cheery, self-denying manner, she felt uncomfortable drawing attention to her own vulnerability. She wanted to know what the dream meant.

As a Catholic she was sustained by her faith and expressed a view that, should Alan die, it was God's will and she could accept it. Though he had epilepsy, she was not unduly worried about it; modern anti-convulsant drugs controlled it successfully and he was doing well. The dream, though, reflected her unspoken concern, and the presence of her mother in the dream was comforting but surprising. Helen feared that it was an omen of some kind. Maybe her training alerted her to clues that her son's condition was worse than she consciously thought, or maybe she was in an anxious phase. Perhaps the symbolic image of the water-filled grotto at Lourdes, that place of miracles, might have led Helen to express fears about her son's safety in relation to water, but we did not have time fully to explore the dream details.

I remembered the dream when a colleague of Helen told me the sad news that her much-loved Alan had as a result of a fit drowned while in the bath. So had Helen been reacting to subliminal clues or was her dream precognitive?

Sometimes we don't want to 'see' a situation for what it is, so our dreams are symbolic. Evelyn, however, rarely has much symbolism in dreams. One of eight, she grew up on a council estate in Glasgow and now lives on a similar estate in Bradford. She has four children under seven and runs round from morning to night devoting herself to their needs. She has no time for herself – indeed, would not know what to do with such time – and in her dreams it is always her children who feature, as in this one:

'Martin, my youngest, slipped out of the back door. One of the other children had left it open. I stood screaming on the back doorstep as I saw him run into the path of a car.'

Evelyn had been worried about the safety of a fence separating her house from the road and had been on to the town hall to get something done. Her dream revealed directly her anxieties about her children's safety.

When I last saw her, at a community centre which she had been cajoled into attending, she looked much perkier. She had been moved into a less crowded house in a quiet avenue, 'And do you know,' she said, 'I've never had that old dream again. My Martin is all right in my dreams now.' She beamed with pleasure as she gathered one of the other offspring to her.

Humorous dreams give Martha something to smile about.

'I dreamt my thirty-one-year-old daughter was a baby again. I tucked her up in, not her cot, but in a roasting tin of all things. I made sure she was comfortable and then I popped her in the oven and switched it on. Half an hour later I went back to check her to see if she was 'done'. She had rosy-red cheeks and was pouring sweat, I thought she was basting very nicely!'

Martha realizes that this dream relates to her central heating, which is constantly turned up full blast. Her daughter complains about the house being too hot when she visits, but for Martha it is just right, so in her dream she casts her daughter as a little child who just has to put up with it. As she says, 'I've given up trying to please everyone else, I'm putting myself first for a change.'

Carolanne wakes herself and her husband up with her dream-prompted, uncontrollable giggling. A recent dream featured her husband and son:

'We were sitting at the breakfast table in our kitchen. In my hand I had a piece of toast with holes in it and thought of a lovely joke. I put the toast next to them and said, "The father, the son and the holy toast."'

I hate to admit it, but I laughed too!

Marriage

Dreams about husbands frequently reveal the true nature of marital bliss. Laura had horrible dreams of vengeful men hiding when her marriage was going through a rocky period, but as things got better so did her dreams. However, Alice's dream concentrates on lack of support and poor communication. She could use the dream to bring up the subject with her husband and find out what his views are, as well as using it to examine her own anxieties. Sharing dreams is a way of sharing feelings.

Here is Alice's dream and her comments:

'. . . My son was about five years old at the time. I dreamt my husband, son and I were walking alongside a canal which had thick brown water. Suddenly, my son slipped in and completely disappeared. I immediately yelled to my husband to get him out, but he coolly replied, "He's dead. There's no point." I was frantic but he didn't show any emotion at all.

'It upset me for weeks, it was so realistic. I remember being afraid to take my son anywhere near water for a long, long time, and I saw to it that he learnt to swim very quickly.'

The practicalities of teaching her son to swim were sooner dealt with than her marital relationship. Alice did not address herself to the icy response from her husband. She cast her partner in the role of rescuer but I wonder if she herself could swim and, if so, why she did not dive into the murky depths to save the boy? Has her relationship with the child excluded her husband? If so, what does she want to do about it?

Anxiety about marital relationships is represented in dreams in many forms. There are wives searching for 'lost' husbands, women dreaming of husbands laughingly flaunting their affairs, and dreams, like Enid's in which the husband dies:

'Many years ago, when I was depressed and unhappy about our marriage, I dreamt that my husband had died. I had been trying to think how to escape my problems, perhaps by leaving him. My dream included the feeling of desolation at his loss and helped in my decision to make the best of staying.'

Jeanne, a dark-haired, perceptive librarian, had a valuable dream about her husband:

'I am back in a situation where, it seems, I am promised to my husband, although he died several years ago. I have been tied to him for years. I suddenly realize that I must break the attachment and strike out on my own. I understand that I have failed to gain any real warmth from the relationship. This will mean getting a new job and living in my parents' home again. (They are both dead, so this may relate to finding the real me, which was eclipsed during my marriage.)

'The realization of what has been missed in the relationship is suddenly so clear that I know I cannot go on waiting and expecting that things will change. There is such a feeling of relief at the final acceptance that my love has always been stunted and that there has never been an enthusiastic welcome or concern for me within the marriage.'

Painful though it may be to acknowledge that a relationship has been unsatisfying if not destructive, the recognition of the truth frees the dreamer to move on to a different, more hopeful phase in her life.

Bouncy Rita, wearing a bright-pink jumpsuit and shiny beads, spoke of a recurring dream of being chased by her ex-husband:

'I run up a gravel path, then fall. I desperately need someone to help me up. I panic because no one is there.'

She has the dream about once a week and feels that is about not having found her way yet after a painful divorce. Her dream is quite straightforward in its depiction of her worries but outwardly she projects an image of shaky, brittle confidence.

This final 'husband' dream, while being quite humorous, highlights friction in Rachel's relationship with her husband Ian. Rachel obviously grasps what the dreams message is about:

'I am married to Ian, who works away on the oil rigs every other week. He bought me a Yorkshire terrier because he thought it would protect me when I was on my own, even though I never wanted a dog as I don't like them. However, the roles have now turned. I love the dog and do, I admit, treat him like a baby. I let him sit on my knee – he comforts me . . . Meanwhile Ian has taken a dislike to the dog, saying that it is no longer a 'good dog', more like a baby. I think this is jealousy because he was the same when we had a cat which I cuddled when I could. Anyway, he is always threatening Barny, the dog, with "electrodes in his ears" whenever he is naughty. We got him from the PDSA and I understand they use this method to put dogs to sleep.

'My dream was that we were in a school hall and Ian took the dog to a man standing by a large boardroom table. He proceeded to electrocute Barny while Ian held me back. I screamed and protested violently but had to watch Barny shake until he was dead. Tears poured down my face. The next scene was a few weeks later, when I had to go to the morgue. Barny was put on the counter. I saw him move, held him and he was alive. The strange thing is he had on a child's cowboy suit with a hat, waistcoat and even holsters with toy guns in.'

There are a number of references to children in this dream, as well as to rivalry for affection between the husband and the dog-cum-child. Do they relate to discussion or thoughts about starting a family or unspoken concerns about this subject? Is Rachel teasing Ian by flaunting her love of the dog so that he gets angry and that anger reassurs her? And what about some of the words – 'board-room', for instance. Is Rachel bored? Does she feel 'held back' or frustrated by Ian? Whatever Rachel finds when she gets to the root of the dream, she has hope; all is not lost for 'Barny' is not dead, even though appearances make it seem as if he is. Her dream is telling her that appearances are deceptive; even the dog dressed up as a child is not a child, toy guns or no toy guns!

Children

Conceiving, carrying and bearing healthy offspring is of vital importance to humankind, as it is to any living group which wants to avoid extinction. However, reproduction is also an emotionally loaded act and brings with it enormous responsibilities. It is also one of the most traumatic life events we experience, both physically and emotionally. The pain, the joy and the wonder of childbirth leave an indelible impression. We are never the same after we become mothers:[3]

> Why do we idealise sacrifice in mothers? Who gave us this inhuman idea that mothers should negate their own wishes and desires? The acceptance of servitude has been handed down from mother to daughter for so many centuries that it is now a monstrous chain which fetters them. Every woman, at some point in her life, realises how much she owes the woman who gave her birth, and at the moment of recognition feels intense remorse, aware that she has never really recompensed her mother for the damage done to herself in doing good for us. But as soon as she becomes a mother herself she stands her wish to repay this debt on its head; she denies herself in turn, providing a new example of self-mortification and self-destruction. Yet what would happen if this dreadful cycle was broken, once and for all? What if mothers refused to deny their womanhood and gave their children instead an example of life lived according to the needs of self-respect?

Should your child die, you do not cease to be a mother. With mothering come responsibilities which begin when the baby first seeks food. You, the mother, are the natural source of nourishment and must give the breast or find alternative sources of sustenance for the demanding, seemingly all-devouring bundle of life. This is just the beginning. Is it any wonder that there are many, many variations of anxiety dreams about those to whom we give life? You will recall some such dreams from earlier chapters, but here are a couple to remind you of those feelings of inadequacy and frustration:

'I am trying to catch my children just as they are about to fall. Or else, I am forgetting to do something which brings bad results for other people.'

'I dreamt of being in a small hospital room with my six-year-old-daughter. She was dancing on the hospital windowsill, three storeys up. In trying to save her from falling, I attempted to get out of bed and awoke on the floor. Being too weak to get back, I crawled to where I could reach the bell.'

'There are times when parenthood seems nothing but feeding the mouth that bites you,' quotes Ann Dally in *Mothers*, an excellent book on the ins and outs of the mothering role.[4] What is it that makes us fear more for our daughters than we do for our sons? Is it because the risks of being a woman feel so much greater, as May Sarton says, because of 'the dangers of being caught in a life one did not altogether chooses'?[5]

My neighbour Hilda told me of a dream which Diane, her nineteen-year-old daughter, was crying for her and was tugging at a gold ring tightly entwined around her wedding finger. Diane had just started to live with her boyfriend but Hilda thought things weren't working out too well between them. When we talked about the dream, it appeared that her own distress about her only daughter and her fears that Diane was unhappy had intermingled, 'intertwined', in the dream. She was concerned that Diane would get trapped in a 'marriage', symbolized by the ring, and hoped she would free herself from the bond. In fact, Diane stayed with her boyfriend for a long time but eventually left to marry someone else.

Worries were evident in Cathy's dreams too:

'I think that if you are worried about someone your mind keeps working while you sleep and this affects your dreams. When I was worried about my daughter, I spent all night searching, meeting strange people, asking them if they had seen her, but I never found her.'

Cathy was unable to re-establish the warm relationship she had had with her daughter before a series of events came as a wedge between them. The dream communicates that divide.

We mother our male children in subtly different ways from how we mother our daughters – ways which we are unaware of. American psychotherapist Dan Kiley argues that we collude with the little-boy act. We strive to meet the needs of boys and men in our lives at the expense of our own. Kiley endorses the idea put forward by many recent women writers that we do this because inside most women is a voice saying, 'You'll never get what you want because you don't deserve it.' We run round men washing their shirts, finding their socks and making their dentist appointments because, if they learnt how to do it themselves, they might not need us and then they would leave!

Fiona, a young woman who worked as a nanny, recently married Steve, a handsome boor who is hopeless when it comes to anything domestic. The last of three children, he was waited on him hand and footby his mother. He left his clothes scattered over his parents' house, secure in the knowledge they would be removed and restored to their rightful places once they had been laundered.

Fiona told me of her dreams:

'I am trapped on a conveyor belt going round and round and I can't get off. In another, it's as if I'm trapped in a room because someone has shut the door on me. The light is out too, and both the switch and the door disappear. I hate these dreams; I'm more tired when I wake up than when I go to sleep.'

We talked again a few months after their marriage, when she had taken over the mother's role. She was feeling tired, what with working full-time and looking after Steve. 'I wish he wouldn't leave everything to me and I'm sick of picking up all his things. He doesn't seem to realize that I don't want to spend all my time looking after him.'

Matters were not helped by that fact that her eighteen-year-old brother had come to stay, and, yes, you've guessed it, he too expected Fiona to do all the cooking, cleaning and care-taking. Until Fiona tells them assertively how she feels and negotiates a different relationship, the status quo will persist. Her husband will expect her to be like his mother because that's what he has been taught about women. Fiona's dreams reflect her unconscious recognition of the situation.

When Vera dreams of flying, it is usually because she is fed up with looking after her daughters and longs for some escape route.

Conveniently, she manages to soar above her responsibilities for a while. When she is less tired and life is going smoothly, she does not need the dreams and does not have them. One particular dream of flying, though, concerned Vera's daughter rather than herself and it captured those feelings of amusement and irritation that energy-packed youngsters sometimes evoke:

'I had this dream when my elder daughter was four years old. She was a thin lively, cheerful child. I dreamt that I opened one of the double windows on the first floor of the house in which we were then living, and my child was laughing, calling to me and playing about in the air, at the level of the bedroom windowsill. The view of the houses, street and trees was otherwise perfectly normal. I was not surprised by her mid-air antics, but cross with her because she would not come in from play. I kept calling her in and at last began to lean further and further out of the window, trying to grab the end of her green and white checked cotton dress as she floated past, scolding her for keeping out of my reach. At one point she stood treading the air as if it were water and laughing with glee at my frustration. I can recall this scene as vividly as many of the real life memories of this period; it was so typical of her as a child and she is now twenty-nine!'

With five children under fourteen, Liz used to get very angry with her situation, particularly when her husband was working away from home and she was left with all the childcare as well as the house maintenance. One night after a fraught day she had this dream:

'I was looking down on an old man who was sitting by a black stove smoking a pipe. A kettle on the stove was boiling away. He said to me, 'You've got to let steam off sometimes.'

She found the dream really helpful, almost as if it had given her permission to express all that anger she had been suppressing. The images reminded her of a peaceful kitchen she had known in the past, while the old man made her think of Jung, about whom she had been reading. She did let off steam; she wrote to her husband and told him how much she disliked having total care of the children for almost all the time. He seemed surprised, since she had never before voiced her true dissatisfaction. They are now discussing possible alternatives. They may not find any quick solution but, as Liz said, 'At least he knows how I feel and he doesn't assume any more that my whole aim in life is to be a mother and a wife. He sees me more as a person in my own right now.'

Fran

Many women are still financially and emotionally dependent on men. Striving to escape the web which entangles us even as it supports us is no easy matter. Some of us want to establish relationships with men as equals, while others such as radical separatists want to set up completely independent, all-female social structures. Fran belongs to the former group. Married for more years than she cares to remember, her dreams came at a time when she was becoming dissatisfied with an unhappy marriage and was afraid that she could not survive alone.

Two of her dreams are worth recounting at slightly longer length than most included so far, for their vivid symbolical depiction of the struggles she went through.

Dream 1

'I was in an old house with my husband and we were looking to see if we could renovate it. I discovered that it had a cellar and I wanted my husband to come and look at it. He said he would come soon but right then he didn't have time. He would not loan me his torch so that I could go alone. I waited for him for a long time and he kept saying he was busy; then he said it was time to go home. He got into the car but I didn't go with him. I went to the cellar alone.

'At first I was very frightened because there was no light at all there and I had to feel my way down the stairs in the dark. As I went down it got lighter and at the bottom it was almost like being outside in daylight.

'The cellar was full of strange things like an old-fashioned set of fire irons on a stand but, instead of the usual brush, shovel and tongs, it had a knife, fork and spoon. There were lots of toys there, including a beautiful wooden rocking horse. I stood at the bottom of the stairs and suddenly the horse started to move towards me. It frightened me and I ran back upstairs. When I got to the top I looked back.

'It was still very light down in the cellar and seemed nice and peaceful but there was still some feeling of menace. I went outside to find my husband. He was gone but it didn't matter. I found I had the keys to the house and I went back inside.'

This dream straightforwardly shows us the present state of their relationship. The old house, their long marriage, is in need of renovation. In order to make the relationship good again, to restore it to its earlier, more acceptable state, there has to be some repair work. Meanwhile, Fran has discovered a previously hidden part, the 'cellar'. This may relate to herself or to the relationship, but the conclusion is the same whichever way you interpret it.

'Cellar' is often used in Jungian terms to symbolize the emotional foundation. It is as if Fran has discovered a new aspect of herself which she wants her husband to see and share, but he refuses. He rejects her overtures. He is 'too busy' to explore with her and, what's more, he will not allow her to use his 'torch', he won't throw any light onto the situation. He will not go with her and, in his refusal to lend her the torch, indirectly tries to stop her. Eventually, still not having found time to respond to his wife's requests, he gets into the car and leaves her alone. Fran gropes her way forward, 'in the dark', in totally unfamiliar surroundings just as in life she was contemplating finding her way as a person alone: a nerve-racking proposition, especially after eighteen years of marriage during which virtually all the decisions had been made for her.

But, contrary to her fears, she finds more light the further she goes down and, apart from the horse, the objects she sees are comfortable domestic ones. These will have particular significance for her and may be helpful symbols in gathering her resolve but, at all events, they are not disturbing. However, the horse comes to life and frightens her, so she retreats; but she escapes unharmed and is not so upset that she dare not look back. She reaches safety and considers what she has seen: it was quite acceptable though there did lurk some danger. Finally, she is alone, her husband having left, and she is quite calm about the whole situation. What's more, she has the keys to the house.

This dream shows her courage in going into the dark unknown. The next example reveals her courage in the face of much more overt opposition.

Dream 2

'I was on my bike, preparing to cycle on what I knew was going to be a long journey. I had a lot of luggage piled on the bike. My husband was standing beside me and telling me I was too old for journeys like that. I tried to ride away but he grabbed my arm and I fell off the bike. As I fell, one of my legs came off and I sat on the road crying. My husband was shouting at me about how he told me so, and I tried to stand up but kept falling over because I had only one leg. I could balance if I held onto the bike but he kept trying to take the bike away. Then he stood there holding the bike out of my reach and I was crying. But there was a wall near me and I found I could hop along if I held onto the wall, which was better than falling over. I continued to cry though, because I wanted my leg back. I was coming to the end of the wall but I could see there was another wall if I could just hop across the street. While I was trying to get myself together to let go of the first wall, I woke up.'

Fran's growing awareness of her husband's feelings about separation is evident. In the dream he tries to remove all sorts of support that will allow her independent action. He does everything to dissuade her from her 'journey', but she is determined. We see a woman resolved to make her own way and overcome all handicaps. She cannot stand on her own two feet, but still she fights using whatever comes to hand to lean on. She is not cowed down but assertively makes her own way and we leave her considering how she will cross the next hurdle, the road. This dream shows Fran tenaciously holding onto her goal; despite the setbacks she will not be defeated.

Friends

Going to Africa was a daytime dream for Cynthia. She had never been there but her parents, who originated from Guyana, had told her a lot about it and she longed to go to a place where she could be a person, rather than a black, first. I didn't know this when she started to draw her dream.

When I asked her to draw her dream, (a technique described in Chapter 1), she drew herself and her boyfriend at the side of a small lake filled with red fish. She held a lantern aloft while he pulled fish out of the crystal-clear water. He did this very roughly at first but stopped when she complained about his cruelty. Cynthia then showed him how to do it and everything was again harmonious.

The dream lake represented pictures of Ghana which Cynthia had seen. Sam, her boyfriend, used to live there and knew all about a way of life which was totally alien to her; she felt like 'a fish out of water' when he talked to their friends about it. However, she had been able to 'throw a light' on many situations in which he had felt uncomfortable and uneasy. His rough, blunt ways in the early days of their relationship had led her to wonder whether they could make a go of it. At the time of the dream she was deciding whether to return to his home with him.

As I mentioned in Chapter 4, fish are often linked to conception and birth, so I asked Cynthia if she was thinking about having a child. She laughed as she replied that she and Sam had been talking about children the day before she had the dream. She had said she would have a child if she liked Africa and if he did not revert to his rough ways. The last I heard of Cynthia, six months after she drew her dream, she was in Ghana and trying to get pregnant!

Vicky, who regularly works on her dreams, told Cynthia about her experiences:

'Dreams are fantastic. They make my life so much richer, and my relationships. They get rid of tension, like when I dream of having a row with someone I cannot face in my waking life. They are my problem-solving kit which comes built in and with no plug to put on!'

Vicky gave an example to clarify what she meant. One morning she woke from a dream in which she had been feeling jealous towards her baby sister. She had not seen her sister for some time, nor was she planning to, but that old feeling of rivalry prevailed. She knew there must be a message in the dream so she thought about what was happening that day which might concern jealousy. She quickly realized that John, a friend from college, was visiting her and that he had also become attracted to her flatmate. All her possessive feelings came to the fore and threatened to ruin the day, never mind the relationships.

Vicky had to take action to correct her pernicious jealousy. In the past she had felt stuck with taking care of her flatmate, and that had resurrected unpleasant childhood memories. Bravely assertive, she decided to tackle the problem straightaway. She spoke to both John and her flatmate saying that she realized the jealousy was her own problem but that she wanted their understanding while she sorted out those feelings. She also voiced her anxieties about possibly being excluded. In the event, her openness brought all three of them closer together.

My friends are very important to me and I'm certain that without their warmth and support there are times when I would have given up. When I was a single parent and trying to have a social life as well as complete my evening course M.Ed. while working full-time, my friends were wonderful. They responded to my needs whether they were for company or to be left alone, and were always there when I wanted to talk. Such friendships are of incalculable value. I was lucky, I felt secure enough in their love to know I could be myself and they would remain my friends. For Joan, however, this was not the case:

'I have a series of dreams in which I meet an old friend with whom I fell out; always I am still wanting her approval. In some dreams she greets me warmly in others she is cold and aloof.'

Joan has unfinished business here and the dream shows the need to complete it.

Verity's cherishing of her friends finds expression in her dreams in an unusual way. For years she has dreamt that she has a special house with its own private chapel. For her, it is as real as the physical house in which she lives. In her dreams, when her friends visit 'for the first time', she takes them to see the beautiful, tranquil sanctuary. Why is this place so important to Verity? It is easy to see the compensatory role of her dreams when you listen to her story:

'I have had a very unhappy marriage. My husband has subjected me to all forms of mental and physical cruelty. Twice I had made up my mind to leave him. On the first occasion I had an accident and couldn't go, and the second time I found I was having my second baby after a gap of ten years. I went through a very hard time after my second son was born, which probably explains why we are so close and why I dream of him so often. But my husband! Every time we have a quarrel, he packs up and goes; he went to Africa for seven years after one row. However, he always comes back. I cannot take action and get out of this marriage but I get a lot of strength from my trust in God and spend a lot of time in churches seeking help. My dream chapel is a joyous refuge.'

Many women cannot recall dreams about friends because they seem to remember best those dreams which have left a strongly negative or positive impression, while forgetting the middle-of-the-road, pleasant dreams where friends are likely to appear.

Notes

1. D. Cirincione, *et al*, 'The Functional Approach to Using Dreams in Marital and Family Therapy'; *Journal of Marital and Family Therapy*, Vol. 6, 1980.
2. Marilee Zdenek, *The Right-Brain Experience*, Corgi, 1985.
3. This comes from Sibilla Aleramo, *A Woman*. It is quoted in Elizabeth Wilson's *Only Halfway to Paradise: Women in Postwar Britain: 1945-1968*, Tavistock, 1980.
4. Ann Dally, quoting Peter de Vries in *Mothers: Their Power and Influence*. London, Weidenfeld and Nicolson, 1976
5. May Sarton, *A Reckoning*, The Women's Press, 1978.
6. Dr Dan Kiley, *The Peter Pan Syndrome*, Corgi, 1984 and *The Wendy Dilemma: When Women Stop Mothering Their Men*, Arrow, 1986.

7

The World of Work

I work at home when I clean, cook, look after the children, wash, iron and do all those domestic chores that having a home and family involves. I also work at home in another way, for I write here; and, in the quiet, set-aside hours, I see clients for counselling. I work outside the home when I run training courses in interpersonal skills, assertiveness training and management practice. And I teach in many further educational establishments. Many women I meet say apologetically, 'I don't work, I'm at home with the children.' Being at home with children and running a house is probably one of the most demanding jobs there is, as well as the most tiring and most rewarding. But the point is, it is still work, even though you don't get paid for it.

Workaday worries

It will come as no revelation that many anxiety dreams concern work. Dreams about workplace encounters reflect specific problems at work and with colleagues and give pointers about the ways in which those difficulties can be resolved.

Maria, obviously feeling very strongly about her job, began:

'I work in the despatch section of a biscuit factory. It is boring work among petty-minded, unintelligent people; that is the reality. In the dream my days were spent at St Joshua's mental hospital, the local asylum, although I have never been there. The interior resembled the biscuit factory, with the beds arranged in the same pattern as the packing tables at work. The inmates looked just like my colleagues. I was completely hysterical, screaming, 'For God's sake, will someone get me out of this fucking loony bin?' but no one listened or took any notice. Everyone just stared blankly as though I was making an unnecessary fuss which in no way concerned them.'

Maria was well aware of the significance of the dream for she concluded:

'It showed up my despair and helplessness in a more intense light than I can admit to myself in the daytime. I find it difficult to tell people about my problems because I fear the reaction "Oh. You're only drawing attention to yourself," so I tend to keep quiet. I just bottle things up.'

In the dream Maria is screaming out loud for some attention; she is desperate for someone to recognize her anguish but she is met with blank unresponsiveness. Her dream graphically encapsulates her frustration and anger about her job and indicates the need to do something about it. Such vivid dreams are important personal signposts.

Seventy-seven per cent of women work in the service sector, which includes clerical work, teaching, nursing, catering and personal services such as hairdressing and cleaning, so most of dreams reported here come from women employed in those fields.

Teachers have anxiety dreams about school which might surprise the pupils. Having taught in some fairly tough schools myself, I particularly appreciate the sinking feeling in the pit of the stomach that I sense in Jo's dream:

'My class at school have gone bananas and I am having no effect in calming them. In another dream I am in charge of a group of people. I know the instructions I have to give but the group will not stop talking and listen to me.'

Other teachers dream of 'kids rioting all around', of being completely unable to cope, or of being unable to communicate because whatever language the dreamer uses the other people use a different tongue and cannot understand her. Lyn's experiences reveal how vulnerable and exposed she feels: before term starts she dreams of going into class with no clothes on or having to go to the toilet in front of her students.

Nancy, a quietly spoken Irish woman who moved to Manchester with her husband, thought her anxieties about work blown out of all proportion in her dreams. She was fairly new to teaching at the time and her gentle, unassuming manner led many people to ignore her or to bully her, as I observed for myself. She described one dream to me:

'I told a senior teacher at school about a book I'd read and

131

enjoyed. The next moment I was in a room full of people and he was saying, "Go on, read your favourite part." He kept saying it over and over again, "Hurry up. You said you enjoyed it. Read it! . . ." All the time I was frantically thumbing through the book and couldn't find a part to read. I could see the words of the book but couldn't read it to them. And still he continued to say, "Read it! You said you enjoyed it."'

The waking reality was that Nancy was under a lot of pressure from the senior teacher and felt that she could not live up to his expectations. After this dream she realized just how much she felt dominated by him. Such dreams are helpful in drawing attention to bothersome situations, for in facing them we have a chance to resolve the difficulties rather than using up vital mental energy in repressing them.

Roma, a skilled secretary, found herself spending more and more time using word-processors while her manager became less and less involved with her as a person. Like Nancy, she did not realize how affected she was by her working situation. She came to feel that she was merely an extension of the machine. Eventually she began dreaming of being in a concentration camp with her boss, who had become a dictatorial camp commandant. He bullied and screamed abuse at her while she tried to placate him and cater to his every demand. The distressing dreams continued until her boss was replaced, but when Roma was told she would not revert to her former secretarial position because she was too valuable to lose from the processing work, she cracked up. She lost her balance control, was unable to walk in a straight line and could not co-ordinate hand and eye movements. The stress, quite apparent in her dreams, had continued unchecked and now affected her physically. After being unemployed through sickness for two years, Roma is just beginning to get back on her feet.

I had a dream about work which truly depicted my inner fears about a very tricky situation but I ignored the dream and suffered the consequences. I call it my 'above head level' dream.

I was working on an innovatory scheme which involved a great deal of liaison with headteachers on the one hand, and teachers who were part of my team on the other. All was running smoothly except in one school where the headteacher was not playing his part properly; in fact, I felt he was deliberately blocking progress and not keeping to his part of the contract. I tried every way I knew to resolve the difficulties, but, as he would never tell me what his position was, I was left powerless and frustrated. His patronizing attitude didn't help much either, especially since he indicated that I shouldn't really bother my head with these matters but should do whatever he decided – not a role I was appointed to fulfil! In desperation I decided that I must express my disquiet in my report for the next meeting of inspectors, advisers and others involved in monitoring the scheme. As he would be there too, I saw it as an opportunity to air the difficulties and get some kind of clarification about what was happening.

I spent ages writing and rewriting a draft report since I was very aware of just how dangerous it was to question the authority and autonomy of the head of a school. That weekend I had a dream. I was in a school walking through one of the corridors when I came across a cleaner washing down the walls. My waking self knew that at certain times of the year walls are washed, but only to the level that the cleaner can reach, which leaves a sort of 'tide mark' where the cleaned part and the dirty part meet. This is to save money and is a practice I've seen many times. However, in the dream, I asked the cleaner why she was only cleaning up to that point and not doing the whole thing properly. She replied, 'You can only go to head's level.'

I did not listen to that dream. I went 'above' the head's level. I sent out my report in the usual way prior to the meeting so that everyone would have a chance to read it, and felt satisfied that I could give plenty of evidence to validate my points. I never got a chance. I was summoned to see the assistant director of education, and carpeted for what I had done. As he said, 'Only the director of education could write a report like that.' When I said I could prove all my claims, he replied that he had no doubts about that, but the fact remained I could not go above the head. The headteacher concerned was furious and demanded the report be withdrawn – a demand to which the assistant director agreed. My team was withdrawn from the school and numerous minor dramas were played out. As a footnote, about a year and a half later there was a series of events which vindicated what was written in the report.

Climbing the career ladder – or not

Chrissy, a lecturer in her early forties told me her story one evening at a counselling workshop. Married to a man fifteen years her senior, she had found the last two years quite difficult ever since Tom, her husband, had been made redundant. After much discussion, they had decided that he should not try to find another unskilled job but should take over responsibility for the care of their seven-year-old son and manage the running of the house. There were teething problems adjusting to the change in roles but on the whole all was going smoothly. Chrissy loved her job and Tom seemed happy at home. However, she was troubled by this recurring dream:

'The lift keeps going up and up and I feel that the building is endless in height. A great feeling of fear as the building seems to sway. An overwhelming fear of actually getting to the top and being so high up. I've had this dream for many years and it is almost identical each time it occurs.'

We worked on the dream and what came to light was that she felt out of control and progressively more afraid the higher she climbed the career ladder. Her working-class parents had tried to dissuade her from academic pursuits, saying she would 'get above her station' and that she would 'come a cropper'. These messages, still skulking at the back of her mind, came forward in her dreams to disturb her peace of mind. Another bit of her, as revealed in the solid casing of the lift, felt quite capable of dealing with the problems that might be encountered in going to the top.

Chrissy's conflict between being a career woman and being a woman as defined by her parents – staying at home, looking after the family and carrying out the usual traditional duties – had obviously not been satisfactorily resolved even taking into account the events of the last couple of years. She still felt guilty about her career and was frightened that she was not truly capable of fulfilling the important position she had achieved. By looking at the different parts of the dream, Chrissy realized that her fears were unfounded and that she could choose to accept and build on her skills and refuse to be hampered by the outmoded messages that constrained her life. Chrissy and Tom are now doing fine and there has not been a repeat of the shaky life dream.

Nursing is demanding, poorly paid and emotionally draining. It produces its own nightmares, be they subconsciously repeating the day's work over and over again or, as in Nan's case, regularly dreaming that she is on night duty and unable to finish all her work in the allotted time. Overburdened nursing staff have a lot of anxious work dreams, especially at times of financial cutbacks in the medical profession. Tricia, now a hospital sister, had her first such dream just prior to her SRN examinations, though she finds it recurring now her hospital is so chronically understaffed:

'I dreamt that I was in a graveyard and all the tombstones lifted up and the bodies which were falling to pieces were chasing me. Now whenever I am under a lot of stress or feeling very worried I have this dream.'

Ruby, a psychiatric nurse, described how it was for her:

'When I first started my job in mental health, I woke up screaming and banging the wall, trying to get through to my friend in the next room. I slammed the wall with my whole arm and tried to get up, put on the light and open the door – I could do none of these things.'

Ruby's dream reflected her early, later dispelled, fears about her work, and dramatically highlighted the importance of a supportive friend at times of need. Ruby was unable to voice her waking anxieties for, like Alexandra, she was unassertive. Alexandra, a hospital administrator, has useful clarification dreams:

'I dream of situations where I am standing up for myself and I know that this is because I am too reserved during waking hours but I feel it helps me sort out situations sometimes. And it really helps to get rid of pent-up emotions that I hold back at work.'

It is now accepted that both nursing staff and patients dream about the stresses of hospitalization. Audrey Foy examined the dreams of patients and staff on a haemodialysis unit and illustrated how dreams reflect the fears and anxieties of those in a situation where life itself depends on the successful operation of a mechanical device.[1] More such studies could lead to improved emotional care in hospitals.

When women are promoted, their dreams often reveal worries about the new responsibilities. After she had been promoted to chief clerk, Sandra found that her dreams were about being in situations which she could not control. For Diane, having to come to terms with new technology meant that she was dreaming of going through word-processor procedures even as she slept! While this caused some anxiety, it was a way of consolidating the knowledge she was acquiring. Her repetition of learning in her dreams probably increased her grasp of it – tiring though it must have been, working a double shift!

Forty-one and a half per cent of full-time women workers are in clerical jobs, of which secretarial work plays a large part. Many secretaries epitomize women's role in society; they run round looking after a, usually, male boss, such as Roma's, and are rarely given the respect or responsibility their talents warrant. A number of my female friends working in TV and radio have found that the only entry open to them has been through the secretarial route.

'Typecast', a group of feminist secretaries in London, described how the ways in which secretaries were underrated led to a vicious circle where confidence was undermined to the extent that they were unable to voice feelings of being degraded in terms of skills.[2] The majority of secretaries surveyed in the city centre 'felt they had no chances of promotion and that the attitudes of male management prevented them from exploiting their potential'. Such waste and frustration is echoed in the common dreams in which women feel their 'feet stuck to the ground'.

Forced to move

A colleague of my husband married recently and we were invited to the wedding reception. I had not met most of the guests before and found myself next to Marjorie, a woman in her early thirties. That's how old she looked, but she sounded like someone who had lost all hope of a fulfilled life; she seemed thirty going on ninety! In fact, some ninety-year-olds I've met have been a damn sight more optimistic. She was married to Tony, an architect with an international insurance company. She was at home during the day while her eight-year-old son went to the local school. However, Tony had just resigned from work because they could no longer face the strain of yet another 'company move'.

Each year about 185,000 people in the UK move home because they change jobs or their company requires relocation. It costs the companies a great deal of money but it also costs individuals dear in emotional terms, as Marjorie told me. She had left her infant-teaching job in the south to move with her husband when his promotion meant a change to the northern branch. Unable to get a post in the north, Marjorie was offered by the insurance group a low-paid, fairly unskilled clerical job. She accepted. At least it would give her the opportunity to meet other women and then she might eventually get another job in teaching. She never did, though, because she felt unable to put down roots; if she was going to have to move with her husband's work whenever the company instructed, what was the point? The unwritten penalty for refusal to relocate was no promotion but, more than that, the practice within the company was: if you refused, you resigned.

Marjorie had classic frustration dreams, ranging from being unable to escape from danger because her feet seemed glued to the ground, to being alone and unhappy, to having no support, to travelling and never reaching her destination. She is still having the dreams and will probably continue to do so if she doesn't seize her opportunity and start changing her passive dependent lifestyle.

Cary Cooper, professor of organizational psychology at the University of Manchester, says that many companies are not taking into account changes in society that mean many more women are working and have their own careers to consider. He believes that part of the motivation for requesting moves is to test the commitment of the employee. In the case of women employees the assumption, which frequently works against appointment, is that women will not be mobile. Some companies are beginning to recognize that social attitudes are changing and that women are more assertive, ambitious and career-minded.

Journalist Maggie Meade-King, a specialist on women in the workplace, has noted that in spring 1986 the CBI set up an Employee Relocation Council to act as a clearing house for information and 'a forum to debate mobility policies'.[3] As Maggie says, 'There will certainly be plenty of debate as the old assumptions about mobility are questioned with companies now under pressure to take their employees' private lives into consideration.' Although it might be too late for Marjorie, it need not be too late for other women.

Artistic Creativity

Mouse Katz, artist-organizer of exhibitions concerned with images of women, is inspired by her own vivid dreams. An American living in Britain, she finds that fecund mother-goddess figures leap from her unconscious and are translated into passionate, humorous works. Amy, the weaver we met earlier who spoke of her dream about her mother as a baby (see page 110), uses her technicolor nocturnal images for weavings and paintings:

'They are an inspiration to my paintings as they are often an outlet to images and colours which I am too busy to sit down and create in my waking hours. I can remember them and retain them in my conscious mind like a video tape.'

In other cases, women's dreams are a source of inspiration for the written word. The celebrated author Anaïs Nin described how her dreams fuelled her writing:

> I kept a record of my dreams for a year, for a whole year, and then wrote a book called *House of Incest*, based on the idea that the first love was always within the family, was always, in an emotional sense, incestuous. But what I found was that if you just keep your dreams, and you're not relating your life to your dreams then you fall in love with them for themselves . . . I learned to allow these images to come floating up, to enjoy them, to look at them as you would look at a painting, to permit them to exist. Usually, unless they are guiding us through a difficult moment of our life, we tend really not to listen to them or to put them away.

Having decided to trust the images in dreams rather than fighting against them, she found new inspiration: 'And every novel I wrote from then on always began with a dream, and sometimes I didn't know where it was going to lead me.'

Anaïs Nin was absolutely certain about the central role dreams played in her creativity. Lily is too. She has been writing poetry since her teens. Sometimes she has written eight or nine poems in a year; other years she hardly writes a line. However, on two occasions, she has woken from sleep with a poem flooding through her brain, and has been impelled to get out of bed and write it down. She recounts:

'Only two poems, I know, but each utterly different, not only from each other in every way, but utterly different from any I had ever written before in my waking state – different in style, rhythm and subject matter. One poem was complete, I had no need to change even one word in order to make sense or the rhyming correct. It just came from my mind as easily as if it had been dictated to me. The other was only half a poem and I had the irritating sensation that I'd woken just too soon and hadn't really got the "whole" thing! This too was nothing like my usual style and the next day I pored over it in the hopes of being able to complete it without the "join" being too obvious! I found the words coming easily and sensibly, without much effort, though not with the facile ease that was there in the middle of the night.'

Lily discovered a new way of writing because of her dreams and this happens with many creative women. The mind continues to work, bringing up fresh ideas for consideration. Of course, these are not necessarily as dramatic as Lily's examples but you may be very surprised at what does happen once you decide to use your dreams. By recording dreams and working on them you will find that your dream recall increases and you will discover a more creative side to yourself.

Josceline Dimbleby, the cookery writer, found so much inspiration in her dreams that she called one of her books *A Taste of Dreams*.[5] The first time she put into practice the sugar-plums which had been cavorting about in her dreams, she was truly astonished to find that they turned out beautifully. Such inspiration linked to problem-solving is not at all unusual as you will see later in this chapter.

Working colleagues

Personal relationships are as important at work as they are in other areas of life. It can take time, though, to feel comfortable in a new setting. Kate's dream showed her unconscious misgivings on changing her job after working in the same place for ten years:

'I dreamt about being an outsider looking in. I was always the spectator.'

As she got to know her colleagues, her dreams changed and she began dreaming about them. Now, she says:

'I dream about people I work with and in my dream I get to know them better and see another side to them. If I see them the next day, I feel that they also have experienced this feeling of intimacy.'

Her waking and dreaming imaginations combine to provide a more complete picture of the people she meets, thus extending her understanding of them.

Have you noticed what happens when you tell a person you have dreamt of them? They usually feel more involved with you and often are quite flattered. However, I doubt whether Faith's colleague would have been flattered to hear this dream:

'I had a dream about my work in which I was very anxious. In it there was a woman whom I thought was more successful than me. She was pouring a glass of water and I suddenly realized that what she had to offer me was transparent. I haven't dreamt of her since.'

Blazing arguments with colleagues in dreams are fairly common; most dreamers who recalled these said they were unable, or unwilling, to express their honest feelings at work. Similarly, they dreamt of lots of tasks mounting up at work at times of increased pressure. Instead of stating that they were overloaded or refusing to take on yet more work, the usual practice was to accept the work, then to complain to everyone else apart from the person who had dished out the work.

Not all work dreams are serious – far from it; some are positively hilarious. Jenny describes one she had which left tears of laughter rolling down her cheeks:

'I do have a lot of food dreams but that's because I spent so many years working in catering. I still wonder about the dream in which I had a bedroom in a Bloomsbury hotel and someone had set a dish of meat in the middle of my bed. It consisted of big, broad bones set up like a crown of lamb. All the staff kept coming past and each pulled a bit off and ate it. I tried some and it was delicious. At this juncture the murder squad from the Met. arrived and started to accuse me of killing Oscar Wilde, pointing to the dish as evidence.

'However, I quickly and wittily thought of a defence and managed to persuade them of my innocence. I pointed out that any seaman would immediately identify the structure as carvel-built, which meant that it could not be Oscar Wilde as he was well known to be clinker-built! At the same time I was holding my breath for fear they would call my bluff, as I did not know whether he had been clinker-built or not. He tasted absolutely marvellous – if it was him!'

Clearly a woman with literary tastes!

Problem-solving

The old adage 'sleep on it' carries the wisdom of ages, for it implies that problems can be resolved as we sleep. Dreams work through problems, as Judi relates:

'If I go to sleep thinking about a particular problem, I often wake up in the morning with the solution or at least with the problem organized in my mind. The dreams help me to get my conscious and subconscious mind working together. They help me to realize what I subconsciously want and how to achieve what is best for me.'

That is exactly what happens to me and I includes an example here. A dream group I was working in had decided to look at the theme of animals in dreams. It was late at night and my sluggish brain was not coming up with much. Too tired to do any more, and conscious that the baby was likely to wake up teething, I decided to go to bed. I had a wonderful dream. In many ways it feels like a 'big', special dream because it allowed me to understand an important concept.

I was in a sunny garden working on my dream material. There were two filing cabinets and I had some notes and pictures of animals in front of me. In one picture was a domestic cat and in the other was a lion cub, but each had a piece missing. I wasn't aware of anyone else in the dream but was puzzling over how all this lot went together. Quite suddenly and unspectacularly, a voice said, 'This is what happens. It is quite simple really. You put this part of the cat with this part of the lion and then you have the whole picture. All life has the bad with the good, the wild with the tamed, the dark with the light. That is the paradox.' Then it seemed that a series of images was run through – for instance, a pleasant adolescent boy with a threatening loutish figure, and so on – all the time making the point that this is how life is made up.

I woke up with a sense of wonderment which I can still remember although it happened a couple of years ago now. I thought I understood the Jungian idea of the paradox of life on an intellectual level but it was as nothing compared to the emotional truth of the dream.[6]

At work most of us are expected to be rational and logical and to make decisions on that basis, but often such an approach leaves out the more feeling response to situations. This is not always the best way forward, as Dilly discovered:

'I use my dreams more now and let myself be guided by impulsive inner feelings because every time I have ignored them and decided purely rationally I have regretted that decision. Very often I dream about those decisions and in the dream I know what to do. I try to follow that since it seems to be truer to my desires than what my waking mind and all outer influences tell me.'

In dreams, ideas can find a form of expression that is not readily accessible during waking hours. Gina was having trouble achieving a particular effect in the paintings she did as a hobby. One night she 'slept on it' and had a dream about being with an artist. He told her exactly what to do to obtain that particular effect and then gave her a demonstration. She tried out his advice and it worked splendidly! In effect, what she had been doing was engaging in that right-brain activity we noted earlier.

Instead of problems being hidden away in the deep filing cabinet of the mind, dreams bring them to the fore as if saying, 'Sorry these are not dealt with. There is work outstanding. Please re-present for filing when you have completed task.' This certainly fits in with Evans's computer theory of dreams (see page 21) and shows how dreams continue to work on issues while we sleep.[7]

Dreams may not provide an obvious solution but they often show the right questions to ask. Eloise uses dreams to show her where she should be going and has found them very helpful at decision-making times in her career. After she had a panic-filled dream about broadcasting live for the BBC, where she works as a presenter, she began to ponder her feelings about the job. In the dream studio, as the camera was sending out live pictures, she found that she had forgotten how to read. There was chaos. She asked herself what it was that she did not want to communicate and discovered that she desired some behind-the-scenes work to get away from the pressures of her on-screen role. She hasn't achieved that yet but she is awake to an ambivalent attitude towards her present role.

I met Morton Shatzman at his home in London, where he told me about his fascinating work on problem-solving in dreams. As a psychiatrist his interest had turned to psychotherapy and the use of

142

dreams. He wrote articles for a number of magazines in which he posed problems. Readers were invited to work out the answers; if they were unsuccessful while awake, they were asked to make a note of any solution which came from dreams. A surprising number of respondents found that their dreams had indeed given solutions. One example was along the following lines: 'What is unusual about this sentence: Prussian slaughter brings rout?' You'll discover the answer in the notes at the end of the chapter,[8] but suffice it to say that many, many people were not successful until their dreaming mind worked on the puzzle.

In dream sleep the brain sorts, evaluates and analyses recently acquired information before it is placed in more permanent storage. This helps the dreamer to assimilate new information and adapt to changing circumstances. In some cases, the dream problem-solving mode comes into operation as we sleep, enabling us to find resolutions which have been elusive in waking life. A characteristic of problem-solving dreams is that they wake the dreamer.

After working on her dreams for a long period, Anna noticed that examining in detail each part of a dream led her to new ways of looking at problems. Her method may be useful to you.

Whenever she is stuck and can't find a solution, she 'requests' a problem-solving dream. Some of us do this unconsciously – for instance, when we're getting undressed and say to ourselves, 'I hope I can sort this out', or, 'I'd like to get this resolved before the meeting tomorrow.' We don't 'ask' for a dream but we reinforce the message to ourselves that we want a resolution. Anna very deliberately says, 'I want a dream solution about such and such a problem.' What she has found out is that immediate, short-term difficulties are worked out under the theme of 'food'!

Here's a typical example of a dream which Anna had when she was trying to write a particularly difficult report:

'I was in the canteen where Harry, my husband, works. It was under new management. There were only two meals on offer. Although I asked for the roast chicken, I had to make do with the fried fish. There was a very large quantity on the plate, including chips, and the vegetable was served on a separate plate. The fish was broken up as if overcooked, and there was some danger from the bones. The vegetable was small, whole cauliflower *au gratin*. I ate what I could, but there was far more than I could manage. Harry came in for his food, took the first mouthful of fish and stood up – there was a fishbone stuck in his throat.'

Anna worked on the dream, making connections such as: *food for thought*; *fishy business*; *more than she could chew*; *bone of contention*; *more than meets the eye* (both the fish and cauliflower were coated and somewhat congealed); and *hard to swallow*. Harry couldn't swallow it; it 'stuck in his throat'. Anna realized that there was something about the way in which she had been landed with writing the report that was not right, and so part of her was sabotaging her completion of the allotted task. The dream helped her to recognize what the blocks were about. Anna now understood what was so fishy about the whole thing.

Where next?

Women are taking more responsibility for themselves in the world of work. 'Networking', where women help and inform other women about work and professional issues, is beginning to happen on a wider scale in Britain. In America it has become an important force, enabling more women to reach higher career points. Santa Clara Valley, near San Francisco, has been nicknamed 'the feminist capital of America' because of the high proportion of women there who have been elected to local government positions.[9] Having political clout is a rare phenomenon for women, but in San Jose there has, until recently, been a female mayor for seven consecutive years. Such power has been greatly enhanced by the existence of strong women's networks which help other women into office. Allied to this is the shared realization of the demands made of women in terms of household commitments and, where applicable, child-rearing responsibilities.[10]

Maybe not all women are as assertive and clear about their aims in the world of work as Diane Abbot. In 1985 she was chosen as the Labour candidate in a London constituency, the first black woman to be given the opportunity to be an MP and she recalled her selection board interview when she went for a job in the civil service. When asked why she wanted to join such a body, she replied, to their amazement, 'Because I want power.' Diane had decided what she wanted and was finding a route to achieve her aim, yet most of us tend to drift into the caring jobs because that is what is expected of us.

You can use your dreams to help you act more creatively, to solve your problems and to get in touch with what you really want. It is up to you to evaluate your current work and its place in your life. When I was midway through writing this book, wondering whether it was worth the effort I was putting in, I had a dream. The setting was the basement of a large university library and I found myself at the shelves where books on dreams could be found. There were a few there but there was a fairly large space and, in my dream, I heard myself say, 'Oh yes, there is plenty of room for my book. There's a gap that needs to be filled.' I believe that dream was telling me to get on with it: the work was worthwhile.

Notes

1. Audrey L. Foy, 'Dreams of Patients and Staff', *American Journal of Nursing*, Vol. 70 (1), January 1970.
2. Maggie Meade-King, 'Why secretaries in dead-end jobs need a stepping stone to advancement', *The Guardian*, 13 November 1985.
3. Maggie Meade-King, 'A step in the right career direction can mean a wrong turn for the family', *The Guardian*, 20 November 1985.
4. Anaïs Nin, *A Woman Speaks*, (ed. Evelyn J. Hinz), W.H. Allen, 1978.
5. Josceline Dimbleby, *A Taste of Dreams*, Hodder and Stoughton, 1976.
6. There is more detail about the paradox in Carl Jung's *Dreams*, pages 222-24, in the Bollingen series, Princeton University Press, 1974.
7. Christopher Evans, (ed. Peter Evans), *Landscapes of the Night*, Gollancz, 1983.
8. Morton Schatzman, 'Solve Your Problems in your Sleep', *New Society*, 9 June 1983. The answer to the puzzle is: By taking the initial letter off each word you can form a completely different sentence – 'Russian laughter rings out'.
9. *Western Political Quarterly*, Vol. 38, No. 1, page 4.
10. 'The Feminists of Silicon Valley', *New Society*, 25 October 1985.

8

Why So Anxious?

Anxiety Dreams

Involving violence towards self, i.e. the dreamer	29%
Involving violence towards family	15%
House	6%
Tasks	5%
Transport	5%
Animals	4%
Losing things/being lost	3%
Babies/pregnancy	3%
Work	3%
Falling	3%
Relationships outside family	3%
Toilets	3%
Examinations/tests	2%
Water	2%
Lifts/stairs	2%
Clothes	2%
Devils	1%
Heights	1%
Planes, attacking	1%
Others, including smoking, school, end of world	7%
Total	100%

I have never come across a woman who has not had at least one dream which made her feel anxious. Certainly I have had some dreadful ones, in which my feelings have the run the gamut from mild concern to intense fear, leaving me trembling and in tears, afraid that the dream was real and the events about to take place.

146

Indeed the spectrum is so wide that the theme of anxiety spans the next three chapters.

The largest category of anxiety dreams, 44 per cent, reported in my survey were ones in which violence was threatened or occurred. Twenty-nine per cent, of these involved violence to the dreamer, ranging from murder to rape, and a number of women chillingly reported witnessing their own deaths. Violence is covered in detail in Chapter 10. A breakdown of different causes of anxiety dreams is given at the beginning of this chapter (page 146)

Before I tell you about my most recent anxiety dream I should explain that my husband's given name is John but everyone calls him Styx – a strange nickname that has stuck since he was about five years old.

In the dream I was walking with my husband in a dark, dreary, inner-city street not far from where we live. Suddenly, we saw ahead of us some youths wrecking a car and harassing someone. The figure was indistinct. Styx moved to intervene as I tried to hold him back, saying, 'Don't, they'll kill you.' The youths spotted us and one of them rushed up angrily cursing us and describing what would happen if we told anyone what we had seen. The setting changed and we were inside a friend's house, both shaken by the situation. There was suddenly a loud rapping on the door. I went to answer it and a darkly-clad thug stood there. He repeated his warning, adding, 'I know where you live and we'll get you all.' I was terrified for the kids in particular and went back to Styx. In tears I told him what had been said. In the final scene of the dream we were going to an estate agent's; I was still anxiously looking over my shoulder.

When I woke up, I was sobbing – something that had not happened to me for a long time. The dream remains very vivid; it brought into floodlit illumination fears I had been trying to repress. About ten months before, one lazy Saturday afternoon, I had been breastfeeding Danny before putting him down for his nap. Styx was shaving in the bathroom, but came into the bedroom where I sat, saying someone was shooting an airgun at our chickens. He went off to sort it out and I, filled with an awful dread, hurriedly put the warm, rosy-cheeked five-month-old in his cot, rushed to the back bedroom and, looking out through the window, saw three figures moving from behind the fence towards a house. Styx was running across the back garden. I decided to follow.

Arriving at the back fence, I could not see Styx, though I could see two figures and could hear others scuffling. I shouted, 'What's happening?' but no one replied, so I dashed to a part of the wall I thought I could clamber over. All the time I really couldn't see anything. I ran as fast as I could round to the front of the other houses.

It was four minutes later. Styx knelt on one knee, glasses in one hand, while the other hand, too late, attempted to shield his bleeding head. The sticky red blood poured through his fingers into his dark curly hair, and then, when I reached him, on to my tee-shirt and jeans. A quiet lazy Saturday! I held Styx to me. Three feet from us stood a young man holding a pickaxe handle in what looked like a relaxed golfer's position. 'You bastard. What have you done? What have you done?' I screamed over and over again as he stood there unmoving. Beside him stood another shifty-eyed man in his twenties and a greasy-haired, mousy girl. None of them would meet my gaze. All the time I was holding Styx, desperately wondering what to do and scared that anything might yet happen. Without a word, the pickaxe-wielder turned and walked off with the other two in tow. There was no one to help us as I got Styx to his feet. He could just about walk, and I recall as we slowly staggered home how the blood oozed through his fingers while my tears blurred the world so it seemed that the blood and tears washed together. I was terrified he would die.

Desperate phone calls swiftly brought the police and ambulance and Styx was taken to hospital while I, after being assured that he would be all right, took the police to the scene of the crime. After many, many months the man who had been charged was given a two-year prison sentence for grievous bodily harm. He was, they said, 'a snapper': he had a short fuse and was prone to violence. He kept the pickaxe handle in his house for 'fighting'. I did not know until the evidence was given in court that he kept the handle taped, so he could have a better grip. The guy was imprisoned, Styx recovered, but I suppose I have still not come to terms with it. I cannot make sense of the arbitrary nature of that violence and I want to leave this area which holds no security for me.

My dream indicated the depth of my anxiety about the attack and we are now taking action. The house goes on the market next month, though it is now over twelve months since tranquillity was smashed.

Other women's dreams, can also reveal deep-seated fears. Sal had many disturbing dreams particularly when relationships went awry.

'The bad dreams only started after my first husband left me. For a year and a half after the divorce they became more and more frequent. Since my second marriage, and with a lot of help and support from my second husband, they are less frequent, though he still has to wake me from my sleep sometimes when I am really upset. After four years of putting up with "me and my dreams" he is not quite as sympathetic as he used to be. I sometimes feel quite ill as I cannot get them out of my mind. It has been suggested to me that I wouldn't dream if I kept my mind occupied by getting a job outside the home, etc., but I'm not so sure . . . In a way it has been a help for me to write them down, in answering your questionnaire, even if very briefly. My dreams have become part of my life.'

Sal, like so many others, had been told to forget her dreams, to ignore them. Get a job! Take your mind off things. What a shame that no one had helped her to take note of some of the messages they were imparting. Her vividly expressive dreams clearly warrant further attention, as you can see from the following details taken from the questionnaire:

'Recurring dreams – falling down an endless staircase; confrontations between myself and my ex-husband or my husband's ex-wife. Sometimes they both appear together and always they are threatening me with violence, then they lock me in a small, dark room. Another recurring dream of drowning in a very black pool. I am spinning round trying to get free . . .

'I have dreams in which my parents die or people that I am close to are being abused.

'To be honest, sometimes I am very worried about my dreams. They seem so real that they remain with me throughout the day.'

Sal is crying out for reassurance, help and support. Her dreams reflect anxieties that she cannot, or does not, express when awake, but the emotions are too strong to be suppressed indefinitely. She is not alone. Dreams bring to our attention that which we seek to deny. The question is, are we willing to look and then to acknowledge what we see?

Animals

'Over many years, my dreams have been filled with the images of sharks biting off my limbs,' writes Pam. Though she finds the dreams revolting, the mutilations continue and are likely to do so until she faces up to whatever it is that is tearing her limb from limb. It may be that the shark represents someone who is unfeeling towards her or some part of herself which is destructive and inflicting self-injury.

The image of the shark is significant. Sharks are highly efficient killing and eating machines, built to last and perfectly adapted to their environment. Their streamlined design has endured while worlds have altered about them. They have ridden the changes and survive where so many other creatures have become extinct.

What does this mean for Pam and for other women who have similar dreams of being attacked by sharks or other animals? The most important thing is to work out what the animal means to you. On a simple level it could be that you have had a traumatic experience in waking life involving such an animal – some people have been attacked by a shark and lived to tell the tale. If this is the case, then your dream is probably helping you to work through the truama. However, if you have not had such an experience, then your dream is using the image of the animal in a symbolic way, and we each have our own meanings for different symbols.

I should like to find out from Pam what she thinks about sharks, what she knows of them, what they signify for her. If she has not had any particularly unusual experiences with sharks, she probably has views in common with others brought up in our culture. We talk about 'sharks' when we mean thieves, people involved in sharp practice or those who are generally untrustworthy, being concerned with their own needs at the expense of other people's. A shark might be someone who tries to 'rip you off'. Somewhere, Pam has the key to the dream meaning; in considering her symbols she will discover what it is.

Eileen's dream affected her for some time afterwards and she found it very hard to shake off the uneasy feelings it aroused:

'I dreamt I was sent two young animals and a letter in a large envelope informing me that I had won them. I didn't read the letter but told a friend, who was with me in the kitchen, that it must be a consolation prize. My friend, being a very good cook, set about cutting one of them up. She cooked the body of the animal, leaving the head and legs. They looked like young deer but only had very tiny horns. When it was cooked I just scooped out a handful of meat from the middle of the animal and gave it to my daughter. In the dream she was younger, aged about six, which was her age when her dad died. When I gave her the handful of meat she vomited it out. I tried to give some of the meat to a neighbour but she said she didn't want it.

'I still feel that I can taste that mouthful. It was tender meat, tasty and very soft, but I didn't want to eat any more. The woman who cooked it didn't touch any. The dream seems to be clinging to me and won't leave me.'

Unfortunately, when Eileen wrote after hearing me on a radio programme, she omitted to send her address so I wasn't able to follow up her disturbing dream. Certainly there is a feeling of repulsion here. Having to deal with this strange 'consolation prize', which is no consolation at all, leaves her with a lingering taste. Could it be that there has been no consolation since her husband's death?

An important clue to the meaning of the dream is that it is set at the time of her husband's death, for her daughter is the age 'when her father died'. Her daughter is twenty-two now, so that's a long time ago. Eileen appears to have been unable to resolve her feelings from that time. She can see, feel and taste the meat; her senses are highly tuned and yet no one else responds or partakes in the same way. She alone feeds on the dead deer – her dead 'dear', I wonder? She alone savours the ambivalent feelings of grief. Others – her neighbour, her daughter – do not want to share in her unpalatable 'consolation'. Her daughter is in fact sickened by it. Is Eileen making her daughter sick, in the sense that people say 'you make me sick' when we continue to do something which is disagreeable to them?

In some way Eileen must bid farewell to what has been presented:

151

she can refuse to eat that which she has misgivings about. She could use her own power and decline to accept this 'prize' which is no prize at all. She could read the letter instead of making assumptions. She could begin by asking her daughter and her friend whether they think she has been dwelling in the past and listen to their point of view. She will be able to achieve a lot once she faces whatever is so distasteful.

Being under attack, or being in imminent danger, is the main thread in Cathy's dream:

'I'm in the country at a dog farm. The alsatians have attacked the people in the farmhouse. One man has had his feet bitten off and is dragging himself along. Another lies covered in bandages on the floor. I wipe his nose for him and make a bit of a mess of it at first but just manage it. Everyone has been bitten except me. The alsatians are still around and are trying to bite me. I climb on top of the fridge.'

Cathy is safe for the time being but where is her escape route? The dream shows her as the only one who is uninjured. She administers aid to others, but I wonder why she wipes the man's nose when there are so many more vital services she could perform? What does she see from her cool vantage point on top of the fridge? She has an effective instinct for self-preservation which sets her apart from the others and comes into operation at this time of threat.

Those of us who have pets feel anxious about their being involved in accidents. Carol's is an anxiety dream reflecting her waking feelings:

'An especially vivid dream was the death of my dog. I dreamed he was chasing a car, got caught under the wheel and was skinned alive.'

Even though it is a common fear, Carol expresses it in a highly personal fashion. Her dog is 'skinned alive'. Is that a common expression for her? If not, then she should think about where she heard it last and what she associates with it, and so gain more insight into her dream.

Rats, mice, hamsters and other rodents appear in dreams to the dismay of many. The reaction of self-effacing, dependable Jill is typical.

'I am in the same old house and hordes of large, fierce rats are everywhere, eating through the floorboards to get at me.'

As this was not a one-off dream but part of a series in which Jill was threatened by floods, kept prisoner with her spastic brother and deserted by her flirtatious husband, the meaning is fairly clear. In this dream she feels under attack from all directions. Even her 'ground' is not safe, for the rats can eat through and still get to her. What is below the surface? What is usually kept from view? Notice that it is the 'same old house'. This is a familiar place for her, just as in waking life being a victim is familiar too. She describes herself as 'a forty-eight-year-old ex-beauty queen with a husband twelve years older'. Though her two daughters are loving and spend a lot of time with her, Jill constantly feels she is 'a nobody' or else hates herself. An early childhood dream indicates fear and depression – a depression which, I feel, has never been adequately dealt with:

'I would dream that my brother, who is eighteen months older than me and slightly spastic, would be held prisoner with me and others in an underground cave. We would be beaten and whipped but, despite my screams to leave him alone, they would not stop. I would wake up in a dreadful state and sit up all night because I knew if I went to sleep again it would begin anew.'

Jill's dream reveals her powerlessness yet shows how responsible she feels for her handicapped brother. No one helped her in the dream, just as no one came in to comfort the fretful child as she sat up in bed for the rest of the night. Her parents did not notice her distress. As an adult, Jill still lacks someone to come to her rescue; nor has she developed personal skills to save herself. She continues to have dreams of being in a cave, though now the water is completely calm, closing in and filling the cave. She knows she is going to drown and waits.

Steve Karpman, an American psychologist, used a triangle to describe life positions that people customarily take up.[1] The three points represent the 'victim' position, the 'rescuer' position and the 'persecutor' position. If we are lucky, we move from position to position, but many people get stuck. Jill is trapped in the 'victim' role. She is under threat, does not fight back but waits for the rats to break through and do their worst. She does not act to save herself as Cathy did by climbing on the fridge. Nor does she summon aid as the Senoi would do. (Remember, their idea was to confront danger in a dream, seek dream assistants and make the dream have a positive outcome.) Jill does none of this. She waits for the worst to happen, and if she waits long and passively enough, it probably will. It is her choice.

Jan received assistance when she was under attack from rats:

'In my dream I found myself surrounded by hundreds of rats. From out of this cluster stood a big black rat with soft eyes. Somehow this one rat was keeping the rest away from me. The rats tried to bite my feet and jump up at me. However, this "saviour" rat kept biting them and they ran away.

'A few days later I was involved with friends in some trouble. It seemed to me that the people I was arguing with were the rats in my dream and the person who was sorting it out was protecting me.'

Harriet described the dream ordeal which she has suffered in various forms for years and, almost in passing, gave an important clue to its meaning:

'This is a dream of sheer terror and I'm paralysed. The first time it happened I was sure it was something physical. I just could not speak or move . . . after a while it stopped, leaving me very frightened.

'I am controlled by a huge hamster which has the power to tighten a metal band round my head. Every time I try to regain control of my mind, the band tightens and I give in to it . . . 'I don't have any fears of or feelings about rodents.

'The metal band was a strip about one inch wide placed right around the top of my head rather like a sweatband. The hamster had the same type of metal bands around its wrist and one around its neck, only there were spikes attached all the way round the bands.

'Incidentally, this dream came when I'd just left my husband, so maybe that is why it's so intense.'

Harriet may have left her husband physically but in the dream she is still very much attached. She says the dream began just after she left him, yet it includes a powerful force which has control over her, even if the control is somewhat remote. I wonder if this reflects Harriet's feelings about her ex-husband? Does this rat-like creature represent him? The image of a tightening metal band which encircles the mind, preventing it from following its own will, is revealing. She wakes from the dream feeling physically paralysed, while in the dream she is mentally paralysed. She concluded her letter by saying:

'My dreams about being paralysed are significant in that they make me more aware of my worries and fears in life. I am conscious that my life is going nowhere at the moment and has been that way for some years. I feel frustrated and dissatisfied and my feelings are so strong while I am awake that it is constantly on my mind, so naturally it comes across in my dreams and nightmares.'

Is there a link between the length of her marriage and the period over which she has had this 'control' dream? In it her power and autonomy are non-existent.

Not all rodent dreams are so extreme. Fiona and her sister both have guinea pig dreams. Fiona's are set in the home she lived in from seven years of age until she was seventeen, the place where her formative experiences took place. On her dream return there, she discovers that all is not quite right:

'I go to find my guinea pigs and realize they have not been fed or cleaned out for years. They aren't dead, just very neglected. I wake up feeling really guilty.'

It could be that the dream harks back to an incident in her childhood when Fiona did not care for her pets. She thinks not because, as she says:

'I can usually identify what they represent in my waking life. This is sometimes to do with work I have neglected, or a relationship that I've not been paying attention to. When I have the dream I now know I need to put more effort in!'

Traditionally, snakes have been associated with sexuality and this view was endorsed by Freud. However, not all that Freud postulated has universal support, particularly his theories about female sexuality – see, for example Masson's, *Freud: The Assault on the Truth*. Many women share the opinion of Valerie, who wrote to me from Dundee:

'It really annoys me, Brenda, to hear that snake dreams are linked to sexual problems. I can recall the time my dreams began. My grandfather took me to the reptile house of the local zoo. I couldn't see a single snake and pressed up against the glass in my efforts to peer in closer. I suddenly looked down and to my horror found there was a huge, obscene-looking one curled up in a corner right against the bit of glass I was leaning against – ugh! The feeling still repulses me beyond words. I hate worms too; anything without legs. Penises

I like, and cannot for the life of me see the connection . . . This incident happened when I was about three or four.'

In the two dreams which follow snakes are again the cause of anxiety, but are linked to the actions of others; in both instances, the 'others' are siblings:

'In one of my dreams about snakes, my brother is terrorizing me with a snake. (We had been talking about snakes during the day.) I was crying and ran to my bedroom. He followed me and opened the door slightly to show me the snake. Then he dashed in and threw the snake around my neck. I screamed loudly and woke up.

'In my dream the snake is given to me alive in a sandwich by my brother or sister; or else it is curling up and hissing in very dry, brittle grass.'

Not very nice brothers and sisters! But then brothers and sisters do frequently torment and hurt one another and dreams reflect that side of family life. The one in which the brother 'opened the door slightly' and 'threw the snake' around the dreamer's neck could be to do with early sexuality and fears involved in that early awareness. The setting is the bedroom, he can handle the 'snake' and he flaunts his ability in her face, forcing her to have contact with it by putting it round her neck. It could also demonstrate the inequalities in their relationship: the brother can physically and mentally dominate the less forceful sister.

Being caught in a spider's web conjures up fearful images of being trapped and bound ready to be eaten when the predator wants his dinner. Some women have dreams of being caught in a web while others dream of being surrounded by spiders of differing hues which bite, chase and generally menace the dreamer. One thing I have come across again and again with women who have spider dreams is that they are so terrified by the spiders that, in their efforts to knock them off the pillow or brush them from the bedclothes, they find themselves sitting bolt upright in bed or reaching for the lampswitch. Their fear is so acute that they force their bodies into action before their conscious mind has registered the change from sleeping to waking.

Poppy, a clinical psychologist in the field of drug addiction, regularly works on her dreams. One night she dreamt that her sister was waving a large black spider in front of her:

'I was absolutely terrified of it. Even though I was crying she would not stop teasing me with it. I think that the dream was about something I did not want to face but which was literally being held under my nose.'

Those awful siblings again! But at least this time Poppy's sister is trying to show her something and Poppy is willing to work on it later.

Trying to escape from spiders comes into Diane's dream:

'I was in school and was handed a sheet of paper, as were the other people. In each circle was the name of an animal and in some the name of an insect, including two varieties of spider. When I looked again the spiders were gone. The teacher told me they were poisonous. I sat up as high as possible on a table, then I saw one of the spiders on my foot. I kicked my foot to get rid of it, then I woke up.'

These dream spiders have to be avoided, for somehow they suggest danger for the dreamer. They are difficult to spot, dart here and there, and are certainly beyond most people's control. The insects do what they want and prefer to remain in the dark, but they also build magnificent webs. What does that tell the dreamer? Each will have to decide for herself what the anxiety is about by looking at the setting, the other people present, and what she is doing in the dream. In most cases the dreamer tries to escape, but maybe she needs to turn round and be assertive. Perhaps the message is that the dreamer is running away from things which are quite small, but which have taken on a disproportionate importance. As for the poisonous spiders, what does the dreamer associate with the teacher in the dream? Why isn't the teacher concerned? At least in this case the dreamer kicks out, fights back and then wakes up. She escapes the situation through her own efforts.

In the following dream we see several different animals, but the cat is the most significant. The dreamer must, at all costs, keep that cat:

'I am asked to ride a huge carthorse which is plunging and thrashing. I refuse but feed it, feeling very scared. It goes free and dies because of my feeding. It makes terrible death noises. Its owner cuts it up into terrible-smelling pieces, lots of blood and flesh, and makes me watch. I feel guilty and sick and have to leave. I take my cat with me. The cat leaps on the wrong bus and I have to get her back. I do, but then she runs off hunting in the fields. I see a dog in the distance and run to get her. It is extremely important that I have the cat safe with me. A girl teases and torments me, gives me the wrong cat and hides mine. She is a girl I don't like.

Jane had another 'cat' dream shortly afterwards:

'My cat (again) was touched by some source of evil and its legs and skin fell off. My mother patched it up in black fur with table legs. I was so sad because it wasn't right. Other cats were after it and I was trying to protect it, but it kept getting away.'

Women are sometimes described as being cat-like and, of course, cats have been traditionally associated with witches. In Jane's dreams we see a domesticated cat that desires to run off, to escape and be free. It wants to run in the fields and to hunt, but Jane is afraid for it and seeks to hold onto it, keeping it safe from attack by its enemy, the dog. But, in doing that, she takes away its ability to follow its instincts and be self-sufficient. She turns it into a dependent, restricted creature. How much of Jane has been tamed? Does part of her long to be out there running wild, fending for herself, alive and vibrant rather than sheltered and domesticated?

There are aspects of Jane's first dream that highlight the conflict between the tame and untamed sides of our animal natures. The carthorse, normally a quiet, reliable beast, here thrashes and behaves like an unbroken stallion. And in the feeding there is contradiction. What should nourish the animal causes its death. Jane does not want to watch the gruesome butchering, but she does. The bus comes but her cat gets on the wrong bus. The girl gives her a cat but it is the wrong cat. Everything is contradictory!

The second dream continues the anxiety theme. Again, all is not as it should be. The poor patched-up cat is not accepted by its own species and needs protection. Her mother tries to help but the results are pitiful.

The need for protection is a thread running through both dreams, as are Jane's attempts to save her cat and defuse whatever threatening situation she is in. Vulnerability and a constant source of threat in the dreams indicate underlying anxieties not yet dealt with. There is a very positive side to these dreams, though: Jane is in there fighting. She is doing her best, which tells us that she has the power to change events. She needs to analyse what the cat represents for her.

The repetition of it in her dreams means that she should make every effort to decipher the message. She should work on the dreams as described in Chapter 12, and chart the progress of this dream cat.

Anita had a dream which similarly deals with conflict:

'I am being driven in a car or a taxi. I am in the back, on the left. I am holding apart two black cats: the female with my left hand and the male with my right. The male is trying to get at the female and is squirming and struggling against my hand. The female is saying, "You'll have to open the door wider to let me out."

'I am trying to open the left-hand door with my elbow and manage to open it a little way. Eventually she manages to slip out. The other cat is still struggling and saying, "It's not fair."

'In the end I have to let him go and he follows the female cat out of the door. I'm left wondering if they will find each other again or not.'

After I had worked on this dream with Anita what came to light were her difficulties in feeling at ease with her own masculine/feminine qualities. She finds it a struggle to build relationships with others and consequently feels lonely and isolated. Mixing, making friends, having chats with people – things which seem so easy for other people – she finds formidable, so she keeps herself apart, sees few people other than those with whom she works, and longs for closer emotional contact.

In her dream, the conflict of two sides against the middle is evident; the male and female cats naturally want to be off enjoying their freedom but the middle wants to keep them separated and restrained. The middle part is very controlling, which is just how Anita is when you first meet her. She seems extremely rigid, watches everyone and everything around her, and is aloof and suspicious. All the time you feel she is criticizing. Yet, after many months I found under that iron restraint a warm, humorous person trapped by her own insecurities.

The only way she could maintain any sort of balance was to be 'in control' all the time, because no one would like the 'real' Anita if ever she let herself go. A therapist wrote some lines which summed up Anita. He said, 'Why I cannot show you who I really am is that you might not like me and I'm all I've got.'

Anita lived alone in her flat, travelled each day to her paper-dominated job and watched TV in the evenings. She stayed aloof because she was afraid of being rejected. I believe the female cat gave her the wisest advice when she said, 'You'll have to open the door a little wider to let me out.' Her instinctual, right-brain side gives her guidance in her dream. And her male cat, her *animus* or masculine side, needs some freedom to show its nature. In freeing these different facets of her personality, Anita will find a healthier, more balanced lifestyle.

Here is a final cat dream for your delectation:

'I had a dream of a cat made of chocolate, far too good to resist. Against my better judgement, I began eating the tail, then the legs, but then the cat suddenly came to life: only one leg now so it could not stand and kept falling over. I was crying with horror and guilt.'

According to an old dream dictionary, the ancient meaning ascribed to the cat is as follows:

'If anyone dreams that he hath encountered a Cat or killed one, he will commit a thief to prison and prosecute him to death, for the cat signifies a common thief.'

Somehow that does not fit Thea's chocolate-cat dream. However, if we consider some of the words she used there are plenty of clues. The chocolate cat is 'too good to resist' though eating it is against her 'better judgement'. This is the language of a person who has resolved to do one thing but weakens and gives into temptation. A dieter perhaps? Thea nibbles the extremities first but, horror of horrors, the inanimate chocolate comes to life to reproach her. One little bite seems innocent enough but then reality rears its accusing head. The cat cannot stand on its own legs but keeps falling over. Does this show that Thea finds it difficult to stand on her own feet? Does she weaken at the knees when faced with temptation? The dream tells her that if she goes against her better judgement she will be sorry. That is a message from herself, to herself, and it does not mean that she wants to eat a cat!

Pursuit

Pursuit dreams fall into two main groups: those in which the one pursuing is recognizable as a person or 'thing' and those in which there is the threat and fear of being chased but the source of danger is not identified.

Many of us have, or have had, these dreams. Amanda, for example:

'I have a recurring dream of being chased by people through streets and vast stretches of land. This always causes me to hide in houses or elsewhere until I am nearly caught, then I start running again but don't know where I am going.'

We see the anxious search for a safe place. Amanda seeks refuge and always escapes but does not know where she is going. In waking life, too, she constantly seeks direction. She moves from one guru to another, from one fad to the next, each time moving on once the novelty has worn off. Marie is different, though in her dream she is also chased:

'I am in, sinister situation where if I do anything wrong I will be killed by other people who do not know who I really am. If I give away who I am, I will be killed. The dream usually features a chase in which I get lost or can't run fast.'

Marie knows her destination but she becomes lost. Added to that is a major problem which centres on her identity. If she reveals her true self she will die and, what's more, she has to be perfect, for if she 'does anything wrong', that will also carry the ultimate penalty. She is in a very difficult situation: she has to be infallible and not be 'real'. How much of that reflects her daytime role of playing the perfect little woman who is not supposed to have independent opinions and who pretends to be whatever people around her want her to be, like a chameleon? Perfect mother, perfect lover, perfect cleaner, ideal friend and true carer. And don't let's forget astute shopper, thoughtful neighbour, selfless PTA member, creative hostess . . . It's exhausting just thinking about it. No wonder Marie cannot run fast in her dream; at least she is still moving!

For some dreamers the fear is intensified because, although we try to escape, we are rooted to the spot, as is the case for Gwen:

'I have always been chased. I am running away from something horrific although I never know what. As I run, it is as if I am never getting anywhere, like running on the spot.'

The variations seem endless:

'Hard as I try my feet won't move. I panic. I shout for help. If my husband doesn't wake me, I wake up myself knowing that

I am shouting out. Sometimes I wake up crying.'

'I run and run but never manage to get to my destination.'

While there is a physiological cut-off mechanism inhibiting muscular activity which usually could be seen as causing such paralysis dreams, I believe these dreams are more likely to concern the psychological attitudes of the dreamers: they reflect powerlessness.

What keeps these dreamers in a vulnerable state when they make every effort to escape? If they cannot escape even when expending so much energy, then they should see if there are parallels in their waking lives. When Peter Sutcliffe was loose, attacking and killing women, many women were afraid that they would be the next target. Nadine was among them but, as her dream reveals, she was not cowed with fear:

'My friend and I were in Manchester. We saw the Queen talking to two men and then the Yorkshire Ripper ran towards her. We chased him out of the city centre, through a fair and into a forest. He turned round and killed my friend, so I grabbed him by the shoulder with my nails and felt such power surging in me. I was angry and scared at the same time. Then my nails just cracked and it was agony. He had a beard and was very tall and big.'

Despite his size, Nadine, on probation for cheque card fraud, managed to counter-attack and save herself. Her power surfaced to save her. She also prevented an attack on the 'Queen', an archetypal symbol of the powerful woman. Nadine did not allow hurt to come to the feminine principle. The Yorkshire Ripper was regarded as horrifically desecrating women in general. The women he attacked and killed were not the only victims of his cruelty; women throughout the country were subjected to assaults on the psyche. His actions defiled us all in a symbolic way, but in her dream, Nadine fought off the evil he personified.

Medard Boss commented on this phenomenon in his book *The Analysis of Dreams*, saying that many young women who dream of fleeing from pursuers wish to flee from sexuality and sensuality, yet at the same time desire them. This contradiction is expressed in the strange feeling of being rooted to the spot. Each urge cancels the other out. However, I'm not sure that all such dreams reveal this state of impasse. I rather believe that many express the more general feeling of powerlessness of women in our society.

162

Why run to the police when you are being battered if you are told, 'It's only a domestic, go home'? Why run in the street when you know 'they' can run faster? And even if they cannot run faster, all your experience will have been directed to telling you that 'they' are stronger, smarter and more capable. We have to turn and face the attacker. We must recognize our own power to act independently of the myths about our inferiority that have been developed over centuries. This does not mean the power to dominate others, as power is usually defined, but the power to direct our own lives and decide our own destinies. At present we're still afraid of the 'bogey-man' or the 'madman' who can cut us down at any moment.

Lucy's 'maniac' dream has a grisly ending, which echoes her waking feelings of inadequacy:

'There is a maniac killer pursuing me, always with a knife or an axe. Often I am hacked to pieces before I wake.'

The 'madman' typifies a recurring figure in women's anxiety dreams. Women are chased, quite often through darkened streets, and desperately try to escape. Many of you will empathize with this fear since it is one regularly experienced by those of us who are out after dark, especially in cities. Our waking worries flood into our dreams, even though, as in my dream that I described at the beginning of the chapter, we may be unwilling to acknowledge them in waking hours.

Such dreams can be a way of 'rehearsing' for such an event should it occur. In Roe's case, she finally found her power in the dream.

'I had this recurring dream about an insane murderer chasing me. I always awoke before anything happened but I was still terrified. In the last dream, which was set in America, I challenged the madman and killed him. I have not had any more of those dreams since then, which is about two years ago.'

The fact that this anxiety dream stopped once Roe faced and dealt with her attacker reinforces the argument that, by facing danger, you can develop your own strength and destroy that which threatens you. Many people I have worked with who have had terrifying dreams found relief by talking about and working through them, thus confronting the threat. Frequently the demons are vanquished never to return. The first step, though, is to accept that your dreams are telling you of worries that you must deal with. Then the

163

success you experience in your dreams spills over into your waking life.

Babs, a gently spoken, considerate twenty-year-old, has a sense of her own ability to survive, and justifiably so as it turns out:

'I dream about me, my mum and sister walking through the country at night and a madman is chasing us. I see my mum and sister go to horrible deaths but I always survive or start crying and wake myself up.'

She suffers trauma and fear but manages to escape the impersonal attacker. How does she recognize herself as a survivor whereas her sister and mother die? When I asked Babs about this dream, she associated it with being raped when she was fourteen years old. She was babysitting and some boys she knew called round. She let them in and, as the baby had woken up, she was just about to put her back to bed. She said:

'They followed me upstairs and that's when it happened. Now I have this dream and another nightmare where the rape is repeated and I wake up crying and screaming because I was so very frightened.'

Her dreams tell us that she has not got over that trauma and should get help to do so. They also show that part of her died in that assault: her innocence, her freedom to choose, her view of herself as a whole female maybe. In the dream her mother and sister 'go to horrible deaths'; some aspect of herself as symbolized by her sister and mother was destroyed. Babs should contact a rape crisis line. The women volunteers who take the calls recognize the severe effect rape has on its victims, not only physically but mentally, and know that such scars can last a lifetime. They respond to calls about rape no matter how long ago it happened. It's not too late for Babs to exorcize these dreams.

In some dreams the pursuant is vaguely defined as 'the enemy' or as stereotypically evil – Nazis or alien beings from outer space. This type of anxiety chase dream reflects generalized worries, prompting us to find a means of escape; but first we need to discover what is threatening us, otherwise we may run towards the danger and bring ourselves even more problems. Lois has such 'generalized' dreams:

'This dream started when I was about eleven. I come out of an air-raid shelter and am chased by German soldiers. They never quite catch me but I dream a lot about war and am always in a country occupied by Germans.'

The roots of her fear lie in the childhood experience of being evacuated to the country during the last war. Although she never saw 'live' German soldiers, she was well aware of the danger. Into her subconscious filtered the image of the 'enemy', which has returned whenever she feels out of place, unsure and under threat. The dreams are a good barometer of her feelings of confidence and probably symbolize conflict in her life.

Vera, who makes a point of using her sleep experiences to help sort out problems, had the following dream:

'I made a machine that turned and chased me in circles. I jumped into space to escape it and then I felt free, without any fear. I awoke with these words going through my head: "Now you can start".'

The relief flooded through her when she awoke. She felt that this dream indicated possible freedom from ties that bound her.

Vera, the eldest of five daughters, decided that instead of continuing to go round in circles looking after systems which she had set up, and which made more and more demands on her, she would make the jump. She assertively offloaded equal shares of the responsibility for an infirm father onto her sisters and found some space in which to escape. She recognized her own need for more personal freedom even though she had made the mechanical object which turned on her. She had 'mechanically', automatically assumed that as the eldest she had to do everything; symbolically, she had made the slave-driving machine. The dream intimates that she is ready to start a new phase.

Dreams in which we are being chased but can't tell by what or whom can be very disturbing. They capture that raw terror of childhood; we experience the dread but are powerless to define or deal with that which threatens our very soul. The two dreams which follow are typical examples from the many that have been sent to me:

'I am being chased and am leaving a trail of blood. At the same time there is the sound of a heart thudding and laboured breathing. It terrifies me.'

'I'm pursued by a strange "being". I have never seen it but know that it would kill me if it caught me. It would drain my blood away, leaving me zombie-like.'

Forgetfulness

When I am particularly stressed, one of the first signs is a pervasive feeling that I have forgotten to do something. I'll be doing one thing, such as writing, and will suddenly find that I'm wondering what the date of my next dream workshop is, or thinking about plans for a new series of counselling sessions or whether I've sent off a cheque for the electricity bill! It's as if the system has been overloaded and I need to take more 'rest time' in order to process all the information, and prevent the stress from becoming difficult to handle. If I act at that stage, the chances of its taking on physical dimensions such as tension headaches, sickness, sleeplessness and palpitations are minimized.

Ethna's dream has all the signs of being stress-induced:

'Some vague task that I have forgotten to do will weave in and out of dreams all night and often recur for weeks. Very vivid. I wake up convinced that there is a real task to be done and only convince myself with difficulty that it is not real. The anxiety remains, though, and I keep wondering what it is that I may have overlooked.'

After a dream of forgetting, it is useful to try and identify the cause. Is there any reason why you might have wanted to forget? Quite regularly we conveniently forget to carry out a task which we did not want to do anyway. Dreams of forgetting may be telling you that you would rather avoid a particular issue. Of course, on the simplest level, you may have a lot to do and to remember at one time, and your dream is saying, 'Slow down, otherwise you're going to forget something, then we'll be in trouble.' In this way the dream is acting as a warning which should be heeded. I think that many of those dreams which are about forgetting some vague, unidentified task indicate this type of stress.

Losing things and being lost

It is quite easy to see how dreams about being lost reflect fears of uncertainty about where we are going in our lives. Maggie, a computer programmer from Luton, has dreams of being disorientated:

'I dream that I am in a building and cannot find my way about or my way out. It appears that the more people I ask the more lost I get. In my dream I go where I am being directed but the directions are never right.'

Her dependence on others is of no use to her. The dream tells her that she has to look to herself to find her own map, for, even when she does as she is told, she is unsuccessful.

In these dreams the presence or absence of a helper is important. Do you find someone to help you easily, or can no one point you in the right direction? If there is no assistance coming from outside, it probably means that you feel isolated and left to fall back on your own resources, as is the case with Naina:

'I frequently get lost. I'm with people I know but they offer no help. I'm so frightened I just want to wake up but the dream seems endless. Although I know it's a dream, I keep running to find my destination. I always wake up worried.'

She feels alone in London, where she has been a student for two years. She has still not adjusted to living in a capital city which can seem so callous in its indifference to human needs.

Another of Naina's dreams emphasizes her unease:

'I'm lost in a big city. It's dark and raining. No one about and I don't know which bus to catch or where to get it. There is no one around to ask.'

Both the dreams show her as isolated and lost, literally and metaphorically. They are pushing her towards self-reliance and independence rather than reliance on others, or, more likely, they indicate that she has not received the support from others that she desires. Once again, the person who has the key to the problem is the dreamer herself, not some 'expert' with a book of definitive explanations.

Anxiety about losing objects should be examined in a literal way. Check to see if you have lost the object about which you dreamed or if the catch is damaged, on a watch for instance. Having done the reality testing, then consider what the object means to you. Who gave it to you? Would you in fact be glad to be rid of it?

Patty, a Welsh physiotherapist, had spent many hours recording and working on her dreams. She discovered that numerous dreams of burglars stealing her possessions and of losing her handbag were connected with losing her identity. I can appreciate her fears on a purely practical level having had my bag stolen recently: it was as if my identity, as verified through credit cards, library tickets, driving licence and other assorted paraphernalia, had been whisked away. I felt somehow exposed for the next week or so as I adapted to a new bag with new identity 'tags'.

Losing things is usually considered to be an unfortunate event over which we have little control. However, this is not always the case. In colloquial usage there are many examples of 'losing' things in an active as opposed to a passive context. For example, women are described as, 'losing' their virginity, as if they have left it on a bus. This does not express the active role of most women who decide to have intercourse and 'lose' their virginity – their choice is not obvious in the language used. In your dreamwork ask yourself if you have really lost this thing, whatever it was, or did some part of you deliberately leave it behind? Losing things may be a way of discarding out-dated, worn-out values and ideas, which you may be much happier without.

Losing people – children, lovers, parents, and so on – indicates worry about emotional relationships. Mary paled as she recalled her dream:

'I dream that I have lost someone very dear to me and I am desperately looking for them. I see someone who looks like the person. They turn around but it isn't them.'

As I said earlier, many women have dreams about having been entrusted with the care of children who have subsequently been lost. Were they indeed lost or were they accidentally-cum-deliberately left behind? Women have many conflicts in relation to children: whether to have them or not; whether or not they should work outside the home; whether they should stay in an unsatisfactory relationship 'for the sake of the children' or leave it and face criticism from outside as well as their own guilt. Maternal guilt is one of the most widespread negative emotions women experience. There are so many contradictory views on the 'right way': the 'right way' to bear children, to feed them, to educate them, the 'right way' to be a good mother. No wonder we have conflicting attitudes to one of our most essentially female preoccupations.

The burdens of childcare often become tiresome, or indeed

overwhelming, and leave us very little time to meet our own needs or replenish our own drained resources. At such times it is easy to feel that life would be easier if the child in question were not around. When she wishes her little daughter would 'get lost', Christa dreams of losing her in a large store, though not permanently! However, such feelings are not acceptable in a 'good mother', so they are quickly pushed down into the subconscious. But, they find an outlet in dreams, as Harriet knows:

'I have a recurring dream that I have a young baby but I keep forgetting to care for it. The baby is always happy though, in spite of the neglect.'

If you have a variation of this dream, consider what part of you the baby represents. Dreams in which babies are forgotten or overlooked are frequently about an aspect of ourselves which we are failing to nurture. It is vitally important that you take responsibility for yourself and make every effort to ensure that you are giving proper attention to your physical and mental health. Consider Lisa's dream:

'I was given a bag with various compartments in it. There was a baby-sized, wizened old man inside with a nappy on . . . I take the children to school and show the bag to a friend, saying, "Look what I got last night." The friend sees nothing. The old man tells me that only I can see and hear him. He is talking to me all the time. Each time I open it he is older and more threatening. He says he is not going to go away and that I can't get rid of him. He also keeps saying he wants feeding otherwise he will die.'

An auxiliary nurse, with two children and very involved in the traditional role of wife and mother, Lisa spends all her time working. If she is not working on night shift, she is cleaning, cooking, or ferrying kids. She grudgingly admits to having no time for herself yet used to take pleasure from tending an allotment. Her father – 'the old man', as she called him – taught her how to garden and grow beautiful produce. She misses it, and it shows! She was surprised that she imediately 'knew' that it was the 'old man gardener' side of herself that was in danger of imminent demise.

As you now know, nothing in our dreams is arbitrary, even though we may have difficulty in understanding the significance of all that occurs. The bag in Lisa's dream was given to her by a patient she had nursed. The old woman had annoyed her by telling her not to work so hard but to enjoy herself whilst she was young. Lisa had not liked to admit that most of her life was work with little if any time for play. As the family are not desperate for money, why can't she allow herself to do what she really enjoys before the 'old man' wilts completely? The insistent dream tells Lisa that she really ought to do something about getting the balance right before it is too late.

A film-maker who fought for many years to have her work recognized, first by her family, who considered it a trivial pursuit, and then by media moguls, who initially rejected it, has found that over the years she has had many dreams in which a baby girl features:

'I am often in the same place with a little neglected child, a girl, who is terribly bright and a wonderful conversationalist. Her parents take no interest in her. Her "nanny" urges me not to overstretch her brain, but I know I have to awaken her to all life's possibilities, and she is such a sweet, cuddly, clever little girl. Sometimes I hold her up to the mirror and say, "We both have the same eyes. No one else has eyes like ours."

'I also have a dream of curing a dark curly-headed girl by holding and embracing her. She has fits but I hold on and feel very powerful.' Peg's upper-middle-class childhood world of nannies comes through in the dream, as does her wonderful sense of personal power. She knows she is apart from those around her, and is determined to embrace life. Not for her the constraints imposed by others: she will resolve the difficulties, she will 'cure' the child. Notice her method of self-therapy: 'embracing and holding' the little girl. She accepts the free, unadapted child within; she does not reject herself as so many women do. Peg defines herself and feels good about herself. She has discovered her own strength despite the rejection she encountered.

Children in dreams may symbolize the childlike, infant part of ourselves, the part which is still dependent and needs to be cherished. If you have a dream where a baby is left with you but you lose or neglect it and then feel guilty, your dream may be telling you to look after yourself more. Sit down and try to work out which bit of you is being neglected. Nurture yourself.

Examinations and tests

Some dreams indicate understandable anxiety about a forthcoming test, be it the traditional exam at school or another stressful situation such as an interview. For many of us there is an almost Pavlovian response: we hear the word 'examination' or 'test' and we freeze with fear.

Examinations in most cultures are a sort of rite of passage. If you pass successfully, then you are allowed to go on to the next stage, and in the really important ones you are given a special piece of paper which certifies that you have particular capabilities. Such endorsement provides a label which is frequently used to classify people. When someone passes a final exam, their status changes, perhaps from dependency to independence. Often, anxiety dreams about examinations highlight feelings of immaturity and lack of confidence.

Louise regularly has such dreams at anxious times:

'In the dream I am about to sit an exam and have forgotten everything I know.'

Like Mona, she feels unprepared or lacks a vital piece of equipment:

'Finding myself back at school, I am unprepared for a lesson or an exam, or I'm in an exam but either I've got no pen or I've been given the wrong paper. Somehow I can't get anyone to help me.'

This dream indicates the need to prepare for some testing event to minimize disquiet. If you have such a dream, try to identify a situation in which you are presently involved or are anticipating and which you see as a kind of test. Then consider what it is about the situation which is causing anxiety. Are you prepared for it? Are you lacking in confidence? Does it evoke that same feeling you had when you were a schoolgirl sitting exams on which your future depended? Are you afraid that you won't make the grade?

Quite often the dream examinations described to me are ones which the dreamer had successfully passed years before. Angela's dream offers reassurance:

'The clearest way I have of letting myself know that some situation is causing me anxiety is when I dream of doing exams. It is usually a

Latin exam and I haven't studied an important work that is being examined. However, I somehow manage to get through it, just as I do in waking life.'

Notes

1. Steven B. Karpman, 'Fairy Tales and Script Drama Analysis', *Transactional Analysis Bulletin* 7, 2, pages 39-48, April 1968.
2. J.M.Masson, *The Assault on the Truth, Freud's Suppression of the Seduction Theory* , Faber, 1984.

9

Trials, Troubles and Tribulations

Throughout our lives, anxiety is the dominant theme in dreams. The causes of some anxiety dreams are obvious, as in the case of the smoker who dreams that she had dropped a lighted cigarette on the bed and wakes up groping for it. She wants to give up smoking and in her dreams her mind continues to point out the risks involved in the habit. My own smoking dreams, now I am an ex-smoker, are concerned with finding myself at a party, having a good time, drawing on a cigarette and loving it. I wake up surprised but recognize the wish-fulfilment! I wish I could smoke and that it be good for me: but it isn't, so I don't.

The theme of being late is ubiquitous, so I haven't given it a separate section here. We are late for appointments, scared we will not meet deadlines, worried we won't be there to pick up the children from school; we just miss the train or stand gasping as the boat pulls out from the jetty! Whatever the event, there is a corresponding dream about being prevented in some way from getting to it on time; and usually we are fearful that we will incur someone's wrath. All such worries are tinted by that familiar emotion: guilt.

Here are some typical anxiety themes for you to ponder.

Safe as houses?

The phrase 'safe as houses' is usually inappropriate as far as our dreams are concerned. Too often, houses are broken into, burnt down, or in other ways under siege. If you have such a dream, consider first whether you feel insecure about the place in which you live. Are you scared it may be broken into? If so, you can do something practical to improve the situation. If, on the other hand, you have no obvious waking anxieties about your house, then try viewing the house as yourself, the dreamer.

Take Helen's dream, for example:

'I was in a house which seemed to be under attack: windows shattering, doors banging, the wind howling – and there was a snake in the room. I was very scared so I started to climb the stairs to higher rooms, but, in each one I went into, the snake was always there, wound around the leg of a table or chair. Then the house started to collapse as if there was an earthquake.'

Helen often feels threatened and under attack, as her other anxiety dreams about work, family and her broken marriage reveal. Though she tries to go higher, maybe as she tries to work more on a head level rather than a gut level, she cannot escape what follows her. The intensity of the danger is evident at the end of the dream, when the house is about to collapse. What does the snake represent for Helen? Which part of her psyche is she trying to avoid? She will only resolve the dream by facing the fear and acknowledging it. In doing so, she should rediscover some of the confidence she had before divorce disrupted her life. Unfinished business is sapping her energies.

If the dreamer is trapped inside a house, it is useful to consider whether this reflects a sense of being trapped in everyday life. Helen told me she felt as if there was 'no way out' of her situation, for she had not wanted her husband to leave, and now she wanted him back.

Bernice, a town planner in Bolton, had this dream when she was going through a stressful period:

'I was in a Japanese-style room with paper walls. I had to get out but couldn't get through the paper. Then two men appeared and showed me the way to the door. This dream was probably reflecting the unhappy state of my marriage at the time.'

Bernice's points of escape haven't been blocked. She is aided by two men who show her the route. The setting is very specific. Does Bernice know a place like this? Has she been to Japan, or has someone told her of such a room? The important point is that the walls are paper; they can be ripped or stepped through, but for some reason she doesn't want to go through that paper. Does the paper equal the 'bit of paper' as the marriage licence is often called? Does she not want to destroy that? In the event, Bernice and her husband managed to resolve their problems after much reasonable discussion over ritual cups of tea – just as in a Japanese tea ceremony.

Unlike Bernice, Liz finds that no one helps her; any access to the room is blocked. If there were someone on the outside who wanted to help, that person would not be able to get through:

'I was in a very untidy room and felt I had to get out of it. I moved through the door into the next, smaller room, looking for the door leading out. Although interconnected, neither room had a door to the outside to let me out or anyone else in. I knew it would be all right if I woke up.'

Liz did wake up in more ways than one. So irritated was she after the dream that she took a number of steps to 'tidy up' her life and to open herself up to other people. Her dream acted as the impetus she needed. Nineteen-year-old Laura needs a similar push. When she told me about her childhood, the symbolism in her dream became easy to understand, although initially its meaning was not obvious to either of us:

'I have been having this dream for as long as I can remember. I am in a room which has no doors or windows and it has plain walls. In the middle is a table and chair where I am sitting. Above me is a light which has no shade and is very bright. While I am sitting there the walls and ceiling start to close in on me. When they get to a foot away from me, I wake up crying.'

There is no sight of the outside world from this windowless, doorless, unadorned room. There is only the unremitting glare of the light, which beams down on the terror of the isolated girl as the harsh world closes in on her. What is the cause of her oppression?

Laura remembers the day when, at the age of three, her mother and father split up:

'I can see my dad fully but I can't see my mum's face. I remember my mum crying and her walking up the street. After that I went to live at my grandad's. I can still remember having a bath in this little blue tub with a picture on the side of it.'

Her childhood impotence provided no way out of that unhappy family situation. It left an indelible mark on her. Since that time she has always felt unsure and afraid, alone and unprotected. She has other dreams in which she has no control over events that will hurt or destroy her. Waking acceptance of that pain has been hard for Laura and she always tries to shrug it off. 'What's the point? No one really listens and I don't want my mum to feel guilty.' Instead, she carries her grief inside. 'I think we dream because in real life we

175

can't express our feelings or what we think,' she says. 'That's how it is for me, I suppose.'

The sense of being threatened comes in many house dreams, even when the visitor is someone you know:

'A recurring dream which started about a year ago . . . It's about my mother. I am asking her to leave my house. I am begging her to go. I point out that she said she would only stay for a short time but she's been there for months. She doesn't pay much attention. The rooms are altered and have her stamp on them and she seems very comfortable. I'm in despair because whatever I say or do makes no difference. Part of me feels sorry for her because she has nowhere else to go but I definitely don't want her in my house . . . The dream always ends with me storming out saying I'm going to look for another house to live in.'

Clearly, this dreamer was tired of her mother's interference and longing to find a way of escaping from it. However, she has been having the dream for some time and has not yet managed to translate that assertiveness into her waking world. Sal, too, fears domination by another:

'I dream of confrontations between myself and my ex-husband or my husband's ex-wife. Sometimes they both appear together. Always they are threatening me with violence, then they lock me in a small dark room.'

If you dream about houses that are on fire, check to see if there are any fire hazards in your own house. Kathy had several dreams about a fire at her home and worried her mother to such an extent that she was eventually persuaded to have the wiring looked at. Some wires under the floor were faulty and the electrician told them the house could have gone up in flames at any time!

If there are no physical reasons for anxiety about fire, consider what the symbol of fire might mean. Is something getting too hot to handle so that it threatens to engulf you? Are you afraid that you may get burnt by playing with fire? For Jean, fire in her dream childhood house was welcomed. Quite often dream settings are places from the past and the events of that time and place hold a key to the dream meaning:

'I dream that I am in my childhood home. The house is very untidy and dirty and I don't know where to start to clean up. A fire starts and everything is burnt. I'm filled with relief for the house is purified.'

The strains of the last thirteen months were showing in Jean's dream. Her mother, old, senile and partly paralysed, had been staying at Jean's house and Jean admitted that death would be a release for both of them. She associated the fire in the dream with the act of cremation, a purifying of the no-longer functioning body. Through her dream Jean accepted that she was under a great deal of pressure and could try to find ways of alleviating it, although she knew that she would be nursing her mother for the forseeable future.

Many women dream about their house being broken into. Ursula, whose dream recurred over many months, thought it came from anxiety about being burgled but, having repeatedly checked the house to make sure it was secure, she found that the dream did not go away. Then she realized that it was herself who was feeling invaded:

'It suddenly dawned on me that I felt everyone was getting to me all the time. If it wasn't one person who was coming round to tell me their troubles, it would be the boss getting me to do more and more research in my own time. I felt as if the whole of my life was taken over by other people. When I recognized this, after that dream had been going on for ages, I made some changes. Now, no more dreams of being broken into!'

For some of us, anxiety dreams can be nightmares. Michelle, a student in her third year at university, has periods of depression which reflect difficult times in her waking life. In her dreams at these times, the colour is generally black and she feels trapped, just as she does when awake. The setting varies; a deserted city street, a dry desert, or a house:

'I was locked in a house in which the interior was absolutely black. There were no windows, all light was excluded . . . I woke to find I had leapt out of bed and was tearing at the walls with my nails. I could actually feel fibres weaving and growing together to trap me and close me in.'

Her 'house' is as dark as the depths to which, in her depair, she sinks; but she does find her dreams useful:

'I often feel that I am at war with them yet I know they are of value to me. I feel that whatever makes me dream is "sulking" because it

177

considers that I misunderstand it. I suppose what I mean is that I am unaware of certain faculties or motives within myself and this restricts my dreaming self.'

It restricts her to the extent that she feels she should respond to the more positive messages that her dreams give but takes no action. However, she wakes up feeling fresh, alive and vital when she recalls dreams, even if they were dull, because they help her, as she says, 'get in touch' with herself.

Doors

Doors in dreams are like doors in waking life; they can act as barriers to keep people out or they can be entrances which allow people to come in. Sometimes the dreamer has control over these doors, whereas in other instances they are beyond her control. Melissa had a dream of the latter sort, as did Deirdre:

'Sometimes I dream that I am at home and someone is trying to break in. I pick up the telephone to dial for help, but however many times I dial the number, it won't connect.'

'I am trying to lock a door that won't lock. However much I turn the key to lock it, it makes no difference; whenever I turn the handle, the door will still open.'

In dreams where doors figure prominently, try to work out why they won't close or lock or open. Is there something you feel you cannot close off, or lock away, or be open to? And if, like Melissa, you can't get through on the phone because it is damaged or broken, ask yourself in what circumstances you have difficulty communicating. Telephones and doors are both means of communication so, if they don't work in your dreams, ask yourself why.

Glenda was not able to protect herself – far from it. She was 'compelled' to let danger in:

'I walk up to a door and am compelled to open it even though I know there is some unspeakable horror on the other side.'

Is she a masochist? Or is she unable to protect herself? Hella also fears what is outside her house but, unlike Glenda, she makes every effort to prevent entrance:

'In my dream, I'm in a lovely big house where I'm trying to secure all the windows and doors to prevent the enemy coming in.'

Hella has this dream rarely, but it is usually when everything is going well in her life. However, she always has a sneaking feeling that misfortune will strike. It's a conviction that 'this is too good to last', accompanied by the thought that she isn't worthy of such good times! Pathetic, isn't it? Many of us are so used to being told that we aren't good enough that we internalize the message and believe it. Such internalized oppression is a major obstruction for women seeking to understand and use their own power.

In a typical anxiety dream the object, place or person you are trying to reach recedes as you get closer. Some examples involving family were given in Chapter 6. Catriona's dream is in the same style:

'I'm in a long room with a door at the end. I walk across but never seem to reach the door.'

It reflects the frustration she feels about the seemingly never-ending task of studying for her articles as a solicitor. She is still striving in her waking life just as she is in the dream.

An intruder forces his way into Jennie's dream house and she finds that, however hard she tries, she cannot scream. She cannot move, nor can she quieten her breath in the darkened room as she lies waiting for whoever it is to make his way to her bedroom. She says that the intruder's motives are violent, never sexual. The daughter of a heavy-handed father, Jennie went on to marry 'a drinker and a beater', who bruised and bloodied her on occasions too numerous to recall. Her dreams repeat the pattern she has, so far, been unable to escape; she is immobilized and dumb, just as she was when the victim of violence. Now, after a period in a battered women's refuge, she is starting anew, but she still relives her powerlessness in her dreams.

Rooms

Houses are made up of rooms, in the same way that people are made up of different personality traits. Rooms have different functions just as we have different roles to play. In the following dreams, the descriptions of the rooms reveal facets of the dreamer's world. Jung believed that the different levels of a house represent the different levels of being in individuals. It is at the deepest level that our most primitive instincts are to be found. Facing such instincts or coming close to our 'roots' can be disturbing, as Lenore found:

'This is a recurring dream. It is a large house and I know all the rooms on the ground floor. There are lots of rooms but I usually just stay in the one room. Other people don't realize that there are many rooms in the basement, one of which is circular. However, I get very frightened and never look any further . . . When I say they don't realize the size of the house, I mean it is big enough to hold two families, two houses in one really . . . I have had this dream on and off for about seven years and I would say that I knew all the house and what was in every room at one point. I have explored all of the basement area but I don't do so any more as I know I'm not going to like what I see.'

It is as if the dreamer has two distinct sides, symbolized by the two 'families' which could co-exist harmoniously if only Lenore would accept it. She has explored the basement, the foundation, and she didn't like what was there. What was so dreadful that it must remain locked away, concealed in the dark depths? She says she usually stays in the one room. Could this mean that she stays in one role which she finds secure rather than using all the other 'rooms' at her disposal? She has retreated to a place of safety and now, conveniently, she does not know what is in all the rooms which she once had the courage to explore. Lenore is cutting herself from her own potential.

Many anxious room dreams reflect lonely isolation, as in Roisin's case:

'. . . In a room where no one remembers me. I am being completely ignored.'

Others pose all sorts of threats. Linda dreamt that she was 'locked in a room and the walls were closing in', while Ina found that, in her absence, her landlady had let her room to someone else. Ina was feeling overlooked and lonely at the time, while Linda felt crushed and unable to cope. In neither instance is the room a secure place. This is in direct contrast to Samantha's dream, which occurs when she is feeling peaceful and secure:

'I am usually alone, wandering about in a very unusually designed house. I take delight in wandering along corridors, up a staircase and finding nice rooms leading off. It is not an enormous house but it's a lovely one.'

As a child she had plenty of space to herself in her home and used to make up fantasies with a friend and use rooms in the house to enact them. She had a very happy childhood and could explore her imaginary world to her heart's content; now, as an adult, she feels that the fantasy structure of the house has remained and returns to her at times when she is most secure in her life. Lucky Samantha!

Stairs and lifts

I met Una at a weekend conference. She was obviously know-ledgeable as well as popular and I was pleased to find myself sitting next to her at dinner. She proved to be an excellent companion and I was somewhat surprised by the dreams she related. She is usually stuck halfway up a staircase because she has lost her nerve and is too afraid to climb any higher or because there is a large space where the landing should be. She is worried that there is no solid ground for her to walk on. In other dreams, stairs are obstacles to be overcome on a journey from one place to another. The journey may be symbolic of progressing 'upwards', be it professionally or spiritually. Una decides to face the danger:

'I'm going up some stairs when suddenly there is a great yawning hole before the next lot of stairs. I only just manage to reach the other side after nearly falling down the hole.'

Seven years later, when I knew Una much better, we talked about the roots of the dream. Traumatic events had so damaged her confidence and trust that for years she had been unable to feel secure either in relationships or in her obvious ability. At that dinner table she could not trust me to explore the dream; she could only describe it.

Carol's dream of stairs at first has a very peaceful, romantic flavour but an immediate clue that all is not well is the images of a woman in a child's body:

'I am myself, in a young girl's body, my own, probably around fifteen. I am playing with a girl and boy. I recognize the girl, who is on a tyre swing suspended on a huge tree in the garden of a beautiful house . . . It is a wonderful, warm summer's day. The sun is bright, the atmosphere carefree and happy. I don't know how, but suddenly I am in the Manor House, which is lofty and traditionally styled with huge oak banisters on a flight of stairs in the east wing. I am being pursued at tremendous speed by an unknown figure, and have the impression that I am being caught up with. The distance between me and my pursuer is constantly decreasing. I know that if I get to the bottom of the stairs I will be safe because intuition tells me that there is a door into a labyrinth which I can bolt and so lock out my assailant . . . The difficulty is that the stairs seem never-ending and I invariably wake up rigid with fear at the prospect of being attacked and killed. In the dream I think it will be by stabbing.'

The characteristics of a chase dream are here linked with details of a special 'Manor House'. At first Carol is happy to be there but this quickly turns to unease. Carol's 'right brain', her intuitive, creative side, comes to her rescue and she seeks the door of escape. By waking up she does not have to face her pursuer. She remains fearful, however, and I'm sure this is because of some unfinished business which continues to cause her anxiety. Also, it seems likely that there is an event which happened when she was fifteen, or around that age, which holds a vital clue if only she would consider it. It is not surprising that the stairs seem never-ending because this earlier event has not yet 'ended', it has not yet been resolved.

When Valerie was at the end of her tether at work, she had this dream:

'I am falling over the edge of the banisters and only just manage to hold on.'

It indicated the extent of the stress she was under. She talked things over with a colleague and began to work positively on the conflicts that were pushing her 'over the edge'. The dream was the nudge she needed.

For some women, the effort of climbing the stairs is removed in dreams; lifts arrive to carry them. However, these mechanical devices have a habit of frightening the dreamer. Sometimes the lift goes 'over the top' or doesn't go where it is expected to, as Pattie discovered:

'The other night I dreamt I was going up in a lift alone. I wanted to stop at the sixth floor but couldn't manage to press the button. The lift went faster and faster and eventually shot right through the roof, throwing me out.'

This lift was beyond her control. It would not go where she

wanted it to, nor would it stop. Does someone else have the power over her in waking life? Does someone else push buttons to direct her? If so, they are pushing too hard, for there is danger that Pattie may well go 'through the roof', or 'hit the ceiling' and be flung aside. Annie has a similar problem, but she determinedly finds a safer way out:

'I am in a lift and it is going to crash straight through the ceiling. It always stops just in time but the space I have to crawl through is very tight. I feel I will suffocate.'

She at least avoids going through the roof, but it is still a struggle. This dream is reminiscent of those which seem to re-enact the birth trauma: it has a quality of struggle through confined space to freedom.

Alison's dream affected her to the extent that she would not take a lift – and six floors up is a long way to walk! She told me what had happened:

'I had a dream about the lift at work but, instead of going up to the second floor from the ground floor, it went down. (In fact it can only go up from the ground.) When the doors opened there was an old oak door. It was very dark and the air was musty. I just jumped awake and, I'm not kidding you, I was frightened.

'When I awoke it was time to get up for work. I would not get in the lift that day, and the day after it was a real ordeal when I did use it. Since then I will not go in the lift on my own.'

What has so spooked Alison that it colours her waking days? Has she noticed something about the lift which makes her think it unsafe? She may not be consciously aware of this, but it might have lodged in her unconscious mind. Or does the lift symbolically take Alison to that deeper, Jungian level of instinct and intuitive, collective communication? That part of her appears to be demanding recognition.

Walls and roofs

The walls and roof of a house provide essential protection. They keep out the worst of the natural elements, rain, wind, snow and hail, and the sun too. They act as a barrier. At home, they provide a private refuge from the outside world. However, in many instances, we are unable to find the security we need; or, just when we think we are safe, something goes wrong:

'I have two recurring dreams. In the first, I can see cracks and damp patches on the ceiling gradually getting larger, so I know the roof is falling in. In the second one, my bed is by the window and I can feel that the outside wall has got a hole in it. It's as if part of the wall is missing.'

I wonder if Sybil, when she had the dream described above, felt as if part of her protective armour was missing? Some source of anxiety is growing more and more visible so that it cannot be ignored. It is symbolized by the small flaws which are becoming larger and more noticeable. If preventive measures aren't taken now, maybe the roof will fall in. The dream is warning Sybil that she needs to identify the source and to take action.

Unfinished business is a facet of many dreams.[1] In Meri's case it is symbolized by her previous home, which she keeps going back to in her dreams, like a dog going back to gnaw a bone. Look how the walls and roof provided her with no protection:

'I have been having this dream for two years now. I keep going back to a flat I lived in many years ago. My furniture is still there, though water is pouring down the walls. Somehow the furniture is undamaged. The council have not been in touch with me at all and I haven't paid rent in all these years, but nothing has been moved. The roof leaks too. I want to take down the curtains and wash them but I don't want anyone to know I'm there.'

Part of her, her mental 'furniture' if you like, has stayed attached to that flat or events that happened there. Everything has been left just as it was and, although Meri would like to wash the curtains, she is afraid of being discovered.

Curtains are a way of keeping out prying eyes and keeping separate the public and private worlds. They are also used as a front. When I was growing up, my mother would go on about the importance of curtains. In our house you put the patterned side out so that passers-by could see it, while we had the duller, unlined side facing into the room! If curtains were clean, tidily arranged and opened every day, that was a sign of respectability. If, however, they were left closed in daylight hours, that indicated slovenliness and a lack of 'standards'.

A particularly cryptic remark came from my mother one day after I had returned from a friend's house at about the age of ten. I had gone for 'tea', and had been given a cup of tea and a biscuit. Clearly I must have been ravenous on my return and, after being questioned as to what I had eaten, my mother said scathingly, 'They're all kippers and curtains' – flashy curtains but too mean to buy good food! So the message was that the outward appearance as announced by the curtains was not the only criterion; what happened behind the curtains was important too . . . But, let's return to Meri's dream.

Meri is afraid lest someone finds out that she is there. Why does she need to hide? What is she afraid of? She should use the dream to discover what needs to be reclaimed from that time.

In this next dream the house seems to symbolize something which has regrettably been lost:

'I have a recurring dream about a bungalow that we lived in when we were first married seventeen years ago. The dreams are never happy ones, though we were happy when we lived there. We sold it because I could not get a job, so we moved back to my home town and have been here for fifteen years.

'In one dream, I went out of the bungalow for a walk and I could not find it when I came back. In another dream, the bungalow was hidden in a wood and it was very run down. In the last dream, both my husband and I were in the bungalow but it was very cold and felt more like a prison than a home.'

Poor Jenny. She is obviously not happy with the way her life and marriage have turned out. Nothing major, it would seem – just a pervading feeling of disappointment. Her house disappears or is 'hidden and run down'. Where is that happy woman of seventeen years ago? She's lost sight of whom she is and is physically frailer – not because of old age but because she feels lack of self-worth. Jenny is 'run down' because she is depressed. Her marriage does not give her the same comfort and meaning that it once did. She seems to be saying that she and her husband are imprisoned by their proximity rather than enriched by it.

Clare's house dream, like so many others, indicates unfinished business from the past:

'I wish I could understand more about my dreams. I am divorced with two children at school and am still friendly with my ex-husband. The other week I dreamt I was in a big house and he came in and put all his belongings into the whole house and just stayed there.'

It feels as if he can move back in at any time without consulting Clare. In the dream she exerts no power and remains passive, even though he takes over the whole house by spreading his belongings everywhere. She doesn't complain; in fact, there is a sense of inevitability about it. This mirrors the situation in waking life. She still consults her ex-husband about every decision and firmly believes she can never really 'leave' him. It is as if there is a chain that binds them together, and Clare has forged it! She has given him her power; she has tacitly given him permission to control her life. Divorce or no divorce, she depends on his mastery. The fact that he may not want it, that he might wish to free himself from the responsibility for her life, does not enter into it. He can 'move back any time'. The dream is very direct in its message: only Clare can make the decision to live her own life.

When you dream about a house, pay attention to the atmosphere you find there. Is it warm and welcoming? Do you feel that it is well cared for or is it dilapidated and run down? Are the outer, protective walls in good repair or are they falling down; indeed, is anyone pulling the walls down? Is it merely a shell? Examine the details closely; they can provide a wealth of information to help you understand your dreams.

If you work on your house dreams, they may be as helpful as they are to Bella:

'The house is a good indicator of my psychological state. It has developed from being decayed, to being burnt down, to being just a wooden frame, and now the top rooms are beautifully decorated. The lower floors are still waiting.'

Gina finds her house, her self, ultimately secure. She has the power to look after herself:

'In my recurring dream someone is trying either to kidnap me or kill me. I run through the streets around my house – it's always late at night – and I get to my house just in time. I'm safe.'

Cars and Driving

Cars regularly feature in dreams. In the waking world, a car is variously regarded as a form of transport, a status symbol, a means of reflecting the personality of the driver; they can even reveal the relative power structure within an organization – the boss has the flashiest company car. I wonder how many people still associate the second car with 'the wife'?

It is always useful to notice who is driving the car in a dream, and the condition of the car, how the engine is running, whether it is going forward or reversing, and to be alert to any special features it may have. Ask yourself in what ways the car represents you. Julia found this a helpful technique.

'When I dream of a car I know it's about the course my life is taking. Recently, I had a dream in which the car was out of control. I am driving but the brakes have gone. I crash.

'This is about events in my life at the moment. I do feel out of control, and I'm scared that I'm not on the right path, but I really don't know how to stop.'

Just as Julia could recognize what her dream meant, so Linda knew that her dream about driving her car at 600 m.p.h. mirrored her over-stressed, frenetic life as a sales rep. for a major cosmetic company. Hans Dieckmann points out that automobiles in dreams are many-sided symbols.[2] They can represent our instincts and drives, our status, our bodies, our technical performance and the view we have of our self. Pat's dreams indicate her feelings of anxiety:

'I am driving a car with my mother as passenger. I suddenly get afraid because I have no licence or insurance and have not passed my driving test. I stop the car, afraid that the police will find out. I have to ring my husband to come and drive the car home.'

Pat's lack of confidence means she has to ask her husband to rescue her. Notice that it is the fear of being caught which worries: nothing actually happens. She is progressing quite well when panic hits and immobilizes her. Her own comments are highly revealing:

'I have wondered if the dream about driving could mirror feelings of guilt at doing something that I know is wrong, and they make me stop the car. I suppose deep down I feel guilty about doing my degree away from home. I come home at weekends. People are always surprised that my husband doesn't mind. I also feel guilty at times because I love my husband as a brother, not a husband. On many occasions when I have dreamt about myself, I don't actually recognize myself.'

She has internalized the oppressive view that her place is with her husband even though, she says, he does not object to her studying for her degree at a distant university. But the dream uncovers much more. She feels guilt because she has no authority to do this – 'no licence'; no protection in the form of insurance; and no qualifications – 'she has not passed the test'. Suddenly she feels inadequate, incapable and scared of her independent actions.

Pat symbolically resumes dependence on her husband. What she associates with the dream, her fraternal feelings towards her husband, tell us that Pat has some difficult issues to resolve before she can accept, and so recognize, her self. She is trying to avoid facing these but her 'car' dream drives her towards them.

Sometimes car dreams indicate that the dreamer is being given more responsibility, as in Barbara's example:

'I have a dream about my sister unplugging the steering wheel and giving it to me. I am learning to drive at present.'

It is triggered by the waking reality of learning to drive, but her sister is the one who hands over the wheel. Barbara understands that her sister feels safe enough to give her that power. A good dream for a learner driver, don't you think?

Isla had a fairly typical car-over-a-cliff dream when she was having problems with her teenage daughter. In it, Wendy, her daughter, is seated in the driver's seat of a car as it heads over the edge of a high cliff. Isla is unable to help and looks on in pained silence. She does not see the car plunge into the water but wakes herself up, so fearful is she of the outcome.

When this dream occurred Isla had been troubled by Wendy's relationship with a man. There had been family arguments, shouting and veiled threats from both sides, and Isla had concluded that she must hold her peace, say nothing further and leave Wendy to learn for herself. It was difficult to stand back in that way but anything else would lead to a complete breakdown in their previously sound relationship. The dream shows Isla standing back, observing the action but not intervening. She sees a car which is not being correctly guided but which goes headlong into danger. This exactly mirrors the feelings she has about her daughter's conduct: her daughter is trapped inside the dream car, just as she is in the relationship with her lover.

Elaine had a lot of 'car' dreams, including ones in which she found herself in a cul-de-sac bounded by high walls. Those dramatically portrayed her life at the time, as did this dream:

'I was in a car which plunged into water. The car was going under but I managed to escape out of the window, and I swam to safety . . . I think this was about a relationship which I did swim safely from.'

Her relationship was getting beyond her control and she just managed to make the break to safety. However, some women feel completely dominated and cannot summon the strength or support to successfully set themselves free. Pauline gave me a graphic example of this when she described a recent dream. Since the dream she has been having trouble sleeping. This was not an acceptable alternative to her usual, easy-going dreams of James Bond:

'I was sitting in my friend's car when a man approached and kept taking the keys from me. He then shut me in and drove off. I tried to escape but couldn't. He drove me down an unmade road and we got to a house in the country. Then I was kept in and, though never assaulted, I was terrified and tried to escape. The only windows were six inches high with orange glass and I couldn't get out . . . then after a while I was let out to go to work but had to come back every day. "He" picked me up from the office and I got no freedom.'

So disturbed was Pauline by this dream that, crying and shaking, she woke up her flatmate. She said she was afraid of 'male domination' and, as a second-year mechanical-engineering student, was finding relationships with men on her course quite threatening. By openly discussing her experiences she was more able to deal with them.

Let Susie have the last word on cars:

'I have car dreams where I speed and go through red warning lights and sometimes the car breaks down. I have heard that cars are phallic symbols and may represent the men who drive them. I think this could hold some truth. When I fell out of love with someone I adored, his sports car turned into a child's pedal car in my dream. A pair of his trousers also appeared, faded and full of holes. In a later dream, the chap's car appeared as a battered heap, full of dents, broken windows and completely wheelless.'

Falling

If you hit the ground in a falling dream, so it is said, you will die. For those of you who believe this, let me reassure you that I've talked to women who did hit the ground, and they lived to tell me all about it! Some women find that, instead of crashing into hard ground, the surface becomes a soft cloud or springy moss. However, most women find these dreams distressing and unpleasant.

There are hundreds of variations on the theme: 'I dream I am falling down pits. Spinning and spinning and never hitting the bottom. I feel that it is hard to breathe, as if something is pushing against my chest'; 'I am falling down a long, bottomless tunnel sometimes.' The dreamer is pushed 'over the edge'. Often we try to escape, as Jilly does:

'In my dreams where I am falling off cliffs, I try to wake myself up as I get to the edge so that I stop myself falling.'

She does manage to prevent herself falling because she has sufficient power over what happens to her. With Jo it is a different story:

'I am in a car. There are faceless people in the dream, too, who get out of the car but I am left in as it starts to roll off the cliff. As I am falling I seem to be able to feel my heart start beating faster but before I reach the ground I awake crying.'

Everyone deserts her and no one cares for her welfare. She is isolated and only avoids knowing the outcome by the tears of despair which awaken her.

A common underlying factor for the dreamer who has falling dreams is the impulse to give up, to let go, or to escape difficult situations by not making the effort to cope. This is often linked to hostility towards the self; the dreamer's anger is turned inward. Instead of directing angry feelings outward to where they belong, women usually turn them inwards, blaming themselves for problems. We find it difficult to assert ourselves so we take the flak, carry the bad feelings around inside and frequently become depressed. Have you ever wondered why rates of depression in women are so much higher than in men? A significant factor is that we do not express anger but repress it.

Clothes

Have you had the dream of being in the street or some other public place, only to discover that suddenly all your clothes are missing? If you have, you are not alone. Many women have anxiety dreams in which clothes or the lack of them, are the central feature. As you recall, these anxiety dreams often begin in childhood.

Sometimes the clothes are inappropriate, which is what happens in the case of Vivien, a reluctant teacher:

'Every term, before school starts, I dream that I set off for school either naked or in totally the wrong clothes. As I walk along I realize I have time to change, and rush back only to find I've got the wrong clothes on again. When I try to return to school, I find the roads have all changed. The familiar route is now strange: there are dead ends and wrong turnings.'

Blue-eyed Bridget, an Irish friend of .mine, has struggled over many years to shake off traditions and expectations which are no longer acceptable to her. She's changed a lot since she left the small village in Wexford to take up an art course in London. However, her dream tells her that she cannot strip all the past away: her early experiences are a second skin which will not easily be peeled off:

'I am trying to cross a river, taking off my clothes in order to swim more easily, only to find further sets of clothing underneath. Thus, I never actually achieve this.'

For these dreamers there seems to be a strong need 'to change'. The clothes are causing anxiety since they prevent the dreamer from getting on with what she wants to do; they act as a hindrance. In dreams the persona or 'image' is often represented by clothing. Clothes are suited to events and occupations, and provide a form of protection. They can conceal disfigurements and emphasize attributes. Clothes allow us to express our feelings and also give us something to hide behind.

In Morag's dream she has no control over her 'image', no matter how often she tries to change it:

'I was wearing a bright pink dress down the road and I was constantly going back home to change it, but I kept coming out in the same dress.'

Her brightly coloured attire draws attention to herself and Morag cannot alter matters. She should ask herself what is significant about the dress that she is overlooking. She won't get her own choice of 'image' until she has sorted it out.

Sometimes we find surprising new clothes in our dream wardrobes but mostly our dreams of clothes are unsatisfactory. Is this how we feel about the image we project? We need a protective outer layer to guard the sensitive psyche but it should work for us rather than against us. In the following dreams, when the outer layer has gone, the dreamers feel embarrassed and exposed:

'I am in the middle of a crowded street trying to get on a bus, hoping I won't be noticed.'

'I am losing my knickers in a public street. I pull them up only to watch in dismay as they fall again.'

'At times of stress I dream of being naked as I walk along.'

Dreams of nakedness repeatedly reveal a feeling of vulnerability. As usual the setting is important. If you find that you are unexpectedly naked in the dream street, does it mirror a fear of public exposure? Are you afraid that some hitherto hidden aspect of yourself might come into the open, that you will be 'stripped naked' for all the world to see? Of course, such dreams will have different meanings from different people. For some, the anxiety may be tinged with pleasure.

To be naked in a dream can mean that you are your natural self stripped of pretence. If this is the case, how sad that so many of us feel badly about it and experience the dreams as being anxious. Have we been so conditioned about how we 'ought' to be seen or 'covered up', that we ourselves can no longer countenance our natural state? Perhaps we are too afraid of what will happen if we are unclothed, since we are told that that the mere sight of a naked woman is supposed to cause unbridled passion in men. In Nina's dream she is in her element, water, but that proves dangerous.

'I'm under water in a swimming pool, where I can breathe, and I am naked. There are a lot of men also naked. They have long hair and beards and all are skinny. They start mauling me.'

Long-haired, bearded, skinny men hold some particular meaning for Nina. Here they are intrusive and uncaring about her feelings. She, happy and totally at ease in this aquatic environment, has her tranquillity broken. She is 'mauled': used and abused for no reason, it seems, other than that she is there. Her relaxed nakedness is not safe. Perhaps she needs to 'swim' elsewhere. There will be places where she can be totally herself without being subject to 'mauling'.

If you regularly have dreams in which you are without clothes, try to make a note of when they occur. See if there is any pattern in the timing which could be linked to times of anxiety, overwork, lack of confidence, weight gain or problems in relationships.

Teeth

More often than not, dreams of teeth make those who hear them clasp their hands to their mouths to prevent anything drastic happening to their own teeth. There's an empathetic shudder as we listen to dreams such as these:

'I'm walking up a never-ending staircase and my teeth are falling out one by one. There is a woman laughing in the background. The dream is so realistic that I check my teeth on waking up.'

'. . . All my teeth dropping out or my mouth is full of loose teeth.'

'I have a short dream which can occur within any other dream. I realize that my teeth are crumbling just like chalk pieces. I put my hand up to my chin and they fall out into my hand in brownish-white flakes and crumbs. I have natural teeth, by the way.'

Having ensured that your teeth are not in danger of falling out in reality, consider what message your teeth dreams are imparting. Are you scared of 'showing your teeth', which is another term for getting angry? Are you concerned that something that has been part of your life for a long time is in fact becoming detached? Frequently, dreams of losing teeth occur at times of separation from those to whom we are very attached. Teeth are also important elements in how we look and how we appear to the world; witness the advertisements which show pearly, shining white teeth with no hint of decay. Do our dreams of crumbling, dysfunctional teeth indicate some 'decay' of which we are unaware? Do such dreams indicate worry about 'losing your looks' or 'losing face'? Once again, you, the dreamer, hold the key to the significance of the dream.

Zena found that her dream was directly related to physical causes:

'I used to have a dream where my teeth were growing longer and falling out. It was most disturbing. While awake one day, I discovered that rubbing the inside of my lower teeth down the outside of my upper ones, created the same feeling. That discovery stopped the dream.'

Clarissa, however, after racking her brains, and having a dental check-up, could find no physical basis for her dream:

'My teeth are crumbling in my mouth and the bits get bigger and bigger in my mouth until I feel as if I'm choking. I can feel them building up inside me.'

What Clarissa did notice, though, was that she had this dream at times of stress. The dream teeth block up her mouth, stop her communicating and almost prevent her from breathing. How often when this woman feels angry does she bite back her words? I wonder if she sometimes feels that the effort nearly chokes her?

Ellen came to a group I was running for single parents and told us of a dream in which her teeth fell out. She began by asking if it was true that to dream of swallowing one of your own teeth meant that you wanted to get pregnant. When I replied that I didn't think that was the case but that it meant different things to different people, she thought about it for a bit and then described her losing-teeth dreams. In the first dreams there were only a few teeth which became loose and then dropped out. But over time the dreams have involved more teeth so that in the last dream there was one, solitary tooth left.

Ellen remembered that when she was living at home surrounded by her family she had none of these dreams. However, when she moved away to college leaving many close friends behind, the dreams began. She said that, at first, she had felt panic and fear, and some disbelief, but the last few dreams have left her really low. In waking life she felt very isolated and vulnerable; most of her time was spent with her toddler and she had little adult company. She had financial restrictions because of low income on state benefit and, apart from shopping and attending the group, which met one afternoon each week, she had no social contacts.

In talking about the dreams, Ellen was able to express herself in a way that had not been possible previously. Marie spoke for the rest of the group when she burst out, 'Oh, Ellen, why didn't you say? I thought you just preferred to keep yourself to yourself. It would be really nice to see you more often. I'm glad you finally told us.' And the other women went on to talk of events she could join in.

Toilets

Searching for a toilet is not an activity that brings shouts of glee; rather at such times we are are usually in need – often, knees-crossing, bladder-bursting need. Joan's is a fairly representative example of a toilet anxiety dream:

'These dreams are all about desperate hunts for toilets which always turn out to be locked, blocked or otherwise unusable. Eventually I wake up dying to go to the loo.'

Similarly, Toni's dreams have a physical trigger:

'Many and varied are these; they include water flowing, oozing, cascading . . . with this, I am trying to use a most unsuitable loo. It's too low, too public, too far, and I'm having great difficulty. Needless to say, I always have to visit the bathroom and the dream wakes me up.'

As mentioned before, it is always best to look for the most obvious message, for dreams are not there to deceive the dreamer but to be of help. Joan's 'blocked loos' prevent her from urinating but force her awake so that she meets the physical need of her body, and the same is true for Toni.

The following dream is another example where there is an obvious physical trigger:

'One dream I've had many times recently is finding filthy, stained toilets and reacting to them with absolute disgust. In fact, no matter what the dream, the dirty toilet situation would arise. This dream intrigued me for ages and then the interpretation came to me in a flash. Looking back, I find it hilarious to think of all the Freudian interpretations I tried for size on this dream! The culprit was my very own toilet, which had recently become stained with limescale because of the practice of emptying teapots down it several times a day. I would think to myself, now I really must get this dealt with. I'd tried various solutions without luck and consciously had tried to remind myself to ask a friend how to deal with it. Obviously, I'd gone on remembering it in my sleep.'

Physical need may prompt some toilet dreams but this is not the case for Bibi, who told me of an isolated dream she had:

'Using a public toilet with glass walls all around so that passing traffic can view me quite clearly. I am embarrassed by this but have to "go".'

She overcomes her hesitancy, though not without cost. She is ill at ease and open to the anonymous world that passes by. It probably means that Bibi feels uncomfortably exposed at present.

Karen's dream forms part of a series:

'I have a recurring theme of "No privacy on the lavatory". In the last of this series, we were staying in a hotel and I was sitting on the lavatory, which was part of our room. There were several people there, cleaners and so on, who, I couldn't get rid of. I got up to go to another lavatory and I realized, as I walked away, that my pants were down and my bottom was bare. I was mortified. I went to another one and the situation was the same. Eyes were on me as I sat on the lavatory. It was terrible.'

There are many taboos about urination and defecation, and children are still told that anything to do with them is 'dirty'. Many women feel embarrassed about using the toilet in public places because it is not considered 'ladylike' to draw attention to 'secret' natural functions. Maybe men don't have this fear because their acts of urination are 'out in the open', so to speak, not hidden behind closed cubicle doors.

Inhibited by the same worry about 'public exposure', Tina found that her friends provided the antidote that she needed:

'Several in which I wanted to go to the lavatory, found it difficult to find one, and when I did it was so exposed and unprivate I couldn't use it. Lately, though, I had a dream where although it was exposed, I did use it surrounded by friends. I felt this was good.'

In frustrating toilet dreams, the dreamer is being prevented from doing something which is natural to her because of fear of public scrutiny. Such scrutiny carries with it the possibility of public

196

disapproval which, as we know, causes women great discomfort. We have been trained to seek the good opinions of others, particularly males, and so are afraid to risk causing upset.[3] Everyone goes to the toilet, even the Queen, so why not come to terms with it?

Irene provides much insight into her own 'toilet' dreams which may be of help in understanding your own:

'In my dream I open the door and see wooden commodes in a line and women sitting on them. I need to pass a motion and I sit on one of these commodes. I hate the thought of "going in front of these people", so I pretend it doesn't bother me. Then I successfully urinate. I can hear it and so can the women around me. I hold back my motion. I don't want them to hear and smell me. Then I can smell the foulness of the air and this room sickens me.

'On other occasions I enter a room full of "public conveniences" with modern facilities and head straight for a cubicle, but when I go in the bowl of the toilet, it is filled to the brim with water and excrement. I think to myself that I cannot possibly go there so the only alternative is to use one of the commodes. The commodes are in a line and visible to all. I choose one as far away as possible from all the other women and go there, but it's an agonizing, humiliating experience. I never relax and feel awful. I wish I could get out. Then, on looking down at the floor, I see it is covered in water. The clear water flows all over the place and I have to walk through it, feeling very uncomfortable doing so.

'When I wake up the dream is never a stimulant to use the toilet. I dislike the dream so much that I have tried to control it, to change the direction, but I never can. In waking life I find it impossible to go to the toilet, even to urinate in public lavatories. I keep thinking I may be interrupted. I think this stems from a childhood experience, but I cannot think what it is.'

Irene's dreams contain elements that are easily identified as stemming from her waking life, such as her inability to use public lavatories. However, they also indicate concern about other people's opinions of her and her own fears of upsetting others, hence she chooses the toilet as far away from the other women as she can. She keeps her distance – I wonder if she is aware of doing this during her waking hours? And if she does keep her distance, is it because she is a bit afraid of other people and thinks they will comment on some unacceptable aspects of herself? If that is a fear, then she will feel it is safer not to reveal those parts in the first place and so avoid any risk of rejection. However, what Irene may well discover, should she take the risk of exposing the hidden parts of her character, is that we all share those very characteristics about which she feels so troubled.

Toilet dreams usually reflect anxiety, but for some women such as Leah, they become a symbol for something more:

'In the past the typical dream would entail a lengthy hunt through some place I used to know well, but I could never find the loo. It was never where I thought it was. Eventually, however, I would find a loo but there would be no privacy and no relief. Always when I woke up I would find I needed to go to the toilet – hence the lack of relief in the dream! But now the need has become a symbol for some other kind of elimination, because not only can the dream continue beyond the point at which I find the lavatory (or some suitable substitute), but also on waking there is no marked physical need to account for the dream.'

Leah gives a long example of a dream which involved travelling to another planet in a spaceship. Just before disembarking she found that she had to use the potty:

'Our guide entered the ship. He disapproved of what I was doing but accepted the necessity for it before I was fit to go among his people . . .'

Here we see a different attitude for Leah can use the 'potty' and she is not deterred by the onlooker, nor does she become frightened by his disapproval. She completes her task. Other dreams continue the development of the theme, so that elimination of 'waste material' has become a significant symbol for Leah to work on when she uses her dreams to encourage self-knowledge.

There were many other anxiety themes reported by women who took part in my survey, as you saw from the list on page 146. However, far and away the largest group was the one which had anxiety dreams about violence to themselves or their family. We will consider those most disturbing dreams in the next chapter.

Notes

1. Maggie Scarfe, *Unfinished Business: Pressure Point in the Lives of Women*, Fontana, 1980. This book gives vivid case histories to show how women are affected by emotional relationships and explains in more depth the concept of 'unfinished business'.
2. Hans Dieckmann, 'The Symbolism of the Automobile in Dreams', *Analytische Psychologie*, Vol. 7 (1), 1976.
3. Colette Dowling in *The Cinderella Complex*, Fontana, 1982, has some interesting things to say about how women are dependent on the good opinions of men and how this affects our perceptions of power as well as independence.

10

Violence Most Foul

Dreams reflect the emotions we harbour in the deepest recesses of our soul and psyche. They show up our strengths, our weaknesses, our tenderness and our viciousness. We all have negative and positive aspects, and once we can come to terms with the less acceptable bits, the sooner we can achieve a healthy wholeness. It is very difficult to own those rotten, selfish, miserly, grudging parts of our own character which are easy to recognize in other people. For women, accepting the violent, angry part of ourselves is a particular struggle. We have been conditioned, taught, socialized, call it what you will, to accept that we should be all that is indicated by that little nursery rhyme. People who accept the stereotyped view of women as 'sugar and spice and all things nice' will be amazed at the level of violence in women's dreams. The question we have to ask, though, is why so much of this violence is turned towards the dreamer herself. Are we so conditioned that we accept such violence and are incapable of fighting back? Is it that we are not permitted to inflict pain on others, even in self-defence, because all women are the eternal giving mothers from whose breasts the milk of human kindness flows? A simple but effective question to ask yourself, if you have violent dreams in which you are hurt, is: 'Why do I let this happen?' If you answer it honestly you will be on the way to preventing terrifying dreams of the kind described below.

Battered and beaten

Laura's dreams are violent and frightening:

'There are shootings, explosions and cuttings. I remember being cut in half with a great sword which split me from crotch to head while I was still standing. My blood shot out in a wide arc.'

Studying her dreams enabled her to begin to understand. She wrote:

'I'm a pacifist and try to live without hurting others. I feel these gruesome dreams allow my violence to express itself. I always feel better for them because they release of tension. Having been a battered baby, then a battered wife, and having stopped this pattern, I feel that any residue of masochistic behaviour is catered for in my dreams and no longer in my waking life.'

I've found that the most violent dreams are experienced by women who were physically abused as children. There is a reason for this, as psychologist Dr J. Hall, who has made a detailed study of the clinical use of dreams in therapy, states:[1]

> It now appears clear that the repetition in dreams of actual traumatic situations helps the ego overcome severe experiences of helplessness and passivity by reliving them in dreams until some form of mastery can be achieved by the dream ego.

In other words, by repeating the pain, your dream is pushing you to consider the 'unfinished business' and deal with it once and for all. The methods for achieving this are described in Chapter 12, but the first step is to accept that such dreams are communicating important information to you.

Norma, a volunteer on a project for handicapped youngsters, came to a day course on dreams. She struck me as a fairly brittle woman with a strident voice and edgy air. Physically she was very well cared for: smart sweater and pants, careful make-up and shiny blonde hair. She turned out to be sixty-three but looked younger. She was married to a man whose spinal injuries had left him paralysed from the neck down. Initially I wondered if she would selfishly dominate the group, but she lapsed into thoughtful silence as she 'drew a dream'. Her picture led on to descriptions of other dreams which were usually too unpalatable to be faced in the light of day. However, there, in that safe group, she had an opportunity to share them:

'In my dreams I kill people by stabbing them: my sister, my children, a lady at work, my friends. I am violent and hit, kick and bludgeon my husband and children. I watch cats attack my mother-in-law and gouge chunks of flesh out of her. I chop up bodies and even scoop out the flesh from a mutilated hand. When all the flesh is out of the fingers I put them on my own finger ends.

'I watch my daughter cook – trapped in a glass-doored oven with no handle. I am forced to look upon a dead face and as I am screaming and protesting the scene changes and I am surrounded by my family, who are sitting in complete silence.'

No support is forthcoming from her family, but then there never has been. Her father beat his wife and children, threatened them with knives; and each year, it seemed to Norma, another child would arrive. One sister, born when Norma was fifteen, committed suicide in her thirties and that felt like yet another turn in the unremitting cycle of despair which is an inescapable part of her life. Alcohol is an important factor in 75 per cent of all cases of wife or child battering and abuse, and Norma's father was no exception. The regular drinking bouts preceded the equally regular beatings.

As a child, Norma went to eleven different schools in eleven different neighbourhoods, never putting down roots. She said:

'I couldn't do anything about my father. Yet I'm like him. My mother used to tell me, "No one likes you because you're just like your father." So I had these macabre dreams and fantasies. When he died, still beating her, I used to go to his grave and imagine the body decomposing. I hated him, yet I'm supposed to be like him. My mother used to say she was just a body with a pinny on: nothing but babies and house. There were ten of us. In my dreams I'm always screaming, but it makes no bloody difference!'

After all these years, Norma is haunted by those experiences which severely damaged her on a psychological level. Anthony Storr gives one of the best descriptions of the effects of such abuse that I have come across:[2]

So long as the good and the bad are separated, children can tolerate violence, death and other things which might be expected to disturb them. But to discover that the person one believed was on one's side is actually malign is to enter into so unpredictable and unsafe a sphere of experience that children become alarmed; just as an adult might if he discovered that the injection which his doctor was giving him were poisonous rather than therapeutic.

Both Norma and Yvonne were beaten as children and the effect of that trauma persists, though they no longer experience violence in their relationships; there is still the need to express the violent side they know exists. But why didn't their mothers leave? Let Yvonne, who finally took refuge in a Women's Aid house, tell us how it was for her. Her feelings about power, or the lack of it, her place in society and her role as a woman raised issues for us all:[3]

> You are under so much pressure when you try to make a break from your man. At least when you stay with him you are looked on as a wife and mother, you have some kind of status. Once you have been parted you lose that and feel as if you are at the mercy of every official you have to see. You have all the decisions to make about yourself and the kids on your own and nobody to help you with this. You are just under so much pressure that no matter how violent your man was, or what you have gone through with him, you tend to start thinking and saying to yourself 'he wasn't really that bad'. The other thing is the fear that you have that he may be round the next corner all the time. You can't relax. At least when you live with him you know where he is . . . I would say that it's these pressures that drive women back to men.

A report by the Women's National Commission published by the Cabinet Office in 1985 endorses the view that violence against women is seen by the police to be the woman's fault, especially in domestic disputes.[4] They found evidence that the police tended to dismiss women victims as, for example 'a nagging, hysterical or sluttish housewife'; such a woman is considered to have contributed towards the man's violence. The report advises police to concentrate on implementing the law rather than making their own value judgements.

My friend Carol asked me to spend an evening with her literacy group. She'd been telling them about my interest in dreams at one of their learning-to-read sessions and all eight women were keen to see me. I didn't know anything more about them so I wasn't aware that Mavis and June were sisters, but their shared experiences emerged in the dreams they talked about.

As a child Mavis had a recurring dream about a red heart being stuck with pins while she sobbed and sobbed. In another she was chased round and round the outside of her house by a man who grabbed her as she rushed to the door. She never reached safety. June dreamt of going to visit a neighbour in whose house she took refuge. Her father answered the door with a huge knife in his hand.

Both June and Mavis had chosen a dream from childhood to draw, yet I had asked them to choose a recent dream if possible. It was as if they were, without discussion, both compelled to return to painful images of childhood. They too had a brutal father and, in both cases, their dreams stopped when their mother finally took the decision to leave. Neither had ever spoken of these dreams before and they were surprised to share them. They hadn't talked about their childhood memories much but later some of their powerful writing was published in 'Hidden Depths'.[5] June's account below and to Anthony Storr's remarks show the professional and the victim speak the same language:

> My mum and dad always argued ever since I can remember. Even though we didn't see him being violent towards my mum very often, as soon as the arguments started my stomach would turn over and I would feel very sick with fear.
>
> Very often my dad wouldn't come home for his tea and we knew he had gone straight to the pub, and the trouble would start after he had had a skin full. It was around that time that my mum decided she could avoid the trouble and a good hiding if we were out when my dad came home. So, around 9 o'clock she would say, come on kids, get your things on, and we knew we would spend another night outside in a field or in someone's shed until about 5 a.m. Then we would creep back into the house and sleep on the settee or chair for an hour or two before going to school . . .
>
> Eventually after seventeen years of marriage my mum left my dad and we came to Manchester. I was so happy at the thought of leaving not the place, but my dad. Pickmere was a beautiful place to bring up a family, but after all the violence I saw there as a child I would never like to go back. The mental scars of childhood last a lifetime.'

Mavis wrote of another incident:

> There was one night which I remember vividly. Dad was late as usual, so rather than go out my mum came into our bedroom and locked the door. We all sat there waiting for him to come home. Finally, we heard the back door open and it didn't need a breathalyser to tell us that he was drunk. As he reached the top of the stairs we could see my mum was trembling. I remember her telling him that she would speak to him in the morning when he was sober. My dad wasn't going to take that as an excuse. He promptly kicked the door, which came crashing down on top of the bed. At this point my mum crouched on the windowsill. She told my dad that she would jump if he came any closer. He said that she was frightened. She wasn't, though; as he started towards her she jumped seventeen feet to the ground.
>
> She was three months pregnant at the time. She carried that baby until she was eight months, then gave birth to a seven and a half pound stillborn baby girl. She also received seven stitches in her knee as a result of

her fall. My dad told all his drinking friends that she had been trying to fly.

Mavis and June were as powerless as their mother; this inability to prevent hurt is a regular feature in dreams of violence.

Lydia, a young middle-class woman from Sussex, described a recent violent dream:

'I was with my husband in the car, talking about the shopping we had done. I got out of the car and went up the stairs to the front door, but I never got to the top because when I turned round to look down at the car I saw my husband was still inside. Somehow, I felt frightened. I called to him but there was no answer so I went down.

'He got out and told me that there was something wrong with the engine. Next, we seemed to have forgotten about the car and were both going up to the house. As we were doing this, one of the car doors opened. I screamed. My husband went and shut it. It happened again but this time I saw a figure of someone sitting in the driver's seat. I felt terrified but my husband could not see it. I could. He just thought there was something wrong with the car but all I could see was this figure in the car. Then my husband suddenly dragged me down the road.

'All of a sudden, we were in a garage. My husband was asking a man about the car, I was standing against a table. I could still see the car with the figure in it, then it got out. I felt a desperate urge to scream but I knew no one could hear me.

'The dark figure proceeded to climb the stairs and halfway up turned towards me; it was my husband. Although he was standing next to me in the garage, that evil figure was him too.

'As I watched, the figure looked around and walked back down the stairs after looking over at me. I again looked over to the car and this time saw a small girl. The man figure looked over at me and laughed. The girl figure screamed so loud I felt myself go cold. All I could do was watch. He opened the door of the car, got hold of her hair and dragged her upstairs. The dream ended there, but the most frightening thing for me was seeing two of my husband.'

The dream message is given twice over: she is assaulted in the dream by her husband, and the drama is repeated as the girl figure is attacked by the dark male figure, who is also her husband. There is no provocation in either case. The scene moves from the mundane shopping chore to violence; and one minute the girl is quietly sitting in the car then she is sadistically abused by Lydia's husband look-alike. There is no rhyme or reason for this unpredictable brutality, but it does show an awareness of two sides of her husband. I do not think Lydia has admitted this to herself in waking hours but in sleep she is too frightened even to give voice to the fear. The 'girl' inside her does, though. She at least has enough strength to pierce the passivity with her screams, futile though they are.

Lydia's dreaming mind, not content to run the drama through once with Lydia witnessing the transformation and being subjected to the abuse of her husband dragging her down the road, repeats the message. It shows the abuse of the girl again by her husband/dark figure. Such a dream stresses the need for the dreamer honestly to face her suspicions.

Stabbings: a cut-throat business

Angela's dream and her explanation of it pinpoint the ways in which violent dreams can be seen as helpful in developing self-awareness, though this can be a very painful process:

'I dream that a man is walking towards me, no face but dressed in a shirt and tie. He puts out his hand to shake mine and has a razor blade concealed in his hand. I am cut to shreds. He walks away.'

The callous indifference with which Angela is bloodily slashed by the anonymous man suggests inhumane cruelty. It leaves us with the feeling that this woman doesn't matter, that she is merely there to be acted upon, certainly not to be considered or consulted. Does Angela feel that she is inconsequential and dispensable or does she think that other people see her in this way? She has already done some thinking about this dream and its meaning for her:

'Although I have another recurring dream of being chased by a man with a knife, the one about the man with the razor blade really bothers me. It might have something to do with my job. I was in publishing and marketing, travelled all over the world and worked hard to get to the top. I loved it but then I had a nervous breakdown. For me the dream means the cut-throat business I was in, but in a subtle way: hand not throat. I'm not in work now but I still have the dream . . .

If I knew what my dreams were all about, I might not be frightened. As it is, they make me keep my distance in case anyone thinks I'm a crackpot.'

Fear of being thought strange or 'a crackpot' prevents many women from talking about their dreams. Angela's dread of disapproval or scorn imprisons and hinders her. If she could find someone she trusted to whom she could talk about her dreams, she could gain a great deal of relief.

In Angela's dream is the image of a faceless man whose shirt and tie give him outward conventional respectability. He approaches with a gesture recognized worldwide as a civilized greeting. In fact, didn't handshaking originate as the mutual clasping of wrists to ensure that the person you met was not carrying a dagger with which to injure you? In the dream the usual becomes horrific – Angela is assaulted when she should be treated civilly; she is rejected when she was expecting acceptance; and the hand offered in trust is now 'cut to shreds'. She is left isolated, no gestures of friendship remaining.

Angela's trust is misplaced. She is let down, abused or abandoned even though she is obviously 'cut up' and 'bleeding'. The dream draws attention to the way in which other people are becoming faceless to her, or suggests that she is becoming facelss herself in her drive to the top of her profession. More likely, it tells us how hurt she is by someone who has not met her expectations. Dreams can warn us of impending disaster and help us to identify times when we need to take a different course in our lives. However, in order to read the signs we have to learn the language – a language that has been forgotten by most people.

Murder

Killings are things that we read about in the newspapers. Each year in England and Wales there are about 500 killings, and in 40 per cent of them the victim is either related to, or the lover of, the killer. We are much more likely to kill, or be killed by, someone we know than a stranger. There are many anomalies in the judicial treatment of women murderers as against treatment of men, as Robin Lustig points out.[6] He wonders 'whether our predominantly male judiciary are always as mindful as they might be of the "provocation" caused to wives by their husbands. Too often, it seems, the women who kill their men are referred to as "evil" or "wicked", words which have an unpleasant medieval ring to them.' On the whole, women offenders are treated much more severely than their male counterparts, perhaps because their behaviour challenges the whole notion of women as passive, malleable creatures. The dreams of murder described below certainly reveal overwhelming rage.

Anger, undisguised by any civilized veneer, erupts in Helen's dream:

'I once dreamt that my former husband, while I was still living with him, turned into a pig and I cut his throat with a huge knife. I was very scared of my own violence and the dream was gruesomely gory.'

The nightmare made Helen realize how maddened she was by the relationship and she eventually left. She was glad to get out, but the threat of separation or desertion by husbands is frightening for many women.

Childhood experiences of being pushed to be independent at a time when we are still emotionally in need of support and reassurance lead to insecurity. Think of the girl who is encouraged to become 'little mother' to a younger brother or sister when she has strong needs of her own which should be met. In order to gain approval, to be thought a 'good girl', she acquiesces and buries her own needs out of sight of others and, probably more importantly, out of her own sight. Later, the woman feels as if no one really cares for her, no one truly loves her, and that one day she will be left. Lo and behold, in her dreams her husband leaves her. He is the person to whom she has transferred her dependence and still she has fears of being let down, of being pushed away.

Hannah's dream expresses this well:

'I dreamt that something was threatening my husband's and children's lives. I was hunting for it. Eventually I picked up a knife and turned round, only to realize that I was the would-be murderer.'

She thought danger was coming from outside – other people, other women, the nebulous 'enemy' – but her dream tells her that the danger is within her. She has aggressive feelings which can hurt and destroy. If we don't recognize our own needs and communicate them, we are in danger of damaging our relationships. In waking hours unfocused fears can be repressed more easily. Rationally we can tell ourselves that we are loved and cared for because the outside reality shows this to be the case – unless it patently isn't, of course. But the haunting feeling that we are unloved or unlovable may surface in dreams.

As women we are taught to be self-reliant and capable on the one hand – i.e. 'the little mother'; on the other we are told that we should lean on and rely on men, in the form of fathers or husbands. We are taught, very subtly, that we should put their needs before our own and that we shouldn't bother them with our emotional excesses, which are socially defined as jealousy, depression, possessiveness, and so on. We in turn tend to operate on that level and don't communicate our needs openly enough. When we do, there is a chance of genuine dialogue and emotional exchange. We can be real instead of playing games which lead to confusion and dissatisfaction.

A number of women dream of their own deaths. Anna's dream of being electrocuted was so vivid that she woke up utterly condemning the use of capital punishment. For Gina, rescue was possible since, in the dream, her father had told her, 'Don't worry. I won't let them hang you.' She was to be hanged for a crime she hadn't committed, but after three unsuccessful 'hangings' she was freed. Two points to note here: her father did not fulfil his promise; and, like many women, she was wrongly accused and convicted. In some dreams women are found guilty for crimes that have not even been committed. That's when you know you are on to a loser!

An anonymous man is responsible for Betty's death:

'I have a recurring dream where I go to my old school, go into the toilets and fill up the sink to wash my face. A man in a black and white suit pushes my head in the water. I escape, then find myself on the field, and the same man comes behind me and strangles me. I can actually feel myself dying.'

I wonder whether Betty's dream is connected with painful episodes when she was at secondary school. She was told when she was thirteen that she would not be able to have children and went through a very depressed period. That news meant the end, the death, of one aspect of her life. Like all her girlfriends, she expected to marry and have children but the latter possibility was then removed.

Nightmares often come at times of stress and if you dream about someone being murdered ask yourself if you harbour hostile feelings towards him or her. You may be so unwilling to own those angry feelings that you transfer them to the 'murderer' in the dream, which is what happened in Kate's case:

'I twice dreamt that my young brother was murdered and his body chopped up. At some point it became me who had killed him.'

Eventually the dream directly revealed her hostility.

There were few dreams about sisters reported in my survey. This may be because such dreams are not particularly dramatic in nature and so may be more readily forgotten. Or it could be that our relationships with sisters are taken for granted. Only two women related anxiety dreams about sisters; both happen at times of conflict:

'I frequently dream about being confronted with violence. For instance I dream about my sisters and I am planning an evening out and getting ready when a murderer steals into the kitchen. We try to hide as he comes upstairs. He massacres my sisters while I remain hidden behind the wardrobe.'

'A dream of murdering my sister and her realization of what I was doing.'

Malevolent mothers

The relationship girls have with their mothers is supremely important for emotional development. In that relationship we learn how to be women, we learn what is acceptable for girls to be and what is not allowed, we learn of the roles women and men play.

The learning process varies for each of us since our mother have different experiences and expectations. The message I picked up from my mother, albeit unconsciously, was that men were the bosses but women could manipulate things to get their own way; so I believed that women did have power even if it was not immediately discernible. Without being aware of it, I learnt to play the devious games Eric Bernes describes.[7] The kind of games I refer to include 'You're-so-big-and-strong-and-I'm-merely-a-weak-woman-so-will-you-change-the-car-tyre?' and 'If-I-don't-get-my-own-way-I'll-sulk/cry/be ill'.

From our mother, with whom we forge the first, closest physical bond, we must learn to become separate; it's hard for the child and it's hard for the mother. We have to grow under her guidance then detach from her in order to be women in our own right. Some women experience this as rejection, which causes difficulties in later relationships. The daughter sees her mother's attention being taken by her father; it seems to the child that he has first rights. She learns that her mother also puts her own interests after those of others within the family. Thus girls accept an inferior place because, for some never openly explained reason, women are not as important as men: that is a very early lesson and, despite logical arguments to the contrary, it is still a deeply entrenched, widely held one.

Other relationships within the family – for instance, between mother and brothers, or mother and father – cause fears that there is not enough love to go round, so we feel left out. This may lead to withdrawal on the part of the girl-child and later the woman. She will keep part of herself back in case she has a rival for any relationship in which she has a great investment. More and more is being written about the significance of the mother-daughter relationship – one recent study I would recommend is Eichenbaum and Orbach's *What Do Women Want?*.[8] The importance certainly comes out in women's reports of their dreams.

Ursula wrote of her 'recurring, stressful' dream and provided some personal details which help us to understand what it is about.

'I am twenty-three and have lived in this bedsit since I was eighteen. It is quite close to my parents' home. The dreams started about a year after I moved here. They are always of my mother and they are always of the same type. For some unknown or trivial reason she is very antagonistic, verbally hurtful, demoralizing and disparaging towards me. In one particular dream I was sobbing for she told me that she had never really loved me, although she was deeply upset at my elder sister leaving home to get married, because she missed her badly.

'I have three elder sisters and one younger one, and in some of these dreams one or other of them is deliberately provoking my mother to be even nastier. I am really puzzled by these dreams . . . but according to the rest of the family I am more like my mother in personality than any of them. Maybe there are parts of my mother's personality in me that she doesn't want to be reminded of. Things she wishes she had done at my age, perhaps, that I could still do – that is, have a career – although I don't think she would do any different if she had her time over again.'

Ursula's dreams throw up a number of conflicts frequently found in the mother-daughter relationship. Ursula still needs her mother's love intensely and fears unprovoked attacks. Somehow she will have to confront the troublesome issues which lie below the surface. Though she writes elsewhere that she and her mother and sisters have 'a very good, close relationship', her dreams indicate that there is something amiss which must be dealt with.

Hilary rarely dreams of her mother:

'The last one was set back in time. I was in a hospital. My mother was a nurse trying to save my life, but I died.'

Here the mother is seen as a helpful, caring person who, though she tries, cannot save Hilary. Maybe she doesn't have the power. Maybe Hilary was going to die anyway and no one could have done any better. Whatever the reason, the mother was unable to protect her. Frequently, in dreams, death means change: the change from one part of life to another, the change from childhood to adulthood, perhaps the change from an unsatisfying way of life to a more satisfactory one. In the transition from being a dependent child to becoming an autonomous individual, one of the most painful realizations is that our parents are not all-powerful and cannot protect us from the big wide world and all its tribulations. The dream could be helping Hilary to come to terms with this. Growing up is a painful process whatever the age at which we do it.

Consider also, should you have a dream like Keeley's, whether the words are significant. They usually are:

'I have recurring dreams of being smothered or strangled. Sometimes I drown. These dreams tell me who to avoid. In one my mother was suffocating me. She frightens me in real life.'

Keeley found it very difficult to break away from her over-protective and domineering mother. However, she did not have the same waking physical persecution that Jean had when her mother became mentally ill. The threat of attack in Jean's dream reflected an incident which actually happened the day before her mother was hospitalized:

'I dreamt she was after me with a knife in the street at the back of the house where I live now. She was running after me and shouting at me.'

It was lucky for Jean that she was away from home that day. She found out from the police later that night that her mother had come searching for her with a knife!

It is hard to be a parent at times, but in these dreams the dreamers feel betrayed, rejected, deserted and psychologically abused by the parents. Non-physical violence can be every bit as terrifying as physical torture, as in the rejection overtly presented in Jenny's dream:

'In a recurring dream, I am at home with my parents but they don't want me and I am trying to find somewhere to live.'

Edith's dream is also simple and direct:

'This morning I woke up dreaming my mother and her boyfriend were eating tons of ice-cream and wafers in my father's house. It was a lovely sunny day but they would not share their ice-cream.

In real life neither of them works. My mother says she wants an easy life and certainly she's got one in some respects.'

Meanwhile, even 'in her father's house', Edith is not wanted. They will not share with her emotionally. She is excluded.

This longer dream, described by Fiona, brings out a number of issues:

'This is the most vivid dream I can remember. I felt a terrible pain in my ears. I discovered that my mother had stuffed my ears with cotton wool and stuck something through my tongue. I was very angry about this.

'I went into hospital and discovered both my parents were lying there in beds. My father was covered with a sheet and he half threw it back to reveal a very hairy body. My mother was reading a book on shellfish. I told them I was discharging myself from hospital and my father said bitterly, "I have waited all my life for you to come here and now you're leaving." By this time the pain in my ears had disappeared.

'I might add that my parents' marriage was not a happy one, and they are now, belatedly, divorced. I feel these dreams hold the key to my feelings about my family. But I wish they were more pleasant and not so disturbing.'

213

There is an air of 'sickness' in this dream. Mother prevents daughter from hearing and talking; she prevents her from using normal means of communication, which angers Fiona. There is the image of 'discharge': Fiona is 'discharging herself'. She is signing herself out of this unhealthy place and by the end of the dream the pain in her ears has disappeared. She manages to assert herself and, although she may wish that her dreams were less disturbing, they are putting her in touch with family relationships she has not yet come to terms with. There are certainly ambiguous messages in a number of the dream images – for instance, in the father's gesture of invitation and revelation.[9]

Fire in dreams destroys and purifies. It also provides an impersonal means of obliterating those who cross us. As I've said earlier, though, dreaming that a person is killed does not mean that you actually wish this to happen in waking life, nor does it mean you will cause such destruction; rather, such dreams reveal that you may have hostile feelings which would be better dealt with than left festering and fermenting to erupt violently.

As an adolescent, Mandy hated her parents for a while and her antagonism found an outlet in dreams:

'I dream that I am out on my paper round and come back to find my family have died in a fire and only the dog gets out.

'In another dream I see my parents' home as a sheet of newspaper, burning, with me outside unable to do anything. Other dreams are about accidents and deaths in my family where I would be left on my own.'

Finally, she is left in peace and quiet, and the dog, who never caused her bother, conveniently escapes death!

Sadistic sexuality

'I dream of people I am fond of being tortured. With female friends this takes the form of being raped or having an abortion while they are still awake.'

Jo said that before she was a feminist she used to dream frequently of being raped. She declared:

'You know, reading back in my diary it was horrible to realize that my attitude to being raped wasn't to be angry or anything. I just

forgave the bloke or made friends with him. I didn't think this was
odd at the time, but now . . . I'd really bought the submissive line.'

A father usually provides a girl's first experience of masculinity.
We learn through him, or through our mother's interpretations of
him, what it is to be a man in the world. We learn that he is different
from us physically and that different things are expected of him.[10] A
little girl is taught that boys and men behave in a way which is largely
discouraged in females. From her father she also learns how to get
along with men; how to win their love, how to gain their approval
and how to be an acceptable woman. Her brothers are also important, of course, but we will consider their role later. So father's, or
father figure's, attitude to a daughter's sexuality is very important.

For some women dreams involving sexuality and the father-
daughter relationship are particularly distressing. Some are based on
actual events while others are veiled in images, as in the following
example:

'I was sitting with my father and sister. A gold chain which my
lover bought me, and which I'd lost in real life, I suddenly discovered in the dream. I had eaten it and it had stuck in my throat,
though half of it was still in my mouth. My sister tried to think of a
way to ease it out gently but my father grabbed it and yanked it out
forcibly, tearing the flesh in my mouth . . . I was so incensed that I
got my sister to pin his arms behind him so that I could punch him.

'This was an unusual dream, in that I don't normally attack him.'

Annie's other dreams give us more information:

'I am being chased by my father and there is an unpleasant under-
current, usually sexual. In another I am vainly trying to find space in
my childhood home. All the doors and cupboards are ajar and I don't
have any room for myself.'

In the first dream we see a number of images which may be linked
to her father's attitude to Annie's sexuality. Her father rips the
lover's token from her mouth in a gesture of violation. There is
no compassionate gentleness in his approach. The image of the flesh
in her mouth being torn is akin to the tearing of the vagina when
rape occurs. On some level Annie may be feeling that her father
is sexually interested in her, even if this has never been explicit.
Her dreams are showing concern and anxiety about it. Luckily,
Annie gets sisterly support and can vent her anger. She confronts

her father in this dream, which is a very positive act.

The recurring theme evident in the next dream is harrowing for Clare to deal with. Her father, as she says, has been dead for three years:

'One which stands out is where he sexually assaulted me. The setting was where I live now. He was next to me on the bed and was wearing his usual dressing gown. I was facing the wall and he was behind me. He was smiling and had hold of me tightly by the shoulders, rubbing against me. I was upset and trying to pull away. I half woke up, feeling sexually aroused and confused. In the dream there was the impression that he was not going to penetrate me.'

Stephanie has similar dreams:

'I seldom have nightmares or anxiety dreams. The only ones of this kind have been recent and have recalled past memories of sexual assaults by my father.'

Her dreams address the horrific abuse of power which occurs in father-daughter incest and she has to find some way of working through the trauma.

These anxiety dreams may be based on actual incidents or may stem from imagined sexual advances from the father. Sexuality in dreams has been dealt with in some detail in Chapter 5, and further consideration of incest is included there.

Suicide

Self-inflicted death raises issues about the right to control one's own life, attitudes towards mental health and 'balance of the mind', and feelings of despair, both in the person who commits the act and those who are left to grieve. In dreams suicidal acts again reveal personal concerns and conflicts, as Sarah describes:

'I had a terrible dream in which my younger brother committed suicide by hanging himself. I awoke with profound feelings of grief and helplessness. There was a lot of friction and rivalry when we were growing up.'

Most dreams about brothers deal with the death or rescue of the brother. As we are growing up, we learn that we are different from our brothers physically and that others have different expectations of us. There is a tendency either to eliminate that which is different or to incorporate it. In this anxiety dream the former occurs:

'I go to visit my mother, who is now dead . . . I see the shop across from our old house burned to its shell and still smouldering . . . The doors suddenly burst open. There are people fighting. I turn around and there is my brother lying in the gutter with blood pouring out of his neck. I look for someone to help and there are his wife and daughter, but they just walk away, very slowly . . .'

The dreamer is deserted. By herself she seeks help while those who should be most closely concerned renounce their involvement. Is this how she sees her brother's marriage? Does she believe that she is the only one who cares for him? And what are those people fighting about? The old house may have been pulled down but the shop, the place of buying and selling, though it has been burned, is still smouldering. I wonder what has been left smouldering in the dreamer's mind that she should have this dream. As she concludes, 'In this dream I was breathless, wanting to help, but I couldn't. I still keep thinking of it. The thoughts won't go away.'

In fairytales and myths we see girls either rescuing or killing their brothers. Maybe, it is necessary to 'kill' the brother in order to obliterate feelings of sexuality towards him. The ambivalent nature of brother-sister relationships may influence relationships with other men, and continue a puzzling love-hate pattern. It could be helpful to examine your present relationships with men in the light of how you feel about your dream 'brothers'.

You're tearing me apart: family dynamics

'When I had this dream I knew it was time for me to leave the man I had lived with for many years. The worst and most memorable part was where we were arguing and then suddenly he was standing with my daughter's injured body dangling from his hand. I knew instantly that her injuries were caused by us tearing her apart. It was sickening.'

The dream was the final straw for that dreamer; there was no denying how far the relationship had deteriorated, and she left. In other dreams women see themselves being hacked to pieces with axes, being shot or shooting others, cutting, chopping and torturing. In the vast majority of dreams, though, women are the victims, not perpetrators of violence. And the setting is usually within the family.

Conflict in families is common; what varies is the extent and intensity of the conflict and the way in which we deal with it.

Maeve's feelings of powerlessness were buried deep in the raw experiences of childhood. Brought up in Ireland, her family were poor, uneducated and brutal – not intentionally brutal, just ignorantly brutal. She told me of a dream she had had since childhood and drew me a rudimentary, childlike picture:

'I dreamt I was in a church. Dead bodies, without any clothes, were piled up on the window ledges. I was locked in the cold church and I couldn't get out. No matter how hard I tried, I couldn't get out. I woke up screaming.'

Where did such a dream come from? She did not know when I asked her, only that it had returned again and again. It started when she was twelve. Had she ever seen a dead body, I asked. 'Ah, yes! Once.'

When she was twelve, Maeve woke up next to her mother, whose bed she shared. She couldn't wake her mother. She was cold. Frightened, she ran for her father. He sent her into the kitchen and then sent the other children to join her. Her father never told her that her mother had died, and for years she was afraid to ask where her mother had gone. Finally, she dared to ask. 'She's under the ground. Finished. Dead. Never speak of her again,' was the stark reply. Maeve never did, but you can see how the dream expressed that isolating pain.

If in dreams you are attacked, cornered or literally torn apart, ask yourself what it refers to. In a group I was running for wives of prisoners, one woman dreamt of being cornered by crocodiles in a modern block of flats. There appeared to be no way of escape at the time and she woke up in a panic. The dream had occurred some months before when her husband, addicted to heroin, had become a snarling, wild 'snapper'. He was unable to control his violent moods and eventually his wife sought refuge with her friend in the blocks of flats in the dream. He followed her there, and so 'cornered' did she feel about what was happening to both herself and the children that she refused to give him the alibi he demanded to get off a stealing offence for which he was to be tried. The dream had puzzled and frightened her but she said it really made sense now, considering all the strain she had been under.

Taking back the power

Healthy rebellion, heroic conflict and robust retaliation all indicate an assertive stance on the dreamer's part. When, in dreams, we fight against flood, fire, attacks and threatened injury, we are constructing a positive role for the protection of our future and it's a very healthy sign! This isn't rebellion or violence for its own sake but in response to aggression. In taking control of what happens, we take back the power to run our own lives.

It doesn't always work, of course. Danae, disappointed as she is, still tries to stand up for herself. She's just not found the most productive way yet:

'There are lots of dreams in which my boyfriend tells me he doesn't love me any more. I find him with nude, semi-nude or fully dressed women, often his ex-wife. I can never remember the exact details of the dreams but one thing about them is that, when I hit him in the dreams, it doesn't hurt him. Often I want to kill him and am not strong enough.'

Her ineffectiveness in putting across her disquiet when awake spills over into her dreams. On neither level can she get through to him and her anger is building up to a point where she wants to hit out but she feels her strength is inadequate to affect him. Other dreamers are more effective.

Vera is moved by intense determination to a verbal attack. She succeeds and feels terrific!

'I often dream about my mother. These go in phases. In the last series I was shouting at her, not very nicely. That finished with a dream of my grandmother. I was paralysed but summoned up every bit of strength to tell her to get lost. It was wonderful but terrifying.'

Cassie, who has just moved into her own terraced house in Burnley, has found that, with her new independence, her dreams are changing. In Cassie's dream there is still threat from her father but eventual protection from her mother. Here the mother is a successful rescuer, unlike the mother in Hilary's dream:

'I dreamt that someone's neck and shoulders were covered in scratches. In the dream I was lying in bed when my dad walked in. He switched on the light and went for my neck and shoulders with a razor blade. The only way I could stop him was to pull at his nose.

My mother came in and pulled him away. When I woke up I felt it had not been a dream at all.'

Linda used her dream to clarify her family dynamics:

'I used to have a real nasty one about being attacked by demons: a cat with a woman's voice, a dog with a man's. I would be rendered helpless by a hideous saw-like buzzing inside my head and they would savage me, sometimes to death. I would wake up feeling freaked out and shaken.

'After a lot of thought, I realized that the cat and dog represented my parents. The last time I had the dream I fought back and escaped.'

Women are much better at fighting for other people – their children, lovers, parents – than they are for themselves. This fits in with the role of women as carers and it causes less dissonance than when they are fighting just for themselves. Arifa rescues her brother in this dream:

'I have violent dreams where my brother is attacked by a number of men. I arrive and shoot the most prominent member of the gang at point-blank range. The dream is very specific: I'd do anything to kill the person who threatens my brother.'

Her filial loyalty is commendable. In fact she feels closer to her brother than to any other member of her family, for she cannot confide in her parents, with whom she lives. Her brother, now living in Germany, is no longer there to support her and, after a particularly disturbing recent family row, she dreamt that he was there comforting her. In her dreams she can protect and save him.

Power in relationships is often one-sided, not necessarily because one person seizes it all but often because a woman gives away her rights. Frequently, by adopting passive forms of behaviour, women deny personal strength. Jan invests almost all her power in her boyfriend, seeing herself as weak and helpless. Living alone with her three-year-old daughter, she is fearful and desperate. It is only since the child's father, her boyfriend, moved out that she has been having these terrifying dreams:

'Once I draw the curtains at night the fear just builds up; sometimes to the point where I sit there staring at the door expecting someone to appear around the door any minute. Please don't laugh, it's terrifying.

'When I finally get to sleep, it starts. They smash the front-room window, or sometimes the front door, and it's just so violent towards me and my little girl. I wake up screaming and sweating. I've told my boyfriend, and he just says, "If there's going to be a break-in, there's going to be one, so stop thinking about it." I have to say that, when he stays the night, I'm all right. I feel better just telling you about them.'

Her dependence on the man in her life, the man who has moved out but who stays over now and again, leaves her terribly vulnerable. The dreams show her utter powerlessness for she has retained no obvious self-protective armour. Jan's dreams will only stop when she finds enough support to help her take control of her own life. As it is, investment in another has not proved successful; he is unwilling or unable to protect her from her fears.

Dr Rossi, in 'Dreams and the Growth of Personality', goes into great detail about the ways in which dreams show how successfully or otherwise we are dealing with life.[11] He views violent, disturbing dreams as indicating that there has been a block or retardation in the individual's psychological development. He says, 'Being defeated by frightening images means that some aspect of one's individuality is overwhelmed.' We can see this in Jan's alarming dreams, and Rossi argues that it is only by a successful confrontation with those negative forces, those fearful attackers, that an expansion of awareness will take place, thus allowing the dreamer to forge a new, more positive identity.

Confront the fear. Take it on. If you cannot do it alone, talk to people, gather support in your waking life and seek expression of those fears which your violent dreams push you to acknowledge. The first step might be to read about assertiveness for women in Anne Dickson's *A Woman In Your Own Right* and then to attend a class. You have nothing to lose but your fears.

Notes

1. J. Hall, *Clinical Uses of Dreams: A Jungian Interpretation and Enactments*, Grune and Stratton, 1977.
2. Anthony Storr, *Human Aggression*, Penguin, 1976.
3. 'You Can't Beat a Woman: Women and Children in Refuges.' Available from: Women's Aid Federation (England), Northern Office and Publications, 116 Portland Street, Manchester 1.

4. 'Violence Against Women', report by the Women's National Commission, published by the Cabinet Office, London SW1.
5. 'Hidden Depths', writings by writing and discussion group, Princess Road, Manchester.
6. Robin Lustig, 'Till Death . . .', *The Observer*, 14 October 1984.
7. Eric Bernes, *Games People Play*, Penguin, 1967.
8. Luise Eichenbaum and Susie Orbach, *What Do Women Want?*, Fontana, 1984.
9. Polly Toynbee, 'For 28 Years the Children Didn't Tell', *The Guardian*, 18 November 1985.
10. See Robin Skynner and John Cleese, *Families and How To Survive Them*, Methuen, 1984, for details about the ways in which children model their own sexuality on parental behaviour and the ways in which this process can be healthy or damaging according to how we operate within the family.
11. E. L. Rossi, 'Dreams and the Growth of Personality' (Ph.D), Pergamon Press, New York, 1972.

11

Psychic Phenomena and Dreams

Throughout history, dreams have been regarded as a source of information about future events, as divine warnings, or as communications across distances, and now experimental work can be cited to support the existence of psychic phenomena.[1] I did not fully accept that I had telepathic or precognitive dreams until I had been recording my dreams for some time, and was able to check later events with dream entries. One particularly vivid example of such a dream came before my sister died.

I dreamt that I was in a church where a requiem mass was being held. I knew that the mass was for a member of my immediate family because my two cousins were there and I only ever see them at major events such as weddings or funerals. When I awoke I was miserable and all that day and most of the next I felt wrapped in a cloud of gloom. The intensity of the sadness was particularly strong because my life was going well; no one in the family was ill and I had no obvious reason for despair.

About three weeks later, on my sister Rona's birthday, there was a telephone call to say she was in intensive care after a brain haemorrhage and that her condition was critical. The news was especially shocking because my brother-in-law was ringing from an American military hospital in West Germany to which Rona had been air-evacuated from Saudi Arabia. Although I realized there was little hope that she would regain consciousness, I flew to be with her for whatever time was left, and hoped against hope that she would recover.

I learnt that, at the time I had my dream, Rona had suffered a minor clot in the brain which her doctors had not been able to diagnose. As the subsequent headaches had not subsided, they decided to fly her to West Germany, where the most advanced care in Europe was to be found. As the wife of a retired US military man, she was entitled to the whole works but, in spite of all their advanced CAT scans, they were unable to locate that first aneurism. If they had, they might have operated to prevent the fatal second one.

None of us in England had known that she was even slightly ill. Her last letter had been about a month earlier but the post from Saudi was not totally reliable and, anyway, she was so busy running a small restaurant with some other women that we had no reason to think that she might be ill. Rona was due to visit us on her way back to the States and I had been looking forward to seeing her. I did see her before she died. I had a chance to talk to her, to express my love. She did not regain consciousness and died about five hours after I arrived at her bedside.

Rona never wanted to bother people when there was anything wrong and had told her husband not to let us know. After all, she had been getting better and there was a possibility that she would be allowed to leave the hospital after a few days. The second brain haemorrhage prevented that. My requiem mass dream happened at the time of the onset of her fatal illness, and for me the two events are inextricably linked.

I know that many other women who have telepathic, precognitive and warning dreams experience anxiety. The more I work on dreams the more certain I am that they reveal layers of ability and forms of communication which are not readily explicable in our highly rational waking world.

Julie offered sympathetic support when she told me of her dream:

'I have had similar disturbing dreams before a disastrous personal event, such as my brother's death. I dreamt of a funeral in a church where even the altar cloth was black and there were waves beating against the stained-glass windows.'

Coming from a family of spiritualists, though not one herself, Julie was not surprised by having a death premonition. As she said, 'I believe my own dreams reflect my subconscious awareness that "something" seems set to happen.'

Sisters have telepathic dreams. 'Hearing' cries of pain when the other sister is hurt, predicting pregnancy and communicating both joy and distress through dreams is fairly common. Linda, a mature student of mine, described two such dreams:

'Just before my sister died of a massive lung haemorrhage and before I knew that this was possible – although I knew she was ill – I twice dreamt about blood. In the first dream, someone was bleeding and blood flowed under the door.

'The second dream was more vivid. It was about someone giving me a blood transfusion and my feelings of desperation as I tried to tell them that it wasn't me who needed it. No one took any notice, and I was in despair.'

She was not able to say at the time who the blood was for, but the death of her sister two days later caused her to recall her uncannily accurate dream. She remembered other extra-sensory perceptions between herself and her sister, though she did not take such abilities for granted, as do a lot of women. Brigid McConville's book *Sisters* tells us a great deal about the bonds we have with our sisters, and she provides many examples of telepathic waking, as well as dreaming, communications.[2]

Dream warnings

If you record and work on your dreams, you may discover, as I did, that some of them precede unhappy events. Joyce dreams of a devil before there is a major family disturbance and now she can 'gird her loins' for the turmoil that is likely to come. Polly had an unpleasant experience with Joel some years ago and regards his presence in dreams as a warning:

'I dream of this clairvoyant and know that I must be guarded. Whenever he is in the dream I feel it is a warning to me since I felt he had tried to take me over in real life. In the dreams I have a feeling that I am being warned psychically that he is trying to get to me. I know I must increase my defences against him.'

There are further examples in psychological and parapsychological literature, as well as newspaper reports of people being inexplicably undermined, in some cases fatally, by 'distant' influences. The Australian aborigines certainly regarded such warnings as real. More recently Filipino and Laotian refugees have died in their sleep after being subjected to nights of terrifying dreams in which they felt they were being attacked and destroyed. In this case, the Federal Centre for Disease in Atlanta, USA, was called in to conduct an intensive enquiry because doctors were unable to find any rational cause of death.

Dr Milan Ryzl, a Czech now working in America, and winner of the Duke University award for distinguished work in parapsychology, has hundreds of accounts of advanced telepathy research in which the 'sender' has been able to induce behaviour and emotions in a 'receiver'. It appears that stories of death by long-distance sorcery may have more than a grain of truth in them! The fact that both the American and Russian military are sponsoring major research projects in psychic (psi) phenomena indicate, that there is a wealth of evidence to support the idea that extra-sensory perception, dreaming and waking, is a force to be reckoned with.

Nina writes of her experience:

'I thought you might be interested in a dream/nightmare I had about five years ago. To cut a long story short, I dreamt that a chap I knew would have a fatal accident in his own car, along a particular stretch of road near his home.

'So concerned was I about this that, when a girlfriend and I saw this same man about a month after this dream, and he offered us a lift, I refused. Though not able to give my true reason to him, I later explained it to her.

'Can you imagine the sheer horror that I felt when this same girl rang about two weeks later to tell me that exactly what I had dreamt had come true, right down to the smallest detail. There was a deathly silence over the phone, while we both took in what had happened.

'Another point is that, for about four years previously, I had been having nightmares that have all come true, but this was the most awful as it involved someone dying. It seemed to be the last, thank goodness! I have had many dreams since but, to my knowledge, no nightmares.

'I am absolutely puzzled as to why all this happened and I must confess I was starting to get a little nervous.'

Her nervousness is common. William Oliver Stevens, researching and writing in the 1950s, records masses of warning dreams and this trepidation is also reported by many who sent dreams to him and the Society for Psychical Research.[4] He would support the advice of Lois, an adept at psi dreams:

'I find precognitive dreams and feelings are especially valuable. When there is a warning element, it is important not to ignore it as, although certain events cannot be prevented, they can be made less serious in their consequences by prayer. Other times, accidents and mishaps can indeed be prevented so it is good to get over the alarm, to do what common sense tells you and so avoid "if only I'd acted on it" feelings. People are not given things they cannot cope with; we tend to underestimate our abilities.'

Hella made no outward changes to her life after her dream, but she reckoned it served its purpose and saved her life:

'I dreamt that I was driving along a dark wet road and turned a corner. A car had broken down just round the bend and I crashed into it. Before I did so I noticed a "Kent" sticker and the registration number: KNL 795.'

Two weeks later Hella was driving down a dark wet road and turned a corner. As she was doing so, she suddenly recognized the place from her dream. She slowed down sufficiently to avoid a car with a 'Kent' sticker, registration number KNL 795, which had broken down just there. She'd never seen the car before and didn't know that stretch of road. She told a friend who was in the car at the time of the fortunate escape about the dream.

My sister Marion dreamt three days in a row of a fire in her house. On the fourth morning she opened her eyes to see the shadow of flames playing on the wall outside her bedroom, and there was a smell of acrid smoke. She and the children escaped and the fire was extinguished.

On the day before the first dream Marion's husband had started to rise very early for a new job, but in cooking breakfast he had a habit of leaving cooking utensils and a pan near the pilot light. This was a fire hazard and it finally caused a fire in reality. Marion's dream was more about communication of subliminal information than precognition.

Was it the same for Ida?

'In my dream I went to my bedroom window and looked out into the dark night. Below was the burning shell of our neighbour's house. The image was very strong. A few nights later, I looked out of the window to our caravan burning below.'

Warning dreams come at any time, as Jean discovered:

'My mother appeared at the bottom of the bed and it was as if she had woken me up. She warned me not to book the holiday we planned to go on in three weeks' time; a fortnight later my husband died.'

Jean was so certain that there was a reason for the message that she took heed and did not book the holiday. When women have dreams of an extra-sensory nature, some do listen to them. Experience teaches them of their validity, as you will discover in the next section. However, the problem is in deciding which ones are precognitive or predictive. The only way to find out is to record your dreams and compare them to actual events.

Precognitive dreams

These are dreams which precede a waking event. Somehow, the dreams tell of what will happen in the future and range from the very explicit to the highly symbolic, almost stylized. Janine's 'frozen wave' catches symbolically the idea of a strong living force which has ceased. The massive energy is shattered and scattered and our dreamer is powerless against that natural tide:

'Two weeks before my grandmother died I dreamt I was walking with her on a frozen beach. We saw a huge wave which froze at its highest point and cracked. She fell down by my side. I often feel that dreams are a parallel reality – that what we call reality is less real than dreams – and that maybe there is another dimension, what the aborigine culture calls "dreamtime".'

Carol had many precognitive dreams as well as daytime premonitions, a common characteristic with women who have extra-sensory perception. The daytime abilities are transferred into dream communication and we wake knowing that the dream is special either because it was particularly vivid or because of the colour or the unusual atmosphere of the dream. Sue is quite certain when her dreams are precognitive, even though she has had only about four or five of them. In these dreams she feels that she is herself rather than an observer of the dream action; she is in her own 'flesh and blood' body. Because they have such clarity she usually thinks the events have actually happened. It just so happens that she had told the one she relates below to her work colleagues when the subject of dreams was discussed. That Thursday night she had an amazingly clear dream:

'The details were unbelievable: it was drizzling, early evening, and the street lamps had just come on. I don't recall the crash, just that I was on the crown of the road and thinking, What are you doing in the middle of the road? Suddenly there was this almighty noise and tearing of metal and as I was coming to there was lots of noise and activity. I felt what I thought was warm water, running down my face. In the dream I remember putting my hand up and seeing this red blood on it, but I also recall thinking, You're alive, Sue, so there's no panic. I felt cross with the people standing around. I saw large vehicles and a fire engine. In the dream I was asking someone if there was a fire and was told that there wasn't. Then I looked up and saw my husband David there. I said, "I'm all right, you know. I didn't know that you can hear bones break; you can. Don't worry, I'm all right." I told him to tell everybody to go home. I knew I was trapped, and looked at the reflections of the umbrellas in the huge puddle that stretched almost to the centre of the road. I remember thinking, Have they nothing better to do?

'I woke up from the dream shouting, "I'm all right. I'm all right." David asked me what I was talking about and, although I told him I'd had a weird dream, I said nothing more because I didn't want to worry him.'

The next day, Friday, Sue went to work and told those same colleagues about the dream. Some were dismissive and one or two suggested that she ought not to drive for a few days. Sue considered the idea because this dream had really shaken her but she resolved not to heed it.

The following Tuesday she was shopping in town after work and decided to call in to see her mother. She rang David at his office and explained that she'd be back a little later than usual and would see him at home about seven o'clock. He didn't say any more but when he put the phone down he suddenly decided to go and meet her. Sue then set off on a journey that completely altered the next years of her life.

'As I was going down Moss Lane, dusk was falling. I slowed down to turn right into my mother's road, turning the wheels – something I never do now – and I looked in my mirror. I was on the crown of the road waiting to turn when the lorry behind slammed into me, pushing me diagonally into the path of an articulated lorry. The mini

I was in concertinaed between the two and I had to be cut out.'

So many of the dream details exactly reflected the waking event that I felt the hairs on the back of my neck stand on end as she told me. A passer-by who didn't know her but recognized her as someone who used to call at a neighbour's house rushed round to Sue's mother. David had already arrived and within two minutes was at the scene. As he stood by the car, he saw blood pouring down Sue's face; the pins holding up her waist-length hair had been driven into her scalp and her head had been dashed against the windscreen. David was distraught. Sue remembered saying, 'Don't worry,' and then passed out.

For two weeks, as she lay in hospital, Sue could not recall the accident but one day she remembered the dream. Then she understood just a few of the facts of that dreadful day. At the scene of the accident she had talked to her husband exactly as in the dream as she faded in and out of consciousness. The fire brigade had cut her from between two lorries. People had been standing staring and she had angrily told David to send them away. The lorry driver that rammed into the back of her had seen her just as she had seen the lorry in her rear-view mirror.

When Sue heard the details from the hospital sister, part of her was terribly afraid that, by having the dream, she had set up some auto-suggestion which had then brought the dream to waking life. So desperately in need of reassurance was she that she asked to speak to the policeman who had attended the accident so that he could tell her the cause. There was absolutely no doubt. 'You didn't stand a chance, love,' he said. 'You just happened to be there.' The braking system of the lorry had been checked; the box which held the fluid was cracked and the brakes had failed completely. She was in no way responsible.

Sue had never told David about the dream but did after the event. She had double vision for three months, was paralysed from the neck down for weeks and was told she might never walk again. In fact, ten years later, her right leg is still completely numb. However, she is such a determined, strong woman that she worked unceasingly in an effort to regain normality. Now she's walking, working and, following four miscarriages, the mother of a delightful daughter. After all this time, what still amazes Sue is that David was there at her side and yet neither of them had made any plans to be at that fateful spot that drizzly Tuesday.

Are dreams such as Sue's mere coincidence? Do we dream a lot of events which we believe will happen in the future but which do not, and then forget them, only to remember the rare ones which do come true? But as Sue said, it was a chance in a million that those brakes should fail at that point, causing her to be propelled into another articulated vehicle. Precognitive dreams are infrequent for Sue, but they are common among the females in her family.

If you have such gifts try to accept and understand them. Rather than fighting them, find other people who have similar skills, read about psi phenomena and recognize that you are not a freak but blessed with a peculiarly feminine seeing talent.

Sometimes the impact of a precognitive dream is so strong that it affects waking behaviour. Does that mean that the dreamer responds to the suggestion of the dream, as Sue feared? There may be some truth in that. For instance, Kate was so sure that her moped accident dream would come to pass that she put on not just clean, but new, underwear the morning of the dream! She then had an accident in the manner depicted in her dream, but commented, somewhat cryptically, that on waking she had thought that if she had an accident she'd have a nice rest in hospital. A warning dream she deliberately ignored or a conscious choice?

As I described earlier, dreams of death may be symbolic, representing a change in yourself or the person about whom you dream, or they may be anticipating future events. Precognitive dreams about death abound. Calpurnia, the wife of Julius Caesar, knew that he would face assassination when she dreamt that a statue of her husband had blood pouring out of the mouth and ears; other dreams showed her husband being struck by daggers.

Before she went on holiday to Spain, Sandra dreamt of a Spanish funeral with women in black wearing traditional mantillas. The dream did not upset her but she recalled it when, after a week in San Sebastian, her husband was drowned. He was buried in Spain.

A dear woman I worked with was a constant source of wonderment and joy to me. Rosemary was one of the clerks at a college where I went to lecture and over three years, through bits of conversation here and there, I gradually got to know her. We didn't socialize outside work as she had ten children and didn't go out much anyway.

One reason we became close was that she had a twenty-year-old daughter called Carla who looked like my then fourteen-year-old son Karl. When Carla, her first-born daughter, got married and became pregnant, the common ground increased as, some time later, I too became pregnant. Rosemary and I would talk about the expanding lumps and possible baby names and the like over cups of coffee. She was also very interested in the material I was collecting on dreams and told me of some of her own experiences, including this one:

'I stand outside a church and graveyard. All is dark, trees are bent by the force of the wind and the rain of a violent storm. The black sky is scarred by great flashes of jagged lightning and the gravestones are stark against the skyline. The violence of the storm, the deafening claps of thunder overhead, are terrifying. I stand outside the church gates holding a newborn infant in my hands, yet I am racked by a great and dreadful sorrow, the like of which I had never experienced, for I hold a baby yet I mourn a baby.'

She had the dream from the age of twenty-one until 1983, and it was in black and white, though most of her dreams are in colour. Rosemary then told me of a dream towards the end of Carla's pregnancy which left her with a feeling of foreboding:

'I dreamt that, at dead of night, when the weather was particularly stormy, I found my daughter wandering in the dark in an uncultivated garden. She looked somewhat bewildered and dishevelled and her face was slightly swollen and spotted with blood. I asked her what had happened to her and she told me that the floor had opened beneath her and she had fallen through the hole. She then said, "But it is all right, the baby is not hurt."'

Carla died after delivering a healthy baby son. She held him in her arms after a difficult birth where a caesarean section was performed but, left alone in a recovery room, it appears that she vomited, and died of asphyxiation. Such were the anomalies of her death that an enquiry was set up to examine the procedures used by the medical staff who attended the delivery. The results are still awaited.

After my own daughter was born, Rosemary and I used to talk about how her first grandchild was progressing with his dad. I saw the pain that losing a child can bring. 'You never think you'll outlive your children, you know,' she would tell me, and I would search for some words of comfort. We both mused on those powerful black and white dreams.

Marie's dream about her father was quite dramatic in its own way. She dreamt that he was dead and surrounded by wreaths. The following night she experienced lots of death symbolism: images of rotting corpses, departing ships, a coffin; and heard hymns being sung. At the centre of the dream was a woman who had one half of her face disfigured while the other was perfectly normal. The next day, travelling home from work on the bus, Marie noticed a very similar woman, someone she had never seen before. Her father died suddenly, in the early hours of the following morning.

Such dreams involve a layer of awareness that is not readily available to us. Edgar Cayce, an extraordinary writer and 'seer', gives numerous examples of women tapping into this hidden dimension, including extended material from one of his clients named Frances, who had many precognitive 'death' dreams.[5] Cayce saw dreams of death as being preparation for a new beginning or for life in a different, 'other' world. The next dream definitely brought drastic change for all concerned.

Having settled into her role as grandmother, Sylvia was enjoying the generous summer that year had brought. Her twin sons were happily married and Davy, who had moved about a hundred miles away when he was promoted, now had two children; Sarah was four and Emma had just turned six months. The peace of the August night was shattered by a terrible nightmare:

'I awoke absolutely horrified because something had happened to our two grandchildren. It was so dreadful that I couldn't even tell my husband and I repressed it so, except for the horrendous feeling, I don't know what I dreamt.'

Shortly after the dream, the police came and told them that their daughter-in-law had killed the children and tried to commit suicide. She had suffered post-natal depression but Sylvia and her husband knew nothing about it. Now, many years later, Sylvia still wonders why the dream occurred and if she could have prevented the deaths by taking notice of it.

Obviously, there are no hard and fast rules, but perhaps the best course of action is to make contact with the subject(s) of the dream.

A number of women who have experienced similar dreams – for example, dreaming of a friend's suicide – have done so and apparently prevented a fatality. But who can ever know for sure? It's a choice each of us has to make for ourselves. Sylvia's dream may well have been a telepathic communication from her grandchildren.

Telepathy

Telepathic dream communication takes place in a way which cannot be rationally explained. The dreamer wakes knowing that information has been given to her. Of course it is very difficult to know whether such dreams are indeed a form of 'mind to mind' communication or whether they are the product of subconscious knowledge which we have disregarded. Jung strongly believed in the reality of telepathy in dreams but emphasized the difficulty of finding a satisfactory theory to explain it.

Research in different fields may eventually help to supply an explanation. Danah Zohar, in her book *Through the Time Barrier*, shows how quantum mechanics, which is concerned with nature and the properties of matter, has indicated that, in certain circumstances, there is a form of communication between widely separated particles.[6] At present, there is no known mechanism to explain this. Particles appear able to respond to each other instantly, though divided by enormous distances. This has important implications for psychic phenomena in general[5,6] and telepathy in particular.

It appears that telepathy works most frequently between members of the same family or people who are especially close. In Nan's case, it was with her husband:

'I dreamt that my husband sat up in the intensive care unit and indicated that he had had enough – he no longer wanted to live. I was wakened from this dream by the phone. It was the hospital to tell me that my husband was dying. Ten minutes later they phoned to tell me he was dead.'

Megan found her telepathic dreams grippingly realistic:

'A personal friend of ours was loading a dump truck when it suddenly spilt. He was buried under the load and had to be taken to hospital. I woke up screaming and two hours later my husband rang from work to tell me this had actually happened. I was dreaming about it at the same time it was happening.

'In another dream I saw a pitiful scene. My mother, who was in England, (I was in New Zealand), crippled with arthritis in her hips, was slowly nearing her death. In the dream I saw her looking frail, very tiny and bent between two figures. One was an immensely tall man and the other a stocky woman. They were dragging her to a building that looked like a prison or a fortress. I awoke in great distress.

'I was haunted by the dream, though I was sure that my mother was at home, with my step-sister taking care of her. Some days later I received a letter from my step-sister, who was a nurse, saying she could no longer look after my mother and so she and the doctor, a very tall man, had decided to put her in a nursing home. There is no doubt whatever that my mother felt that this was tantamount to being put in prison and that had I been there I could have prevented it. As far as I could make out, her removal took place more or less while I was dreaming and I had absolutely no other warning of this event, not even a hint.'

While unaware of these events at the time, Megan believed that there had been communication. Meera is so sure about telepathic exchanges that she actively harnesses her knowledge:

'I can take care of matters in the dream state that are unpleasant or bothersome to me in the waking state. For instance, if I have to tell a friend something and feel uncomfortable about doing it, I can communicate the idea to them while they are asleep. They will then call me the next morning upon waking and tell me in so many words that they have received the message. Some friends are aware of the telepathic communication, others are not, yet they still receive the message.'

Many of us are familiar with dreams in which a person appears who, we have not seen for a long time and then very shortly afterwards we have a letter or telephone call from them completely unexpectedly. Could it be that communication is happening while we sleep? Caroline is sure it is:

'My dreams often coincide with what other people have been discussing while I've been sleeping. I find out it has happened when the conversation is mentioned the next day. In the last one I dreamt of a man dying and my friend being related to him. It was dreadful;

I felt him walk through me. It was a very strange, icy feeling.'

Caroline discovered the link when she told her friend of the dream:

'The odd thing about this was that the girl in question had, a number of years before, found her father dead, and on the night I dreamt this she had been discussing her father's death with another friend. I had previously known nothing about her father or her domestic situation.'

Not all telepathic dreams are to do with people we care for; some are about absolute strangers or trivial events. Denver psychoanalyst Jule Eisenbud, in *Parapsychology and the Unconscious*, makes out a good case for the reality of psychic behaviour.[7] He attributes it to the development of a group mechanism which controls the behaviour of such species as ants, for instance. While humans are a lot more complicated than ants, and while we pursue individuality, Eisenbud argues that, although the hold of the central-group controlling mechanism is generally relaxed, it can at times be reactivated and intervene in our lives. He suggests that some animal groups are equivalent to a fleet of radio taxis: they can cruise around picking up individual fares while remaining subject to the requirements of their district control centres.

There are coincidences we all experience, such as going to telephone someone but finding the phone rings and it is the person you planned to call ringing you; or thinking of a person whom you haven't seen in ages and then bumping into him the next day; and so on. Eisenbud, like Jung, would argue that such happenings are not merely coincidental. For Eisenbud, they represent intervention by a vestigial psychic intercommunication system – the central communicator is switched on! Jung puts the reason down to a phenomenon known as synchronicity.

Such theories help to explain why we dream about a person or event we have no connection with, as Lizzie did:

'I was in a house which seemed to be under attack. I saw myself in a run-down garden in which stood a dilapidated greenhouse, and all around me I could hear children laughing and playing hide and seek. I ran to the greenhouse as if to hide and tried to climb in through a broken glass window, but I fell to the ground with a piece of glass firmly embedded in the inside of my thigh; blood pouring out of the gash.

'I was screaming for help and shouting, "I'm dying! I'm dying!" I awoke pouring with sweat it was so real, so much so that I told a friend of mine the next day. Later I was reading a newspaper at breakfast and there in front of me was an article about a child who had died in exactly this manner. Every detail was as it had been in the dream. It was such a shock.'

John Donne's lines 'Ask not for whom the bell tolls, It tolls for thee' are particularly relevant here, especially since we understand more clearly now than at any previous time that 'no man is an island'! Psychic phenomena of every description echo that message.

Ruth's dream was the first of many which related to events which had yet to take place:

'It concerned the death of a neighbour. I had simply "seen" him driving his old car and a voice said it would be his last journey. It was a month later he died.'

What enables Ruth to 'tune in' to the future? She knows that her mother had the ability and she was taught to respect her 'odd' intuitions and strange predictive dreams; they were taken as an expected part of life. It was like that for my friend Linda. She told me she was twelve years old before she realized that other people couldn't see and speak to the spirits. She thought they were odd! For Ruth and Linda there was never any pressure to reject or dismiss their dreams or 'visions'. Many other women have such sensitive antennae which they fail to use through fear or because they have lost touch with their own power.

Disasters near and far

As you have seen, not all telepathic or precognitive dreams concern people we know, although the majority do. The lack of a direct emotional link, as Eisenbud relates, does not prevent communication taking place. One woman told me about rushing down a narrow tunnel, panicking and screaming in her sleep, only to a waken to the news of a London tube crash; another explained how her dreams of raging fires were early knowledge of Australian bush fires, while others concerned air crashes, murders and earthquakes.

Doreen dreamt about a disaster which I saw reported on TV. She was standing on the shoreline near where she was brought up:

'It was dark, almost too dark to see the sea. From behind me five dark figures came running and they ran past me into the sea in front. One by one they all quickly disappeared and I was shouting, "They'll be drowned. They'll be drowned." Just then I saw one floating at my feet as if I had been standing in the water but I was not wet. I grabbed this figure and thought, He's still alive.'

Three days later, Doreen listened to the same item of news I saw. On a tempestuous, windy day a man walking along the promenade threw a ball for his dog. The dog went over the edge after the ball into a very rough sea. The owner followed the dog and was drowned. Three policemen and a policewoman in turn made vain rescue bids. Three were drowned and only one was rescued. It was for most people a thought-provoking piece of news: why did so many lose their lives in such obviously impossible conditions, and because of a dog? However, for Doreen, it was thought-provoking in a different way, as she explains:

'I felt terrible, as if I had foreseen this without being able to warn anyone. I am old and have sometimes thought odd things happened. I used to be told by my mother that my grandmother had second sight. Perhaps there is something in this.'

Though Diane tried to dismiss her dreams as mere coincidence, she had her doubts. As with so many other women who have predictive, or telepathic dreams, they started in childhood. When she grew up, her dreams had the same quality as those early ones:

'The first one – well, my husband had to wake me from that one, I was in such a state. Apparently I kept saying, "It's the cow. I can't get it off the railway line." I could hear the train coming at a very fast speed.'

Both were shocked when they heard the news the next day: a train had crashed in Scotland because a cow had wandered on the line. Diane related a second dream:

'I was with my family when I loooked up into the sky and saw a huge aeroplane with its tail end engulfed in flames. I could hear people sobbing and I knew lots of people were going to die. I did not wake from this dream then but in the morning I told my husband that there had been a terrible aircrash. He went downstairs to make some tea and came back later saying, "You're a bit creepy sometimes." An aeroplane had crashed into a mountainside and lots of

Japanese were killed. There it was, the headline news, in black and white.'

This type of dream fits into the category of 'remote viewing', which Dr Russell Targ of the Stanford Research Unit in America has been studying for years. In his book *The Mind Race*, Targ explains how his work was funded by the US Defence Department and intelligence agencies. He has found that certain people are able to describe distant events, locations and objects while in the controlled atmosphere of a laboratory. They 'tune in', just as some dreamers can tune in to other people's conversations.

'The other side'

Getting in touch with people who have gone to 'the other side', who have died, is commonplace for some dreamers. The dead are thought to contact dreamers in order to act as guides, advisers or mentors. Grace wrote of her experiences:

'A few years ago, during a period of particular trouble and difficulty which continued for some years after the dream, I dreamt I was in a large hall. Everywhere was stone: stone walls, ceiling, floor – thick, crudely fashioned slabs of stone, for the most part. Everything was utterly devoid of ornamentation.

'Directly opposite to the raised dais on which I stood, on the lower level, were two narrow doorways – no doors – cut out of the stone. As I stood there, I looked from one to the other of these openings and through the left one I could see a terribly rough and stormy sea. The waves were huge and threatening, the sky lowering. My heart sank as I looked at it. Turning to look at the other doorway, I glimpsed through it a raging fire with tongues of flame leaping at least twice as high as myself. Beside this door stood an old man dressed in a long robe, bearing a narrow rod in his right hand.

'I knew I had to go out of the hall by one of these doorways and was very much afraid. Slowly I descended the right-hand set of shallow steps, thinking, I cannot possibly go through the left doorway, that water will sweep me away and I will be lost. I shuddered at the thought of the fire, but chose that, and as I drew level with the old man he looked at me as if he was both sorry for me and proud of me for the choice I had made. He said gently, "I am sorry, but I will

239

have to burn you." Then he lowered the tip of the rod and I saw that a narrow jet of flame was burning very steadily, rather like a gas jet. He applied it to my arm, but I felt no pain and went past him into the heart of the flames, terrified, yet aware that I was passing through them unharmed.

'On waking, I pondered this dream for a long time. I was sure it meant that had I followed my own inclinations concerning my particular grave difficulties, I would indeed have been lost. As it was, against my will, yet feeling utterly convinced that I was doing the best thing, I decided on a course which had been recommended to me by my friends on the other side. Though it was a real trial to obey, I knew in my heart it would prove to be the correct one. It is too personal to go into, but I eventually came out beyond the fire.'

This feeling of being aided in dreams can be very reassuring, as Agnes relates:

'It seems that the dreams I remember are very significant, as if someone, often relatives who have passed on, are emphasizing I am being looked after. I remember them for years after. They are imprinted on my memory.'

It is probable that some dreams about messages from the other side reflect the important positions that certain people hold for us. The influence of their views and the strong impression they left is revealed in dreams. For Agnes, the feeling of being looked after warms her. Feeling cared for is important for all women, who too frequently have the role of care-taker. If dreams can give this nurturing, then women will be enriched and energized.

In Clara's case the message from the other side came, as far as she is concerned, from Georges Sand. We have no way of 'proving' this. However, for Clara the dream was an important one which helped her to decide her future, which she had been concerned about for some time.

'This took place in northern France. In the dream I was sitting on a park bench idly gazing at the scenery, when I realized someone had joined me. The woman, dressed in a pale lavender, satin ball gown of the Victorian era, introduced herself as Mme Dudevant and told me to take up my pen and write.

'There was no more to the dream than that, but I was intrigued. I asked my French friends if they knew of the name but it was a radio programme that gave me the answer. It was the real name of Georges Sand who, when young, apparently wrote and published several novels, financially freeing herself.

'Taking this dream as an answer to my problems, I decided to write and am still doing so. Indeed, my dreams continue to help by producing new ideas.'

Contact with historical figures can be explained as communications from the unconscious, so we could say that Clara was encouraging herself to write. With Thelma, though, there is no obvious reason why this dream should have arisen:

'We were living in the Dordogne, in France, and I dreamt that I was in part of our grounds which was forest land. I was in a ditch and finding great difficulty in getting out, even though the ditch was not too deep. Looking up, I saw a man standing above me with his hand outstretched. The man was instantly recognizable as King Louis XVI of France. He was dressed in rich, elegant courtier's clothes of his day. He smiled and, taking my hand, gently pulled me out of the ditch.'

Had that been the end of it, we could say that the dream was a romantic wish-fulfilment induced by her new surroundings. However, Thelma decided to explore the grounds and two days later, near the place of the dream, she found a bronze coin. It had the head of Louis XVI on one side and a shield with three fleur-de-lys on the reverse. The coin is dated 1788 with lettering around the edge inscribed quite clearly with his name. Were the dream and the waking event merely coincidental?

Out-of-body experiences (OBEs) and astral projection

Out-of-body experiences happen in dreams and they are frequently accompanied by astral projection, by which the dreamer is able to travel to different places and observe and participate in what is taking place. Unlike what happens in flying dreams, the dreamer leaves the physical body behind while she travels to other places, possibly other worlds. V.S. Staff in *Remembered on Waking* reports numerous OBEs, and Vera's explanation could have come straight from that rare book:

'We can leave our bodies during sleep but not in the physical sense. Perhaps it is the soul that travels. Have you ever read descriptions of people who have died and then come back? Apparently an experience they all remember in common is floating up above their bodies and looking down on the people below in the room. Perhaps the "soul" lives on and, free of the physical body and physical world, floats around in the fifth dimension.'[8]

Could this be what is happening in dreams of astral projection?

Penelope knows she is having an OBE because she sees her physical body below her, on the bed for instance, while she is hovering above. She can then 'travel' and return later. However, it is not always quite so simple:

'I think you will be amused by my reaction to returning to my body after visiting somewhere on the other side. It certainly amused me when I awoke.

'The first time I remember clearly returning to my physical body, I stood at my own bedside looking down at my sleeping self and felt deep reluctance to 'get back in' the body on the bed. I remember thinking how heavy that physical body felt compared with the glorious freedom and lightness of my spiritual body. Then when I began slowly to "fit into" my body and found myself waking up, I remember that my arms felt huge and clumsy.

'The next time, I was again looking down at myself prior to returning to the physical, and I turned to a friend who had come with me – a friend who passed on some years ago. I said to him, "Oh, I do wish I didn't have to go back! It's just dreadful having to walk around in that heavy, clumsy body after being here like this." My friend smiled understandingly, and helped me in, then I awoke.'

I should add that Penelope is a slim five foot four, and weighs about eight and a half stone.

Such wanderings are found throughout history. J. G. Frazer in *The Golden Bough* comments on an accepted belief that the soul of a sleeper escapes from the body and visits places, sees people and performs acts which are dreamt about. In more recent times Carlos Castaneda has depicted the development of extra-sensory perceptions and powers based on ancient American Indian practices which include dreaming and astral projection.[9]

Carol, a spiritualist and long-time student of psychic phenomena, has no doubts about the authenticity of her psi experiences:

'I know that as a child I was aware of things and thought that other people were too but just didn't bother to talk about it because it just wasn't necessary . . . I did feel fear when I realized that I had left my body, but maybe it was a healthy fear because you do have to take care in the astral plane and not get waylaid by lower entities.

'I think it is important to understand about astral travel. The spiritual body, the "subtle" body, starts to detach itself from the feet upwards. Some people say this is changing body pressure. In one such dream I took a trip out of my body. I had my arms outstretched and was looking below me. It was very exhilarating, flying over trees, hills and hedges. It made me feel I had escaped my prison and was free. I felt much better.

'At another time, when I was going through a period of spiritual changes after I felt I was going to die, I travelled all the way to the edge of the Sea of Galilee. I met a being who seemed like the one we know as Christ. He was very, very brilliant and there was a tremendous feeling of knowledge but I didn't tell anyone because I didn't want to end up in a psychiatric ward. Besides which it didn't have the same religious connotations for me as it might have had for some people. I was suspicious about what someone like that was doing with me and why I'd been drawn to that being when I was in such a vulnerable state . . .

'I would like to urge all women not to suppress their psychic lives since the energy, if it is not used well, backfires on them. I hope this is not alarming, but it is our responsibility to learn about it and how to use it. Gradually the fear goes but only if it is confronted, not forcefully, just gently. Lots of women also long to have such an awareness, as it can be so comforting. There is so much fear and ignorance about this area, especially from people who have not had any direct experience and who feel it is "progressive" and mature to dismiss it all and rationalize it in some way.'

Hettie, a frail seventy-year-old, had the following dream, and asked that she should not be considered mad because of it! See how women have internalized the oppression that defines feminine difference as 'mad'?

'I am sure that during some of our dreams our spirit leaves our body and travels. I know it happened to me during a holiday in Belgium. My spirit was met by a soldier from the First World War

243

who explained about the waste of so much life. It was quite an experience, so much so that I can still see the dream in my mind.'

Diane also commented on this subject:

'I am prepared to believe that in our dreams we can practise mental projection, astral projection and perhaps even travel in time. This is open to conjecture but there are large areas of the brain as yet uncharted, and we have a lot more to learn.'

May has had numerous dreams over the past ten years which have left her in no doubt about her capacity for astral travel:

'After a dream about teaching someone to fly and flying myself – over a prison, ironically enough – I realized I was having an astral type of dream. I was awake, that is I could hear my husband breathing next to me, and yet I knew I was dreaming.

'I was very interested and flew on and on . . . I saw a fire across the road with lots of smoke. I knew I had to go through the fire and felt I'd be protected, which I was. I came to a bank of sand and was told I couldn't fly over it. I flew straight at it and was surprised to find I went into the sand quite easily, travelled through it with ease and felt the sand trickling past my face.

'In another dream I slipped out of my body feet first, conscious of my breathing being louder than usual and wondering if it would disturb my husband. I went upwards as usual but at one stage felt rain on my face. I thought I was going up through a rain stratum.'

The sensations of this type of dream are very positive for Fiona:

'I feel they are like mystical experiences. Numerous times I'm leaving my body and feel very free and light. I meet people and find myself in places I've never seen, although they frequently seem familiar. It is in this sort of dream that I see future or past events.'

Vanessa explained at length about the various types of dreams which have helped in her own spiritual development: dreams in which she has visited dead relatives, explored other realms and helped to free earthbound spirits:

'I believe that, despite the fact that most people are unaware of it, many of us lead "double" lives. While the physical body sleeps, the "inside" body continues to experience, learn, travel and develop. One travels in one's astral body every night – remembered as flying dreams, sudden ascents or descents, the descent being the return to the body.

'When leaving the physical body people often experience different sensations: perhaps a build-up of power or vibration before feelings of whirring or rolling over backwards very fast; sounds of rushing wind; and sometimes feelings of terror which jerk one awake.

'I have sometimes experienced difficulty in realigning the astral and physical and felt myself literally manhandled into position – perhaps an astral shove on my feet to get the two bodies to fit.'

Women's mysteries?

Women have been considered unacceptably deviant in patriarchal cultures because their special skills and abilities were seemingly inexplicable. Such a situation is worrying to rulers for that which you cannot adequately explain you cannot fully control. In the past, men's fear of women's intuitive powers led to ridicule and, in many cases, punishment – consider the treatment of witches. Many women, have now also come to believe that such skills are unacceptable; they have internalized the oppression that I spoke of in connection with Hettie's dream. Women are often feared, and what are most feared are their psychic and spiritual powers. How disappointing that we too fear ourselves. What feels like a strength is degraded and we forget how strong we are.

Women reporting 'psychic' dreams for which there can be no rational explanations express worries that they may be considered insane. We have been conditioned to accept the view that such experiences, abilities, skills, call them what you will, are not acceptable. They are a sign of something amiss in the mind. Yet women have throughout history been reported as having, using and valuing such powers. Just because we cannot explain them in fashionable scientific terms, because we cannot measure and replicate the experiences in laboratory conditions, does not mean they are insignificant.

Lorraine was also concerned with this issue:

'I think as much research as possible should be done into the question of "prophetic" dreams, particularly those experienced by women. Prophecy, clairvoyance and dream interpretation are traditionally associated with women and it seems likely that such powers are heightened during menstruation and pregnancy. I cannot remember if I was menstruating when I had terrifying precognitive dreams about the death of my father, but I do know that I stopped bleeding for about four or five months after his death.

'I remember confiding my experience to a well-meaning Freudian who informed me that I had not, in fact, foreseen the death of my father, but, quite simply, had wished him dead. Had my father not died, I would have been comforted by the good doctor's view, feeling that the dream was the result of some repressed antagonism on my part, and relieved that my father was not going to die in the near future. However, it is another matter when the person you have "wished dead" actually dies two days after you have the dream.

'Freud's attempt to rationalize the hitherto unexplained succeeded only in bringing about in me some irrational, primitive idea that I may be some sort of witch. I feel certain that other women have had this sort of experience. It is frightening enough to have such a dream in the first place, particularly if it concerns a member of the immediate family.'

Women who felt that they had dreams which were 'psychic' in one way or another also reported having similar experiences while awake. Helene has sensed the deaths of relatives, heard voices giving warnings, and had experiences of clairvoyancy while awake, and has also had precognitive dreams. She treats such events calmly:

'My dreams come true and warn me of things. I'm sure this is a natural psychic ability all we women have; in some it is more developed than others . . . I believe that psychic ability and dreaming are given to help you live your life and help you over problems.'

Bernadette, a woman who attended a dream workshop, raised an issue which drew attention to the relationship between psychic ability and dreams. Are dreams merely a continuation of waking extra-sensory events? She had had a dream in which a man whose name she was told appeared and she talked to him and had a pleasant time. Some weeks later she met the same man in waking life, though she had never met him before. She said that he too had dreamt of her, though again there was no rational explanation for this. Bernadette wanted to know whether she had been dreaming or whether she had been involved in astral travel into the future. Can we really share dreams? Certainly, close family members have reported having the same dream on the same night, but these may have been triggered by shared waking experiences. Lilian welcomes the idea of further investigation in this area. She has been recording her dreams for over thirteen years and has details of many which anticipated future happenings:

'They are so astonishing that I may not say which reality is qualifying which. I keep very much alert to dream clues as they often provide a warning system or at least a preparation for external events. This raises all sorts of philosophical questions . . . Do I dream something because it is going to happen inevitably and there-fore I apprehend it, or, by dreaming, may I change that future which the dream anticipates?'

The subject has occupied much of Montague Ullman's time. This American expert on dreams has done much to demystify dream in-terpretation and with his team from the Dream Laboratory of the Maimonides Medical Center, New York, has provided fascinating documented evidence of telepathic dreams. In *Dream Telepathy*, which he wrote with Stanley Krippner and Alan Vaughan, he des-cribes both spontaneous telepathic dreams and those which were 'sent' by an experimenter in the laboratory to a subject who was then asked to recall his dreams.[10] The results link parapsychology and dreams in a way rarely attempted by the scientific world.

Ullman has personal experience of psi dreams in which he has dreamt of events in his patients' lives of which he had no conscious knowledge and which has greatly helped the therapeutic process of analysis. Eisenbud, too, reports on the psi phenomenon, showing that there is much more to therapy than the rationally practical aspects that are discussed in Chapter 12.[11]

How do we explain psi dreams?

Déjà vu is a fairly widespread phenomenon. Some people say that their dream is 'broken' when they meet an event in waking life which corresponds to the one dreamt about. Lily describes it:

'I often find myself doing something during the day and I realize that I have dreamt it the night before – then I recall the dream. Only occasionally are the dreams significant.

It may be that the place in the dream and the place we come across in life are very alike; we feel we have been there before or that the events are very similar, but in some cases there seem to be too many identical details for it to be explained by mere coincidence.

J. W. Dunne, one of the earliest aircraft inventors, was so certain that his dreams were predictive as well as retrospective, that he decided to prove his theory scientifically. His dreams were repeatedly verified by subsequent events; he dreamt of a volcanic eruption in Martinique which happened several days later. In 1912 he dreamt of a friend dying in a monoplane between 7 a.m. and 8 a.m., and a friend was killed at that time, in that way, the very next day.

Dunne told his story of precognitive dreams in his book *An Experiment With Time*. He suggested that, in sleep, time does not go backwards and forwards and but all events in one pool at the same time. Dreams circulate in this extra, fourth dimension, and if properly recalled can reveal past, present and future. This fascinating book, though difficult to get hold of, is well worth consulting if you want to examine detailed recordings of precognitive dreams and their subsequent verification.

One of the most rewarding aspects of writing this book has been the contacts made while gathering data. Margaret from Sussex filled in a questionnaire which was so full of fascinating samples of precognitive and telepathic dreams that I wrote to her asking for more details. She replied and, realizing the difficulties involved in tracing literature dealing with dreams and parapsychology, she also sent me a whole pile of relevant books.

Margaret's long history of psychic dreams and waking psi phenomena meant that she was unsurprised by the large number of women who had reported psi dreams to me. She said, 'I have discovered this aspect of dreams is truly a very large part of it and women are probably more willing to tell about such things. I suspect, like mediumship, clairvoyance, etc., there are more women than men so "gifted".'

I give Margaret the final word on dreams and psychic phenomena:

'I do honestly feel that to treat dreams as purely physical phenomenor is utterly mistaken and likely to lead to wrong conclusions, just as treating a person as a mere physical organism does. It seems to me that dreams brought about by chemical reactions of the brain cells or physical organism, by emotional disturbance, or by commonplaces such as overeating, too many or too few bedclothes and so on, are really only the tip of the iceberg. All my own experiences, all I have heard and read of other people's, and sheer intuition, scream out to me that the spirit side of our lives is very much more involved than many suppose or wish to admit.'

Why are we so afraid?

Notes

1. Stanley Krippner, The Paranormal Dream and Man's Pliable Future', *Psychoanalytical Review*, 56 (1), pages 24-43, 1969.
2. Brigid McConville, *Sisters*, Pan, 1985.
3. John Barnes, 'Riddle of Nightmares', *The Sunday Times*, 24 May 1981.
4. W. O. Stevens, *The Mystery of Dreams*, Allen and Unwin, 1950.
5. Edgar Cayce, (ed. Mary Ellen Carter), *On Prophecy*, Coronet, 1968.
6. Danah Zohar, *Through the Time Barrier*, Paladin, 1983.
7. Jule Eisenbud, *Parapsychology and the Unconscious*, Berkeley, Calif., North Atlantic Books, 1983.
8. V. S. Staff, *Remembered on Waking*, privately pub., 1975.
9. Carlos Castaneda, *The Teachings of Don Juan*, Penguin, 1974. This is the first of five books about the author's initiation into the mysteries of sorcery, among other things, including OBE.
10. Montague Ullman, *et al*, *Dream Telepathy*, Turnstone Books, 1973.
11. J. Eisenbud, 'Chronologically extraordinary psi correspondences in the psychoanalytic setting', *Psychoanalytic Review*, 56 (1), 1969.

12

The Use of Dreams in Therapy

Telling the dream

One of the most important aspects of therapy is sharing with another person that which has been hidden; as Nor Hall says, 'Exchanging words is the essence of psychotherapy.'[1] Making the private public, bringing our worries into the open, happens when we talk about our dreams. Telling a close friend, a caring partner or a supportive group is a therapeutic experience.

It may not be long before crucial insights occur which completely change the way you view yourself. That happened when Catriona came to interview me for a radio broadcast.

She arrived, late and flustered, and eventually interviewed me in a fairly insensitive way, so I was not surprised when she asked me if I could help her with some disturbing dreams she was having. Well, she didn't put it like that. What she said was that she was having stupid, bothersome dreams which were ridiculous because, of course, she had no worries, no concerns, and if she had she would be more than able to sort them out. Smile. But could she tell me about her dream?

I'm quite used to this. It's an occupational hazard that I like, fascinated as I am by dreams. Also, it is one of the quickest ways to get through to people, reporters and interviewers especially, to work on specific dreams. So Catriona's dream took shape:

'I dream I am in a room holding a baby. The figures are dark and shadowy. I put the baby on the shelf; it is beginning to shrivel up. I cry out to the people but no one helps. The baby changes from its healthy self into a fish, floundering out of water. It doesn't die but it will do. I have a veil over my face.'

Catriona's super-confident, somewhat condescending mask was beginning to crack. She said she hated the dream and could not understand why it bothered her so much. I asked her to describe the people in the dream, in more detail. 'I think they are all men. They are ignoring me, though. I really need help but they are not doing anything to help.' I enquired whether she explained in the dream why she needed help. She replied that she did not but that 'they should have known'. I asked about the veil; could the people see who she was? Could they see how upset and anxious she was? That caused a pause for thought: 'Well, no, they can't see through the veil.'

I continued to ask very simple questions and gradually Catriona began to reveal that, far from being stupid, this dream was very incisive. Here was a young woman terrified of showing her feelings in case she was rejected. She dared not draw attention to herself in her new high-risk job in case she was found wanting and some other bright, competitive thing took her place. She would not let anyone see that she felt a 'fish out of water' or that she was facing the perennial dilemma of career versus children. Hadn't her mother said to her before she left for the big city lights, 'You'll be on the shelf if you don't settle down soon.' All these worries surfaced in our talk and Catriona recognized her own ambivalence.

The dream fish does not die. Catriona can redeem the situation of she chooses to, but it is up to her. She can be more direct instead of giving veiled hints. Just as she sits apart in her dream engrossed in her 'baby', so in waking life she keeps away from people, then feels hurt when they don't rescue her from herself. Like so many other women, she is not honest and direct in her communication with others but, by turns, manipulative and aggressive, neither of which qualities is very healthy. After an hour and a half she departed, taking with her a surprising knowledge that she had a lot of work to do on herself; it wasn't all 'their' fault.

Kathleen Jenks, in *Journey of a Dream Animal*, describes a dream in which a 'goldfish' appears; this one is struggling in the mud. Kathleen was going through a mental crisis at the time which left her vulnerable to intense emotional reactions. Her goldfish represented her spirit becoming submerged under worries. In the book she charts her own progress through 'the dark night of the soul', and chronicles her signposts in the form of dreams; it proves a remarkable record of a woman journeying through hellish despair.

Caligor and May are sure that 'No matter how much a person

rationalizes or intellectualizes, the symbols in her dream keep right on wrestling with her real problems.'[2] That is exactly what was happening with the keen reporter, but her dreams kept her in touch with the price she was paying. Before she left, Catriona asked how she should record her dreams.

Get the message

The first step in working on dreams is to have a dream and then record it. Dreaming is a purposeful activity, as Jung, Perls, Fromm, French, Evans and many, many more have shown, and you can make it work for you. Freud rediscovered the positive importance of dreams. He pronounced that the unconscious was the undiscovered country into which we try to banish those memories we want to ignore – but that's easier said than done. Memories are not easily dismissed. They come to the surface in dreams and, most important, pulling them back from the unconscious into the conscious can have a vital therapeutic effect.

As soon as you wake up from a dream you should write it down or tape it; do not, whatever you do, think that it is so vivid you'll remember it anyway. You won't. Brilliant dreams have been lost that way.

Having recorded your dream, try to make time during that day to work on the message. Who is in the dream? Where is it set? Does it relate to events from the daytime? What were you doing in the dream? Were you active or passive? How did you feel? Ask yourself about the interpretation, paying particular attention to the emotions and thoughts the dream triggers off. You will have gathered quite a lot from the analysis so far described in this book and this will help you to understand your own dreams.

Make notes of your mood at the time of the dream and any waking concerns that you are aware of. Keep all these details together because they will form a diagnostic record to enable you to understand your dream symbols and your subconscious. Like Lucy, you will be startled; as she said, 'It never fails to amaze me how dreams that everybody thinks stupid really do make sense once you start to learn what various things symbolize.'

The level of activity is also very important, as Corriere and colleagues emphasize in *Dreaming and Waking: The Functional Approach to Dreams*.[3] Less importance is placed on dream content than on the shifts in the process of expression. Thus, how you dream is seen as more important than what you dream. You may find it useful to ask yourself the question that these writers see as being the most important: 'How effectively do you function in this dream?' The answer should tell you a lot.

Symbols: signposts to the psyche

A symbol is never arbitrary; it is an expression of something in the dreamer's history or her cultural and emotional experience. My black dogs (see Chapter 4) are symbols of anxiety but I only know that because of what happened in my dreams. They invoked such fear in me that, since that time, I have been apprehensive of black dogs that fit those dream images. But why black dogs? I made associations with the children's story of 'The Tinder Box', in which black dogs guard the underworld. My 'black dogs' stemmed from my reading about those fearful creatures rather than flesh and blood experience.

There are no all-encompassing dictionaries of dream symbols, nor indeed could there be. In order to include all possible meanings, then all human experiences would have to be included, with permutations to take account of possible links to objects, animal, mineral, vegetable and imaginary.

Symbols are like metaphors or similes which communicate feelings. If you want to find out what is being communicated symbolically in your dreams, then write your own dictionary of dream symbols. Gradually you will learn that when a certain image appears it is linked to specific emotions or issues in your life. It is useful to learn more about symbols especially when confronted with that which is strange to you, yet intrigues and possibly startles. Jung's *Man and His Symbols* is a good resource to extend your awareness in this area.

Let's have a look at a symbol which recurs frequently in women's dreams, remembering that here we will use the term symbol in a Jungian way, to indicate that which is not yet fully known.

Houses, which have been discussed elsewhere in this book, are richly symbolic. Stephanie, a museum curator in Bristol, has worked on dreams ever since she attended a weekend course at a northern university, and she has built up a comprehensive personal dream dictionary. She tells how she uses her knowledge after describing the dream:

'Bricks are being removed from a wall and behind is a concealed room. It has in some strange way been a small partitioned-off compartment of a doll's house, but now it is a normal-sized room. A small window near the ceiling is one I looked through as a child. Now I am on the other side of it, and inside the room. It is dusty and neglected and tiny pieces of dolls' furniture are scattered on the floor. They seem useless but a woman, perhaps my mother, rubs the dust off one piece, and we see that beneath is an exquisite piece of craftsmanship: polished wood inlaid with mother-of-pearl. The value of these erstwhile toys has not been recognized before.

'This dream tells me that part of my consciousness that has been unrecognized, hidden, perhaps glimpsed as a child, but neglected, has value after all. The mother-of-pearl relates to my mother, and my father used to carve wood as a hobby.'

Stephanie is not experiencing a sudden breakthrough but a gradual awareness of the importance of things past. Notice how bricks are being removed from the wall. She is dismantling the symbolic barrier. She has got through to the 'other side', where she can appreciate treasures, to whose positive attributes she was blind before. She finds that, by penetrating the grimy layer built up over years of neglect, she discovers great beauty. This empowers her.

Her enthusiasm for dreams is unrestrained. Without hesitation, she says: 'Dreams are the most helpful things I have found in my life. They explain how my childhood affects my adult life and they indicate what I can do about it. They help me to face things I couldn't otherwise face and thus to sort out problems.'

Various symbols can represent the same thing, bearing in mind the importance of personal associations, so your dreams of being trapped, getting lost, missing the bus, losing tickets, and so on, all point to an inability to make further progress. The dreamer feels hindered, held back, blocked. In therapy the next step would be to discover where such feelings come from and to assist the dreamer to free herself from such hindrances. When the blockage has been freed, the action in the dream changes. A classic example of such movement is symbolized in the discovery of extra rooms in a house, as in Joan's case:

'I stumble across a secret room in our cellar. I find a passage leading to the room in the body of the house, signs which are hidden from the rest of the house. This room is the most beautiful I have ever seen and is stuffed with exquisite embroidered cloths, etc.'

Cathy, engaged to be married and planning the details of the ceremony, suddenly found that she was dreaming about wedding rings: 'Over a period of about six months I dreamt that I was trying to pull a wedding ring off, though I was telling people I was married.' At the time she was beginning to have doubts, and was forced by her dreams to face them. She later broke off the engagement and was very relieved to have done so. She had learnt that her dreams 'echo worries already present or show some that I didn't even recognize'.

Jung calls this coming to self-understanding 'the individuation process'. Such inner growth is frequently expressed in a long dream series where developments can be seen over time, though during the course of the series the overall meaning may not be discernible. You can see this in Patricia's dreams, which are described at the end of the chapter.

Not all dreams are full of symbolic imagery. Dement found that chronic schizophrenics have dreams which are remarkable for their emptiness and sterility.[4] However, most of us dream in symbols at least some of the time. Why? Anaïs Nin explains in *A Woman Speaks*:

'Dreams are a language we have to learn. It's still an indirect language because we can't bear the naked truth, so it comes in the form of a symbol or a metaphor.'

Each of us needs to learn our own 'vocabulary'!

As you have already discovered, I often ask women to draw their dream. By this I mean that they make a visual representation on paper, perhaps using pencil only or maybe using lots of colour. The drawing then acts as a focus and allows much unconscious material to surface. The way we draw, the size and relationships within the drawing, all contribute towards expanding awareness of the meaning of the dream. Hilde Meyerhoff, an art therapist, points out that, in

255

both dreams and art, the unconscious seems to work towards insight by using the language of pictures.[5]

Self-help dream groups

Self-help groups grew out of disillusionment with traditional forms of treatment, usually drugs or dismissal, given by doctors and other professionals who lacked sufficient time for sympathetic consideration. Women suffering from depression, anxiety, eating disorders, phobias and fears found scant comfort in being told that they were being neurotic. I find that time and time again women apologize to me for taking up my time with 'trivial' complaints. Despite the fact we are in a business relationship and I am being paid, women feel guilty about taking time for themselves.

Montague Ullman has pioneered dream groups in America and in an article he sent me he spelt out his own views:[6]

> Two principles govern experiential dream work. First, the dreamer remains in control of the process in its entirety. Second, the group serves as a catalyst, helping an supporting the dreamer's effort to relate his (her) dream. No one, including the leader, assumes an authoritative stance . . . The dreamer and the dream are appreciated in their uniqueness.

The process is quite simple. The dreamer presents a dream when she wants to talk about it. Then the other group members describe any feelings they had while listening to the dream. Next the group might turn their attention to the images appearing in the dream, only this time they consider them from a symbolic, metaphorical viewpoint rather than a literal one. Finally, dreamer and group members discuss what has arisen, as Ullman describes:

> The dreamer and the group work towards making concrete connections between the dream images, the current context and the significant points of contact of the dream with events in the dreamer's past. The group neither pushes nor pries. They supply what they feel are open-ended questions to which the dreamer responds with as much self-disclosure as (s)he feels comfortable. The process generally continues until the dreamer experiences a sense of closure.

Dream groups provide opportunities for women to get together and share in a mutually enriching journey. The destination can never be fully anticipated but much self-discovery happens along the way, as Caitlin remarked:

'Since working with my dreams I've not so much changed as learnt to accept and integrate parts of myself which I had long ago rejected. I feel I'm a more rounded person now.'

My groups are usually made up of eight to ten women who gather together one evening a fortnight to talk about their dreams. Sometimes everyone will talk about a dream while, at other times, one or two people will need to work on a dream at length.

Here is a powerful dream that was brought to one group by Nancy, a thirty-year-old community worker from London. I should say two dreams, since she felt she couldn't tell one without the other:

'I can't seem to think of this dream without a childhood recurring one. In the one I had from the ages of seven to twelve, I am on one cloud, by myself, going one way, while my mum and dad and little brother are on another cloud going in the opposite direction. There is absolute silence and they are waving and smiling at me.

'Anyway, this recurring dream is different now. There is a sort of rolling device, like one of those machines in hospitals that measure brainwaves or heartbeats. There is an arm which moves across the paper making marks which act as a record. The cream paper on the roll is moving upwards. The pen on a metal arm moves smoothly to begin with but then begins to move faster and faster until it tears the paper to shreds. There is a background noise like factory machinery which gets louder and louder. When the paper is all screwed up and the noise is unbearable, I always wake up very upset.'

Nancy was upset describing the dreams and we encouraged her to talk about what she felt about them, what they connected to and what happened between the ages of seven and twelve. Her replies were illuminating.

Nancy's brother was very ill as a child and her parents were totally absorbed in his care. Nancy, being a good little girl, never demanding attention nor complaining that she felt left out, seemed to drift further and further away in her lonely quietness. You can see how this is symbolized in the dream in the silent cloudscape. That cotton-wool imagery dulls any whimpers. Now she is still very quiet but wanting to express herself. It is a tremendous struggle for her and she finds it detracts from present relationships. Her latest recurring dream was commented on by the group. 'It's like everything is smooth and under control at first then gets screwed up,' said one, while another said, 'Things are just getting too much. The noise, the pen going all over the place. It's overloaded.'

The general impression was that all those stoical feelings from childhood were finally bursting forth. This resonated for Nancy. She had never felt before that she could honestly admit how life was for her; she always considered whether other people would be upset, and assumed that everyone else's concerns took precedence over her own. Her recent dreams foretold a change. At last, she was acknowledging how 'screwed up' she felt.

The power-sharing so central to self-help dream groups suited Nancy well. It freed her to express her resentments and pain without being afraid of judgement or disapproval.

Women can take control of their own 'therapy' by working with peers in this collective and reciprocal way. Sheila Ernst and Lucy Goodison wrote an article in the *Observer* in March 1981 on the publication of their book *In Your Own Hands*, an excellent self-help therapy guide. They said:

> The self-help experience has shown that, when each woman is in charge of her own therapy process, deciding how far she does or does not go, such therapy is unlikely to be dangerously disruptive or undermining.

Interesting, isn't it, that professional attitudes to self-help groups have softened to such an extent that doctors now refer patients to them. The medics recognize that time and facilities are unavailable in our overstretched, under-resourced practices.

Initial obstacles in groups I have been involved in were fairly typical: too many people trying to talk at once; too quick solutions to problems posed; too readily proffered pseudo-psychological insights; as well as the usual difficulty of getting some participants to be quiet while the shier ones had a chance to speak. These are easily overcome, though, if there is an honest expression of feelings and sensitivity towards each group member.

Charlotte brought many dreams to the group. Most chronicled her feelings of inadequacy and bouts of depression, but this one heralded a change:

'I dreamt I had a small pinprick in my finger that was bothering me. I located it and, as I pulled the tiny, protruding point out, it turned into a huge thorn. I managed to pull most of it out but couldn't quite get all of it. Drops of blood were dripping very slowly from the wound.'

Through her dreamwork, Charlotte had begun to 'pinpoint' the causes of her present emotional pain. In the dream she is symbolically addressing herself to the problem and, though she does not remove the source completely, she has made some progress. As in the fairytale of the princess who is condemned to sleep for one hundred years after being pricked in the thumb, Charlotte began to wake up as she located the root of her emotional difficulties. She was quite calm about the dripping blood. It felt as if the 'bad blood' was being released, which was healing for her.

When I asked Charlotte if she had any comments to make to other women thinking of attending a dream group or seeing a therapist, she pensively replied:

'The images and events in dreams are symbolic and it takes a lot of time to work out what they mean. This is where other people are useful, especially those who know you, because often they can pick out a meaning that is obvious to them but not to you. Often dreams show up our faults or areas of difficulty which we may not wish to admit; an outsider can often see them more clearly. Sometimes it is quite painful to have such things revealed, but if we take it seriously we can learn a lot about ourselves and become happier, confident, more self-aware people as a result of the changes we make in our conscious lives.'

Pam, who has been recording her dreams for five years, only recently joined the group in question, and explained what she had found while working on her dreams in isolation:

'I started recording my dreams initially because it just seemed terribly important to do so, at a time when I had no other help outside to explore issues that I really needed to look at . . . I realized I could get some understanding of dreams without going to a psychologist or whatever. However, I feel I could have got a lot more out of them if there had been help. So I honestly think you need someone around who has some experience with dream therapy to get going properly. A dream group is a great idea!'

Women who come for therapy have a range of difficulties which are often exacerbated by social factors. Whatever the reasons for emotional pain, dreams provide one of the most important tools in the therapeutic armoury. Examining dreams especially at times of crisis should clarify what I mean. Often, short-term therapy is all that is needed to clear an obstruction, as Nor Hall relates in *The Moon and the Virgin*. But essential to the task of finding out about ourselves is the willingness to reflect, think and engage honestly in the search for meaning. That journey of interior discovery can begin with a vividly germinal dream.

In *A Woman Speaks*, Anaïs Nin explains why we need to learn about our unconscious:

> We should be fearful of an unconscious that inhabits us, that guides us, that influences our life and of which we don't know the face and don't know the message . . . I have much less fear since I confronted my fears. What's frightening to me is people whose unconscious leads them, destroys them and yet they will never stop and look at it.

Nin did stop and look at her unconscious in great depth for she went to Otto Rank, the noted analyst, and even began training to become an analyst herself. What she discovered from her dreams freed her creativity.

Anxiety attacks

Janet wrote in a firm, flat style which contrasted with the turmoil of the content:

'I suffer from anxiety with various symptoms from giddiness, nervous headaches, churning stomach, hot flushes, strange feelings of detachment, but worst of all terrible attacks of panic and mounting tension to an unbearable pitch. This has been happening on and off for the past seven years and I'm now thirty.

'Since being a teenager I have had a recurring nightmare that I was walking along a pavement and slowly responsibilities would mount up and up. This was symbolized by a ball of grey stone getting bigger and bigger like a granite snowball. I always associated those responsibilities with my family, who were very demanding . . . This ball would grow to such a size in front of me that I would wake up in a panic, sweating and convinced I wouldn't be able to escape.'

Janet had this dream when she was ill and sleeping in the sick room at boarding school. Now she has it whenever she is under stress, and particularly when there is a drop in her hormone level, when she stops taking the pill or after she has had a child. There is a physiological trigger which is useful to know about, but there is a psychological aspect too.

At the age of four, Janet was very badly frightened by three boys dressed up in black with masks and it affected her until she was in her twenties. Her fears have become focused in the grey, impenetrable ball, which blocks progress along her dream pavement. Similarly, early terrifying experiences have left her open to sudden attacks of anxiety which paralyse her and temporarily prevent her progress.

Decreased dreaming, as indicated by decreased amounts of REM sleep (see page 24), may well be a factor in various disorders including schizophrenia and depression.[7]

Depression

'A very grey atmosphere of a dream I had made me realize the extent to which I was depressed, whereas my conscious mind would not allow me the weakness of depression. The same dream ended on a note of hope with a fire burning in the grate.'

Characteristically, women who are depressed, like Kitty above, have dreams where the colour is grey or black. The atmosphere is dark and gloomy and the dreamer is unmotivated or despairing. As I've pointed out before, this is not true for everyone; some people have dark-hued dreams and feel happily optimistic.

Dorothy had many disquieting dreams, such as this one, which revealed feelings of depression:

'A great grey mass is by the bed. A terrible sense of evil is calling to take me away. It is so black, has no shape and evil flows from it. I always wake up screaming and crying. It leaves me depressed for days. it drains me.'

Though her outward appearance is quietly self-confident, Dorothy is going through a period of major readjustment. The 'grey mass' dream began two years ago, when she realized that her youngest son would be leaving home to go to university.

For twenty-four years Dorothy has lived with her husband and family, and now her children have all left. She is suffering from the 'empty-nest syndrome':

'I have no skills other than a home-maker. That has been my life. I'm not sure about myself any more. I don't think I could cope with a job. I'm sure to fail. My world has been the home and family . . . I have a very good husband. We have little in common but we get on very well. I have a terrible fear of dying young, also of flying, sailing, high places and being closed in. I need space.'

Dorothy needs space to discover who she is other than the carer and nurturer that she has been so far. Her daytime escape from the 'shapeless' fear that will overtake her is in the form of spy stories and adventure films. Her dreams do affect her:

'I feel I am either being warned of something to come or punished for something I've done, and I'm worn out thinking as to what it can be, as I live such a boring, quiet life.'

Guilt! There it is again. We must deserve whatever pain we get and, if we cannot immediately decide what our sin is, we torture ourselves trying to find out. Or we believe it is because something is about to happen. Notice the passivity. Something will happen to us, something will be done to us, we will be acted upon. When women have a stronger sense of their own power and autonomy, these dreams will be less pervasive. When Dorothy explores further her potential as a woman in her own right, she will learn that failure is not her birthright! Having spent years looking after others, we ought not to assume we have nothing else to offer.

Francis Manley, investigating the effect of intentional dreaming on clinically depressed patients in an American institute, found that significant results were obtained when depressives were taught consciously to influence their dreams using the Senoi principles of confronting and conquering danger, approaching pleasure and achieving positive outcomes.[8] Thirty-five per cent of the experimental subjects were able successfully to change their dreams at least once, and dramatic changes in mood were to be seen in some of the successful subjects. However, anti-depressant medication, that killer of dreams, was a confounding factor.

A nervous stammer was the stimulus that brought Susie into dreamwork. She was referred to a psychiatrist when, completely lacking in confidence, she became acutely depressed. She told me that her therapist had placed great store in dreams but, although Susie found her comments interesting, her interpretations of the dreams were never as revealing or pertinent as those she can now do for herself.

That understanding of dreams unleashed Susie's own power:

'What I have learnt about myself from my dreams has sometimes been painful, but, if approached with honesty and acceptance, has always been of value.'

'Dreams like this seem to repair torn bits of myself' is a sentiment echoed by many women when talking about particularly helpful dreams. Kathleen Jenks recorded her quest for personal identity as she journeyed through the very depths of despair and on to greener and more hopeful pastures. Yet through it all she used her dreams as guides. She comments on the whole process of dream discovery:

> There are times when it can be terrible. But there are also times of radiant beauty and times when one's battered spirit is given a balm that heals in ways no words can describe.

Dreams caused by depression are often nightmarish. Isaac Marks describes a woman he treated for recurring bouts of depression.[9] A recurrent nightmare over fourteen years rapidly disappeared after it was told, 'rehearsed', repeatedly during treatment. The subject was also encouraged to find endings which were more to her liking, which she did. The repetition desensitized her to the fear, and the nightmare stopped. Her case illustrates the benefits to be gained in actively confronting that which you fear most in dreams.

Hannah, too, found sorely needed help, not from a psychiatrist, but from a spontaneous healing dream. When depressed she had a recurring dream of being in an overwhelmingly dull grey place. Very often she heard her own voice weeping above other wailing voices. There was an exception, though, which felt like a gift:

'I went to bed very unhappy and dreamt that I heard the most beautiful song I ever heard. With it there was such light and an experience of joy that I thought I could never really be unhappy again.'

A short but influential dream brought a complete uplift in mood for Hannah. Her earlier dreams of being in cramped spaces accurately mirrored her feelings that the world was closing in on her, but this one shows progression towards a more positive state of mind.

Notice how sound and light modalities are significant for Hannah. Particular sensations are more prominent in dreams for some people than for others. For instance, blind people dream but do not have the visual imagery so important in dreams of the sighted.

Depression is often a reaction to stress or distressing life events. For Tania it was more to do with the birth of her daughter and the result of months of disturbed nights. She told me about how she was affected:

'My little daughter was about six months old at the time and I was feeling depressed for the first time in my life. Up till then I had had depressed moods but they had never spilled over from one day to the next. Anyhow, within this climate, I started feeling anxious about facing up to bureaucrats and decided to practise relaxed rehearsal of the event in those few moments before sleep. On the second evening the rehearsal went right into the dream.

'I dreamt I was at a bus stop heading into town for a meeting with the bureaucrats. Then I was in an office faced by a terribly smarmy, officious man. I was having a dispute with him. The dream progressed in stages. At first I was hesitant, but I remember changing my attitude at that point to a 'No, I'll show him' stance. I proceeded to enrol him in an agreement in a calm and remarkably assured fashion. I even enjoyed my new-found superiority.'

'At the next point in the dream a female colleague came to his assistance but my resolute attitude remained. Both of the dream persons came round to my point of view.'

Tania was quite pleased when she woke from the dream: that feeling of strength had been a rarity of late. When the situation next arose in actuality, she found a complete absence of nervousness. In using her dreams to confront her fears, to combat her depression, she had empowered herself.

Being in therapy

I am never sure where counselling ends and therapy begins. In my therapeutic work I use all sorts of techniques: non-directive Rogerian counselling, challenging Gestalt techniques, dynamic analytic processes, practical-skills work, as in assertiveness training, and art-therapy methods. Whatever the approach, the most important factor is the rapport, the 'therapeutic alliance', between me and my client. When approaching a dream, forget techniques at first, and approach the dream directly.

Poppy decided to train as a therapist and began to see a therapist twice a week. At the onset of therapy she had a dream about a car which was stopped. Car dreams were quite common for her, but this one directly involved her new course of work:

'The car was stopped – it wasn't clear what was wrong with it, if anything; it was just still. I went to ask for help at a house and a woman came out. She was very well dressed, perfumed and feminine – an apt description of my therapist. She looked as if she couldn't or wouldn't get her hands dirty. We found a hole under the back wheels of the car which was full of old rubbish, old clothes and odds and ends. The car was over a great hole in the road. In a sense, what supported the car, the road, was unsound and needed to be cleared out before I could proceed on my journey . . . I felt then I could have a safe ride.'

Her therapist helps her to find the source of the problem which renders the car immobile. Poppy felt good about the dream and saw it as a favourable omen for the therapeutic journey on which she was embarking.

In Gestalt therapy, first used by the dynamic Fritz Perls, every aspect of the dream is a part of you the dreamer.[10] The different aspects don't just belong to you; they are you. 'After all,' Perls says, 'you are the maker of the dream and whatever you put into it must be what is in you and therefore available for constructing the dream.'

Dependency on drugs of one form or another, alcohol among them, has been treated in many ways. Dreams have a role to play in therapeutic approaches to the management of such problems. Emil Makaric, a Yugoslav researcher, found that those undergoing alcohol deprivation frequently had infantile dreams in which they fulfilled their unquenchable thirst for the dreaded drink.[11] By recording dreams and discussing them, patients could explore their needs and gain support to cope with the deprivation. Also, information obtained from dreams contributed to a more objective analysis of the patient and could be used to prevent relapses and suicide. Other research with alcoholics being treated on an out-patient basis has shown that the prognosis is good for those who dream about drinking.[12]

The therapeutic process

Every woman I know who has undergone therapy, a painful and disturbing process, emphasizes the important role dreams have played. Rosalind Cartwright found that those women who could remember their dreams prior to psychotherapy stayed with it for longer than those who had poor recall, thus gaining more positive results.[13]

Dreams can bring clarity in themselves, as Daphne learnt:

'Dreams have helped me move forward, when talking around a subject hasn't helped.'

The emotional impact of dreams has stirred and spurred her onwards. She continued:

'They explain unconscious motives behind my behaviour and sometimes show how unhealthy it was. If I had not studied my dreams I don't know how I would ever have been able to discover what was behind my anxiety and panics.'

Dreams tell of past conflicts, unrecognized current causes of difficulty, troublesome relationships and untapped strengths. The settings provide important clues to the life context of the dreamer.[14] The dreams heal as they reveal. And, in recurring dreams in particular, we find that the core issue, the heart of the matter, is repeated, symbolically or realistically, until there is some form of resolution. Patricia, some of whose dreams are described below, experienced recurring themes: dreams of theft, dreams of her family, and dreams of women.

Patricia

This is the story of one woman who came to see me. Dream work was an integral part of her therapy. Her dreams guided and revealed much, even on that first day when, tense and uneasy, she sat opposite me and began to talk.

Patricia came to see me because she was constantly feeling low, unable to cope with life and isolated. She resigned from a job as a probation officer because she felt overwhelmed. She couldn't see how she could continue to help others when she was so in need of support herself. She had returned to her father's house and was living on social security. The extrovert Patricia had disappeared. She said that her recent dreams seemed more real than her waking life.

'My dreams lately have been about relationships and sexuality. Events and emotions seem more intense and passionate, whereas my waking world is fairly dreary in comparison. They remind me that I am a thinking, living person.'

She told me about a dream she had had the previous week:

Dream 1

'I'd been sent to prison for six months for speeding. I felt afraid but then one of the warders, a woman, began to dance with me. Her thigh touched mine and I remember feeling comforted. I found something sexually exciting about her authority and distance, yet there was this closeness. I remember someone saying how unfair the sentence seemed. I agreed but didn't feel that incensed. I took the injustice and went like a lamb to the slaughter. Eventually I took advice and appealed.'

This first dream about a prison represented how Patricia viewed her life at that time. She was coming to see me so that she could discover a way to escape her restrictions. At the same time, though, she felt very secure in her prison – the routine, the absence of pressure, the thought of just concentrating on herself, were very attractive. She is ambivalent about whether to stay in her known confined world, the 'prison', or go towards freedom, which is her right. She is told in the dream of the injustice of her sentence. Also, there is 'pressure': the advice of her friends who want her to take action and return to their world; the 'pressure' of the other woman's thigh.

This initial dream described her situation. What follows are some of the subsequent dreams she brought to therapy, arranged in chronological sequence. Not all the dreams she described are here, that would take a book in itself, but these indicate the path she trod.

Dream 2

'I was driving my car and my mother was in the passenger seat. She kept pushing her elbow against the gear stick so I couldn't drive properly. I shouted at her to stop but she wouldn't; and she kept pushing over to my side of the car.'

Patricia felt crowded out by her mother, who gave her no space, was always dictating her values and would not 'allow' real feelings to be expressed. Patricia saw the interference with the gears as her mother wanting to control and disable her. Part of her believed that there was great malevolence behind the maternal front, especially since her mother never listened to anything she said.

Talking of her mother led Patricia to mention her friend Sally, who has two children. She is jealous of the children and resents the love they get, and she sometimes feels overwhelmed by a desire to achieve that sort of bond. This is affecting her relationship with Sally and she fears she will lose her support.

Anger and tears were mixed as Patricia told me how hurt she was when her mother brought home a new baby. She was five then and remembered the fine detail of what happened, including being told to go out and play so as not to disturb the baby, even though she had not seen her mother for ten days. Patricia said, 'I decided then not to cry, but it was as if I put a wall up. I didn't want anyone to get near me ever again. She didn't love me.'

Since then Patricia has been terrified of 'letting go', terrified that if she gave vent to her angry feelings they would destroy whoever they were aimed at. Much of her subsequent therapy involved the expression of those feelings in a safe place, where she would not be rejected. Her sense of alienation and separation was demonstrated in waking life by barricading herself in her room at times to keep others away. Though she lived in her father's house, they spent little time together, and she withdrew from the world into the barren space they shared. She described her father as being as 'gloom laden' now as he had been from her earliest memories.

Her parents, now separated, hardly communicated with each other. Patricia recalled that they didn't speak to each other for two years, during which time the children were used as go-betweens. Great emphasis was placed on not communicating emotions. She particularly feared expressing her feminine side because this would make her like her mother. Denial became second nature.

Dream 3

'I was ill in the dream, as I had been all that week in waking life. A woman was standing over me and was trying to put a tube into my stomach. I was screaming that I didn't want it in and tried to stop her. I wanted to tear the tube out but was afraid I would damage myself and pull half my stomach off.'

The setting reminded Patricia of a previous traumatic episode which related in some way to a present difficulty. She associated this with her fear of looking at or touching her navel. When she was six years old she had an operation for a hernia and she recalled her mother saying, 'They'll get a knife and cut you open.'

The distance between them grew. Pat's sense of rejection deepened. Later her mother tried to make it up to her by buying presents and so on, but twenty-one years later Patricia had still not forgiven her. However, this has been punishing both of them, for, as hard as she pushes her mother away, a part of her desperately yearns for the love she missed.

In the dream Patricia was powerless against this intrusive woman yet she wanted to take action. She was not sure how to do so. Also, she was anxious about self-inflicted injury should she be bold enough to act.

Dream 4

'Dreamed last night of two men: one man, A, was saying to the other, B, that B had to die but that it wouldn't hurt. He said to B, "Just keep saying to yourself it doesn't hurt and you won't feel anything."

'So B lay on the bed and A poured hot oil all over him and set fire to him. B was burning and A kept pouring oil over him. B kept saying, "It doesn't hurt. It doesn't hurt," to himself, and it didn't. He lay very still and made no attempt to get up.

'Then there was a quick picture and the man was being replaced by a little girl but A was pulling the bedclothes over her head.'

This dream helped Pat to recognize how two parts of her were in conflict. One part, A, was trying to inflict pain while persuading the victim part, B, it would not hurt. The victim part accepted 'death' passively and did not fight back. Pat was really struggling now: should she lie down and allow herself to sink without fighting the demons in her world, or should she push back the crucial barriers and forge through the pain?

In the last part of the dream the little girl appears. The bedclothes are pulled over her head; Patricia would rather not see and face her dark negative side. In many ways she would like to retreat to closed-off childhood, where she cut herself off to avoid pain. In opening herself up to these feelings in therapy she rediscovered the desperate child who causes her such pains. She talked about her own passivity.

Dream 5

'I was on holiday with my mother but she kept delaying me. She was acting like there were hours available, yet we only had a few minutes to get the train. I screamed at her.

'Then my brother appeared in the dream and said I'd spoilt his holiday and he wanted a refund from me. I felt guilty and resentful that I'd ruined his holiday and didn't want to pay him back any money.

'I woke up feeling black anger, destructive and aggressive.'

Patricia expressed her hostile feelings more easily. She understood that her relationship with her mother had 'delayed' her emotional growth. She talked of her brother whose birth caused her so much unhappiness. She examined the guilt which she frequently experienced in relation to him.

Dream 6

'I was a van saleswoman. I was driving a delivery van and lifting heavy trays to deliver to shops. I felt strong and I was managing very well – to my surprise. I felt really competent. I also had to do the books but the accounts looked very confused and I started to panic. There was a man standing nearby trying to "help" but he only made me nervous. I kept thinking, If he'd go away and leave me to think clearly, I'd be able to sort out the accounts. I awoke feeling very confused.'

Patricia was beginning to feel more strength and personal power, but notice how she still worried about the accounts. Something felt out of balance and she was trying to get it right. She had a flash of panic, which recalled her disabling panic attacks, one of the reasons she came to therapy.

Dream 7

'I was in a rough flat which was frequently burgled and which the local authority had offered me. My sister and mother looked around, saying it had a lot of potential, but I was terrified of being burgled.

'Then the dream moved to Paris and in another room in the same building was a group of women: some, I knew, were lesbians, and one in particular I liked a lot. My sister and mother went out to see the sights and I stayed in to watch the film with some of the women. Next, I was outside walking, with my arm round Diane, a friend I had two years ago. She seemed very small and I was unafraid. I told her how much I missed her and that I'd like to introduce her to my mother and sister.'

The dream opened with Pat's sister and mother discounting her fears, totally unresponsive to her anxieties about being burgled. This led Patricia to speak of other dreams about property being stolen, which were linked to her fear that things would be taken from her. So, in waking life, she deliberately avoided becoming attached to objects and people, lest they be 'taken away'.

The change of setting is important here. Frequently in dreams which are set in a foreign country, or where events are witnessed with a sense of detachment, we discover that the dreamer is beginning to have an outside perspective which allows self-reflection to take place. This proved to be the case for Patricia for it was a watershed in her therapy.

Patricia began to talk about her attitude towards Diane, and for the first time opened up about her sexual feelings towards other women. Shame, external pressure and self-doubt had previously led her to suppress these emotions. In the dream we can see that shift towards a stronger sense of herself; she is 'unafraid' and now wants to publicly 'introduce' her friend. She 'introduces' this part of herself to me, her therapist.

Dream 8

'My friend/I was being raped. She was typing and a man came into the office, a big fat white South African. He took her into another room with a glass door and when I looked he was raping her. She was lying on her back with her legs pulled up to her chest and was completely passive. She said nothing. He wasn't undressed and was inserting his penis into her in a very slow, cold, mechanical way. I was so disgusted I ran out to find someone to phone the police. I ran from office to office but they were all empty and I couldn't find anyone. All I felt was helplessness. I think I did find someone in the end, but I'm not sure.'

This dream aroused anger. 'Why didn't I phone the police myself?' she said. She was irritated by her own helplessness. This was a return to her feelings of being isolated with no one to help. She also related the man to her anger about political events in South Africa. But the negative side of herself was symbolized in the man, for, like him, Patricia sometimes felt she was coldly distancing herself emotionally. She would have liked to disown her sexuality and came up with a powerfully negative image. She was still grappling with issues in her heterosexual past, when she sometimes took temporary typing jobs, and her current homosexual desires.

Dream 9

'I dreamt about going to an art class. After a couple of hours I realized I couldn't do "it" but everyone else could. Disheartened, I went out for a walk. When I got back to the class, the instructor told me not to worry, that I could make a spindle instead. He showed me a finished one and started to cut out a pattern from which I could make my own.'

You can see the progress Patricia has made. Though she withdrew from a situation in which she felt a failure, she didn't interpret it as rejection. She went back and was shown how to make a spindle. Spindles are associated with women's most ancient arts of spinning and weaving, and are symbolically attached to many myths and stories about women. In facing her feelings of failure, by returning to the class, Patricia was given a precious gift.

Dream 10

'I had a very explicit lesbian dream. I dropped off to sleep after reading a hundred pages of Colette Dowling's *The Cinderella Complex*, a book about women's unresolved dependency feelings. While I was reading about dependency and vulnerability, I started to become very anxious and wanted to eat. I ate two packets of Jaffa cakes, one Kit Kat, a packet of chocolate buttons and a small bar of wholenut!! Then I felt sick and threw up, after which I ate another bar of chocolate.

'I then slept and had this dream:

'I was in some kind of encounter group. There were one or two men that I quite liked, the rest were women. One woman I liked particularly was a carpenter and was planing a piece of wood. Also, there was Violet, a lesbian friend from three years ago. I left because the relationship was getting too hot for me to handle. She looked a shadowy figure in the group and didn't seem to see me or look at me.

'As the group ended, I followed Violet to the loo. She heard me following and tried to get away. When I first went in, I couldn't see her but then we saw each other and said hello. I was so pleased she didn't reject me.

'I started to kiss her on the mouth and I said, "I love you. I love you." She didn't resist and we were kissing and holding each other tightly for a while. She wanted us to stay together and I looked at my watch. I was going to make an excuse and go to catch my bus. But it was too late, the buses had all finished. We agreed to go to her boyfriend's – Violet was into men, she wore make-up and high heels, but I knew she wanted me then.

'We went back to her boyfriend's. She was going to explain that we were only sleeping together for convenience and, on the way, we talked about where we would sleep: somewhere a little cold with a window letting in fresh air so the room didn't become stuffy.

'When we got there, Violet went to make coffee and came back in. She sat on a big soft couch, with me on the floor at her feet, and I started to stroke and kiss her knees. I felt very passionately towards her, and powerful. I wanted her so much that I wasn't going to give up. Then I woke up.'

Patricia had come beyond the point of no return: 'the last bus' has gone, there is no going back. For the first time she actually allowed herself to express her passionate feelings honestly, and to talk about her eating problems. Instead of hiding, minimizing or rejecting them, she brought them up openly, in a highly erotic dream. She had come to feel strong, vibrant and part of the world.

Dream 11

'I dreamt about a man I went out with years ago. I saw him at a kiosk buying sweets and I thought he hadn't seen me. I stopped to buy something and turned the opposite way from where he had gone. Suddenly he jumped out from behind a kiosk into my path. I pulled my knee up and kicked him in the groin.'

She said, 'That was something I always wanted to do to him anyway. I always despised him but used to "mother" him.' In exploring this further, Patricia explained how she had never thought of herself as an important person; somehow she never felt real. The most important thing used to be keeping everything under control, especially around her mother. The cost of this was high, as Pat commented, 'I hated my mother and that really screwed me up sexually. I couldn't be who I wanted to be, I was so entangled with her. Now I understand more, I can be me, even though it's still hard.'

Patricia was now no longer passive but actively making choices about her future. One day she came to her weekly therapy session saying that she was aware that she did not need to feel guilty any more; it wasn't her fault that the early relationship with her mother had been so difficult, nor was her mother an evil woman. Rather, Pat accepted that she had had her own pressures. This realization went a long way in freeing her: she no longer had to reject out of hand anything her mother was interested in; she no longer had to deny her own soft, feminine side; she could accept both the masculinity and femininity which made her a whole person. This gave Pat such a buzz of energy that she actually looked transformed.

We met for another six sessions, by which time a great many changes were under way. Patricia moved to London, got a job, found a sunny flat and became much more involved in women's groups. I wrote to her to ask permission to use her dreams in this book and asked if she had any comments to make. She had:

'. . . As for what I gained from using dreams in therapy . . . dreams gave me a basis for exploring "forbidden" feelings – in some ways the dreams distanced the emotions so that I didn't feel so devastated. And, sometimes, they were fun! Talking about dreams gave me clues without it seeming that I was really looking at myself.

'My dreams are much more "flowing" now than when I was seeing you. I felt so blocked at first and the recurrent dreams were variations on a theme. Since I've loosened up, they're less rigid. I still discuss them, though now it's with Katy and it strengthens our relationship and brings us closer.

'I remember work I did with you – one session in particular, when I admitted I might be a lesbian. I had never admitted that to myself. I haven't had many intense insights like that and it was so important to me. I feel so much stronger having accepted it.'

Patricia uses her dreams for herself now. Initially we worked on the dreams together, as a joint task; she learnt the skill of interpreting them herself. It's a skill that will enrich her future.

Notes

1. Nor Hall, *The Moon and the Virgin*, The Women's Press, 1980.
2. L. Caligor, and R. May, *Dreams and Symbols: Man's Unconscious Language*, Basic Books, New York, 1968.
3. R. Corriere, K. Werner, *et al*, *Dreaming and Waking: the Functional Approach to Dreams*, Peace Press, 1980.
4. W. Dement, 'Dream Recall and Eye Movements during Sleep in Schizophrenics and Normals', *Journal of Nervous Mental Disease*, 1955.
5. Hilde Meyerhoff, 'Art as Therapy in a Group Setting', *American Journal of Art Therapy*, Vol. 16, 1977.
6. Seymour Boorstein (ed.), *Transpersonal Psychotherapy*, Science and Behavior Books Inc., Palo Alto, California. Article by Montague Ullman, 'Dream Workshops and Healing'.
7. J. Hall, *The Clinical Use of Dreams*, Grune and Stratton, 1977. On page 78, Williams research re decreased REM sleep and depression is quoted.
8. Francis Manley, *The Effect of Intentional Dreaming on Depression*, The Fielding Institute, USA, 1982.

9. Isaac Marks, 'Rehearsal Relief of a Nightmare', *British Journal of Psychiatry*, 133, pages 461-65, 1978.

10. F. Perls, R. Hefferline and P. Goodman, *Gestalt Therapy*, Redwood Press, 1951.

11. E. Makaric, 'The Importance of Dreams of Alcoholics in their Treatment and Abstinence', *Socijalna Psiijatria*, Yugoslavia, Vol. 7, pages 41-53, 1979.

12. S. Choi, 'Dreams as a Prognostic Factor in Alcoholism', *American Journal of Psychiatry*, Vol. 1, page 130, June 1973.

13. R. Cartwright, *et al.*, 'Focusing on Dreams; a Preparation for Psychotherapy', reported in *Psychological Abstracts*, 66, 1981.

14. Jill Harwant, 'The Life Context of the Dreamer and the Setting of Dreaming', *International Journal of Psychoanalysis*, Vol. 63 (4), pages 475-82, 1982.

13

All This and So Much Left Unsaid

All human emotion is reflected in our dreams and, having been privileged to share so much inner drama, I know there is a great deal more to say on this subject. However, it is impossible to include everything in one book, so in this final chapter, I will cover four major areas. They are dreams concerning illness and health, nuclear war and disaster, sex differences and the empowerment of women.

Illness and health

Unconscious forces influence disease just as the moon affects the tides. Those forces communicate with us in dreams and by listening we may learn much about our physical state. It doesn't have to be complicated. May's dreams of impending illness are quite straight-forward:

'If I am going to be ill, a few days before I dream that all the walls in my bedroom begin to close in on me. Even the ceiling gets lower and it's all very vivid.'

May, a secretary working for a pharmaceutical company, has learnt to respond to these dreams and tries to take life easier in order to minimize the effects of illness. Gwynneth dreams of her late husband just prior to illness and he always appears to be warning her. For other women, hot fiery dream colours of red and orange precede illness. Donna didn't know what her dream meant. She certainly didn't see it as a prelude to sickness, yet if she had been familiar with her own dreams, I'm sure she would have understood:

'Night after night I dreamt I knocked someone down on a crossing. Then in April I was driving along a country road and I just went to sleep. I woke up in a ditch with firemen, police and ambulancemen all trying to get me out. I spent eight months in hospital with terrible injuries and a nervous breakdown. According to the doctors, I was having the breakdown before the accident.'

It's easy to be wise after the event but here we have a recurring dream in which someone is being 'knocked down'. The repetition of negative events in a dream mean that there is some aspect of the dreamer's life which is in conflict. The clues here are that a car is involved and there is one victim, who is left prone. In some dream therapies, as we've already discovered, each part of the dream is the dreamer: Donna is the victim knocked unconscious by the car; Donna is the car that drives on regardless, even though her dreams, and other things I'm sure, have been telling her that all is not well; Donna is the crossing which connects one side with another, but this crossing isn't safe.

If Donna had been in one of our dream groups we would have helped her to look at some of the issues her dreams raised, for her other dreams displayed signs of disturbance too. There were similarities, for instance, to the dream of the man with razors in his hands which we've already examined. However, the dream of knocking someone down was an immediate precursor to her illness. If we paid more heed to our dreams, there would be fewer 'breakdowns'.

Dr Selma Hyman, clinical associate professor of radiation therapy at the University of Oregon's Health Sciences Center, sent me an article on her treatment of a woman cancer patient. In it, she describes how standard cancer treatments of radiation, cobalt and surgery were extended to include dreamwork.[1] The tender account reveals how dreams presaged the discovery of further organic growths before they had been discovered by medical examination, and the dreams show how the patient's psyche was sifting and concluding unfinished business, particularly with her husband and son. Dr Hyman's work highlights the value of responding to and working on dreams as an adjunct to physical therapy.

Some dreams are so influential that events are altered because of them. Nancy, a nurse of many years' experience, had a dream which really shook her:

'I had a dream where I was ill in hospital. I had to have an anaesthetic and died during the operation due to the incompetence of the anaesthetist.

'The dream was extremely vivid but I didn't attach too much

importance to it until I was taken into hospital as an emergency admission a few days later. I was having severe abdominal pain though I had been perfectly well just prior to my admission. The doctors queried an ectopic pregnancy or pelvic inflammation. After various tests they wanted to take me to theatre for a laporoscopy but because of the dream I would not consent. I'm sure they thought they had a crackpot on their hands.

'They started me on antibiotics and put me on bedrest for five days and whatever it was cleared up.

'I'd had another dream just before this one in which my grandmother, who has been dead for twenty years, appeared. I had never seen her so clearly in a dream before. The two dreams really frightened me.'

Nancy declined to take medical advice, going against the grain of her medical training. She interpreted the dreams as a warning and acted on them. At other times in history, Nancy's reaction would have been quite usual. Indeed, there used to be a practice called 'dream incubation' which was directly concerned with achieving insight through the use of dreams. Medical incubation, in which guidance or healing was sought, was widespread, and particularly associated with Aesculapius, the god of healing. Patients would sleep in his celebrated temple at Epidaurus in the hope that the god would visit in a dream and ordain a cure. The Greek 'Hippocratic Corpus' set out the view that dreams reflected bodily disturbance. For instance, in dreams of the sun, moon or stars:[2]

> . . . if any of these celestial bodies appear displaced or changed then such a sign indicates bodily disease, the severity of which depends upon the seriousness of the interference.

Rivers were seen as the circulation of the blood, springs and wells linked to the bladder, and seeing your teeth black in a dream signified general ill-health. Galen (born AD 129) emphasized the need to observe dreams carefully for clues to healing.

Had Sarah's parents observed her childhood dreams they might have hoped for a healing dream:

'My particular nightmare was cowering from an advancing wall with an accompanying wail which varied in pitch and intensity.'

At the age of twenty, Sarah was diagnosed as schizophrenic. She felt persecuted by her surroundings: the walls, the rooms, the very texture of her environment. She told me that, just prior to her 'breakdown', she got her 'waking self and sleeping self mixed up, confused'. She could not distinguish between dreams and reality. Now, she says, she dreams about being happy and fulfilled, though she is not so in waking life. Her dreams compensate for what she lacks in the daily world, offer some solace amid much distress.

Schopenhauer, the nineteenth-century German philosopher, likenned the dream to a brief madness, while madness itself was regarded as a long dream; Dement, echoing this sentiment, observed that our dreams allow us to be safely and privately insane every night of our lives! Acute mental ill-health may be heralded by dreams. Medard Boss, in *The Analysis of Dreams*, described how psychosis is often indicated in dreams even twenty years before the onset of an illness. He cited the case of one young woman who called her family to dinner. Her two sisters, who were sitting on bed, turned to stone, then her mother turned to stone, then her father. She rushed up to him and threw her arms around his neck but he crumbled into sand. This dream recurred four times over a few days and without warning she was taken ill with a severe form of schizophrenia, displaying catatonic symptoms. Boss points out how some schizophrenics:

> . . . have had recurrent dreams of this catastrophic end to their human existence . . . These childhood dreams are distinguished by the fact that they end in absolute hopelessness, in catastrophe and inevitable despair. However, in these ominous childhood dreams it is never the dreamer alone who dies. The dreamer often does not die at all. His whole dream world is annihilated.

Nowadays, treatment for schizophrenia allows much more room for hope than in the 1950s when Boss was writing, but his many examples of dreams preceding the onset of mental illness are worthy of detailed consideration. Paul Bakan, a professor of psychology, has continued research into the whole subject of dreams and mental illness, and he comments:[3]

> Although most dreaming occurs during REM sleep, some people's dreams spill over into non-REM sleep. Such people tend to score above normal on the schizophrenic scale of the Minnesota Multiphasic Personality Inventory, an extensively used objective test of personality.

More recent research investigated the idea that dreams are a response to biological functioning.[4] Selected groups of hospital patients were involved in discussing dreams. There was a significant link between the dream content and the clinical outcome. Bodies such as the Bristol Clinic, which treats cancer patients, have recognized that dreams can be used to induce positive feelings, which in turn affect the mood and response of their clients. Guided imagery, visualization or 'waking dream therapy', all form adjuncts to medical treatment to provide a holistic approach to healing. Use your dreams to heal yourself.

Ann Armstrong, paralysed by polio, has spent the last thirty years on a respirator, but she, like Norah, finds a certain solace in her dreams. Like most paralysed people, she is never disabled in her dreams. Wendy had a terrible car accident last November; doctors did not know if she would walk again and thought, for a while, they might have to amputate her legs. Luckily they did not but one of the changes Wendy noted was in her dreams:

'For a long time, while I was still in a wheelchair, my dreams were almost always the same: walking, legs, feet, shoes, anything to do with my legs. As I began to improve, my dreams changed, returning to how they were before the accident. They were a real boost to my confidence and, somehow, helped me keep going.'

Obviously, what we introduce into our bodies makes a difference to our dreams or our recall. There are numerous examples of fasting or drug ingestion to induce dreams from places as wide apart as the Mayan civilization and the Graeco-Roman empire. However, some practices reduce dream recall. When Jo goes out to parties and has too much to drink, she doesn't remember her dreams; similarly, Erica finds post-coital sleep inhibits dream recall.

If you are one of those rare people who say that you can't remember your dreams, and there is no obvious reason for it, such as having sustained brain injury, you could be lacking in vitamin B_6. Dr Pfeiffer of the Princeton Brain Bio Center, having spent years working on the biochemistry of dreaming, advises taking B_6 to stimulate recall. Where there is an excess of B_6, he says, insomnia may result. The nutrient tryptophane can also aid dream recall.

Fiona sent me a sparsely filled-in dream questionnaire and

commented finally, somewhat wistfully:

'I take sleeping tablets and feel this is the reason for my not dreaming as often as other people.'

This would come as no surprise to Maggie Scarfe, author of *Unfinished Business*, a worldwide bestseller. Before she wrote that book, however, she addressed herself to sleep problems. Her comments on drugs and dreams are very pertinent:[5]

> All sleeping pills, including even the mild, over-the-counter antihistamines, affect REM sleep profoundly; so do anti-anxiety drugs such as tranquillizers, and so do alcohol and amphetamines. Anti-depressant drugs also act to inhibit or erase dreaming sleep.

Barbiturates alter dreams, making them conceptual rather than perceptual, more 'thought-like' than 'dream-like'.[6] And, as if all this wasn't disturbing enough, once a person becomes dependent on such drugs, which may only take a matter of weeks, getting off them is hell – and it plays havoc with your dreams. Maggie continues:

> The dream rebound is what makes it so hard for people who are hooked on sleeping drugs to get off them. The first night there's usually horrible sleep, virtually all REM and full of anxiety dreams and nightmares.

This is why sleeping tablets, tranquillizers and the like cannot be abruptly stopped; in the 'cold turkey' mode, the REM rebound is a terrifying experience, leaving the would-be ex-user afraid that she is going insane. Gradual withdrawal should lead to the gradual renewal of normal dreaming patterns.

Women dreamers who have arthritis may be interested in a report by Theodore Tihansky.[7] He discusses the case of a fifty-nine-year-old unmarried woman with a twenty-four-year history of progressive arthritis which did not respond to traditional treatment. Desperate, she sought an alternative, and through hypnoanalysis and dream interpretation she realized that she had assumed the identity of her placid mother. Her own anger and tension remained pent up inside and her physical symptoms became more pronounced. The realization of her own misidentity allowed her finally to give vent to her feelings and cure herself of distressing physical pain. Using dreams was a crucial part in finding the cause of her illness.

Many women feel that they begin dreaming as soon as they fall asleep, without apparently passing through the preliminary three stages of sleep. Anne, for example:

'I am interested in the REM cycles researchers say we go through, as I personally dispute their findings. I know I always dream immediately on falling asleep and I think we dream continuously until waking. To me, REM sleep signifies immersion in a 'real life' event type of dream and deep sleep brings on a deep, slow considering of the brain upon ideas – no thinking involved, just reflecting. If I am ever woken from a deep sleep I always have the sensation of returning from far, far away.'

One important aspect of dreaming which deserves a final word is that awful feeling of paralysis. I'll just include one example of many:

'It usually happens when I realize that I'm having a dream and want to wake up from it. I find that I can't wake up because a powerful force, like a G force, has me paralysed. I usually try to cry out to wake my husband but nothing ends the terror until full consciousness eventually comes.'

This sensation may be caused by a dysfunction of the recticular activating system in the brain. About one person in twelve has suffered from it and, apart from an uncomfortable sensation, there is nothing amiss. Similarly, sensations of strong images that actually appear to be in the room with you either just as you're falling asleep or just as you're waking – hypnogogic and hypnopompic events, as they are respectively known – are related to physical factors rather than to dreams. However, paralysis when we dream can be very useful.

Freud noted that during dream sleep our bodies remain exceptionally still, as if paralysed. During REM sleep, muscle tone is reduced, especially in the large muscles of trunk and limbs. This ensures our safety during sleeping 'madness' because it allows us to dream without taking action, thus the temporary paralysis protects us. This is not always the case, though, as this report in the *Manchester Evening News* of 22 February 1986, shows:

A woman who had terrifying nightmares ran out of her home in the middle of the night and later drawned. An inquest on 54-year-old Mrs M. L. heard that she suffered from appalling dreams.

Mrs M.L. had fled from her home in the middle of a bitterly cold night without a coat and was later found drowned in a nearby canal, the Macclesfield hearing was told.

A daughter said her mother had suffered with her nerves for years and this had got worse following the death of her son in a road accident.

. . . Coroner Mr Herbert Sidebotham, recording an open verdict, said, 'It could be she had some sort of nightmare and dashed out of the house not knowing where she was going.'

Fortunately for the rest of us, this reaction to a dream is atypical.

Let me end this section with a self-explanatory healing dream recounted by twenty-four-year-old Vanessa:

'A year ago, in the throes of anorexia, I had a very symbolic understated dream in which I was ritually departing. I had to make a descent into a valley and it was all very Jungian. I had to descend through different strata of landscapes which also took me back in time to a pre-Roman period.

'At each stage I took leave of people, friends and family. I was following a stream down. Finally, I came to a vast, still, autumnal lake and, on my own, I had to walk out a long way into the lake on a narrow, wooden jetty. Then I looked down into the lake and saw the body of a girl.

'I was overcome with horror, panic and the feeling of the cold isolated place I had got to. I was terrified of the death I saw figured in the girl and woke up really scared.

'It was the feeling of breaking through in the dream, which I'd been holding off in waking life, that made me take steps to change things.'

Dream messages come in all forms. Puns may figure frequently, as they do for Sandie, for whom they are revealing unhealthy conflicts that need to be resolved. For instance, when she was working as a waitress, she found the restaurant owner very difficult to get on with and thought the sack was imminent. After a particularly fraught evening, she had her 'shot over a trifle' dream:

'I was waiting on a table at which Mrs Meredith, my boss, was sitting. Against all odds, the diners had reached dessert stage. I brought the order and, as I was putting down the trifles, Mrs Meredith jumped up, pulled a gun out and shot me in the chest. I seemed unhurt but said, "You've shot me over a trifle!"'

Another beauty came when Sandie was going through a rocky period with a man whom she later ditched. In waking life she had spent two years making a beautiful hand-sewn patchwork quilt. It was a very special possession and Sandie had put 'fragments' of herself into it in a symbolic way. Her dream really angered and upset her:

'I dreamt Andrew was in my bedroom. Suddenly he jumped on my bed and pissed all over my quilt. I said, "You're just pissing all over me. Get out!"'

She admitted that the dream forced her to accept that Andrew was not committed to her but 'using her as a convenience'. See how the words all link together?

Lucid dreaming

I am worried when I hear that lucid dreaming is supposed to be the big thing of the future. These are dreams in which the dreamer knows she is dreaming and, because of that awareness, can control dreams. Want to go to Brazil? Then become lucid in your dream and fly there! All very well, but what happens to all the material from your unconscious that needs an airing?

Lucid dreaming is being promoted on the basis that people can indulge their fantasies or prevent nightmares – that is, if you have a nightmare, you wake yourself up from it or change it by becoming lucid. Not much mention is made of the fact that the nightmare may be an important intrapersonal communication. I feel it is more important to deal with the source of the nightmare, to root out the cause, than merely to mask the symptoms.

You may have experienced lucidity at its most basic level: in a terrifying dream, you either force yourself to fly away from danger or you tell yourself, in the dream, that you must wake up. However, much recent research by Keith Hearne, who has invented a 'dream machine' which enables you to monitor when a lucid dream occurs, and by Dr Peter Fenwick and Dr Morton Schatzman, of St Thomas's Hospital, London, has emphasized the possibilities of controlling dreams. There are obviously some benefits in this, especially if used in the Senoi way of confronting the danger in the dream, but that as far as I know, has not been the intention so far.

We have enough work to do in learning to listen to and understand our dreams naturally, without having to control yet another aspect of our lives, especially when something like the 'dream machine' involves being wired up to a monitor.

Women Dreaming

My brain, right-dominated as it is, reacts negatively to the idea of traditionally male, left-brain rationality coming along in the form of dream control, so I'm not going to devote any more space to it. However, Celia Green's book *Lucid Dreams* presents a clear picture of this aspect of our nocturnal world for those of you who would like to explore it further. If we could all control our dreams we could escape from the horror in the examples that follow, but would that help us in the long term?

Nuclear-war dreams

Blinding white lights, hiding from the blast and trying to save children and friends: all are common in dreams for many women. The mushroom cloud darkens our dreams as it does our waking lives.

Cassie's disturbing dreams drove her to become a CND activist. The first came three years ago; in it there was great confusion, scorching heat, a blinding light and people screaming and dying. The fear remained with her when she woke. She had the following dream one month later:

'I'm in a house with a friend. We are listening to the radio when a warning comes on that a bomb is to be dropped. We lie down on the floor and cover our eyes with our hands. There is a blinding white flash which lasts for a long time, as does the powerful heat.

'We uncover our eyes to see that the house is still standing, though the windows have been blown out. We seem OK, and go out. Outside people are dead and burning. We search for food but there is none anywhere. I join a long queue of people seeking jobs but the person behind the grille tells me that teachers aren't required; all the children are dead. We have no money left and the city is empty except for dying people. We try to leave the city but my legs are getting weaker, they are sore and hot. I wonder if I have sunburn or radiation sickness.'

Waking issues about her work can be seen in Cassie's dream. She wants to leave teaching, and in a macabre way the dream allows her to do this by wiping out all children at one go. However, the emotional impact of the dream emphasized her deep dread, hitherto largely unvoiced, of nuclear devastation.

'I don't think I dreamt about experiencing the actual "happening" at all. I mean, the bomb being dropped. I just knew it had happened. Everyone did.

'People were milling around, homeless like refugees, desperate, confused and lost. The noise was intense. I was just one of thousands carried along in a wave of bewildered not-knowingness . . .

'The last scene was my standing at a wall staring over the horizon and seeing the silhouette and the land we'd left behind. I have a vivid recollection of the total desolation of the scene. It wasn't black and charred or devastated, just dying – as if all the vegetation had suddenly lost its life source. There were leaves on the trees and plants, but all looked grey and lifeless. A silent, hopeless, abandoned country. I remember the intense feeling of bitterness and loss.'

Sue's dream was one of total inevitability and, even though she fights and campaigns in the anti-nuclear lobby, she feels that politicians do not listen. Her dream describes her sense of futility:

'When we knew the bomb had gone off, time slowed down and, as my mother and father and I ran into the countryside, I kept looking at my watch. Minute by minute, as I looked, I was able to say all the people I knew were dying one by one as the blast spread from each city centre. We ran until my mother could run no further. Everywhere was totally silent. My father said it was useless to run any more, so we turned and walked slowly back to the city. As I looked at my watch, only five minutes had passed and I was able to time when the blast would finally hit us.'

Although such nuclear-war dreams are depressing, they have spurred some of us to action.

When Carol dreamt of nuclear war, though, she and her dream characters were debating whether or not to commit suicide before the impending cataclysm took place. This acceptance of the inevitable destruction of our world is one of the most sinister aspects of these dreams. Linda's dream provides a more detailed example of what I mean:

'People were all congregated together when news came through that a nuclear bomb had dropped. There was no panic but we expected something awful would happen. My friend went to buy some food and I ate it, thinking, 'I have to eat this because soon there will be no food left,' and, 'it must be contaminated.' There was still some running water, which I drank, trying not to think that the bomb might have polluted it.

'Everything was so peaceful – no panic. Walking along the street, I knew, at the back of my mind, that soon the shop windows would be smashed and the goods plundered as the realization of what had happened hit the people. Then I was listening to a discussion on the radio about where the next bomb would drop. It was agreed that the worst consequence of the impending bomb would be the flash, which would blind people immediately.

'I found a newspaper on sale with FALL OUT ISSUE stamped all over it. I thought I should buy it and preserve it as historically valuable. A couple of pictures inside had me and my ex-lover in them. I started to wonder where he was, then I woke up.'

Saddened as she was by the dream, Linda saw that it reflected the way she sees Britain dealing with the threat of nuclear war – that is, largely ignoring it and carrying on as if it was not there. In the dream you can see how she tries to distance herself from events by objectifying them, as when she buys the newspaper. Personal relationships are mirrored. She cares about her lover and knows that, in reality, should the bomb drop, she would probably wonder about him. The enormity of such a possibility numbs her: she finds it hard to take it in and longs to avoid the unimaginable, and so has calm, intelligent interchanges and discussions in the dream; but in reality she knows that emotions, and not rationality, would dominate.

Women who are active at Greenham recognize the need to take personal action, as Sheila Triggs explained:[8]

> This web of awareness inspires the actions that Greenham women are taking all the time. Their actions show both the public and the military that the Greenham base is hopelessly insecure; that cruise missiles, dangerously using our domestic roads, cannot be deployed secretly; that the implementation of our laws is arbitrary: that our prison system is based on revenge not reform; that we must all take responsibility for what our government does in our name.

Knowledge of the probable effects of nuclear war has come to us through articles and films like *The War Game*. Significantly, almost every woman who reported a nuclear dream talked of being with strangers, initially trying to escape to the countryside from the city, silence, feelings of bleak hopelessness, eventual acceptance, sadness and grief. Many women mention falling to the ground, covering their eyes from the blast, 'creeping radiation sickness', and an all-pervading sense of futility.

The dream that concerns Libby most of all is a confused, muddled anxious one, yet it leaves her heart-stricken lest it be prophetic:

'It's as if the end of the world has come. I'm standing hopelessly with a group of strangers, concerned about my children, but always waiting and looking for something to happen. The hopelessness and despair are appalling. In some of these dreams I am walking, slowly, again in search of something but dogged by despair.'

Novelist Prue, living and working in Bristol, had an extremely vivid dream. She hoped it was a story, like those stories Robert Louis Stevenson and other authors claim to have dreamt, rather than a horrible long-term prediction:

'The world had been devastated by an atomic war and this dream concerned the aftermath; though clearly it was some time after, as most material benefits were present, though very restricted, and in both social and legal matters things had undergone great changes. Much of the earth was uninhabitable because of the effects of radiation and in most places people lived under plastic domes so huge that the younger element frequently didn't realize that they were looking at the sky through very fine plastic.'

She goes on to describe the buildings and family structures that existed in the post-nuclear totalitarian state; anything to do with psychic ability, telepathy, mediumistic ability and the like was utterly taboo. The world had become completely materialistic.

Obviously, Prue's interest in psi phenomena is reflected in the dream and she sees future prospects as bleak for the growth of those skills. However, good does come from these dire dreams. They give many women insight into the cataclysmic horror, and in informing us stir up action against the obscene insanity of atomic war. Such disturbances at the possibility of war is not new, nor are such dreams unusual, as Charlotte Beradt's book indicated.

From 1933 to 1939, Charlotte Beradt collected dreams of hundreds of Germans. *The Third Reich of Dreams* shows how totalitarianism insidiously warped a nation. The dreams, like those of the nuclear holocaust, reflected the anxieties of ordinary citizens and showed how deeply government directives and propaganda had penetrated a nation's psyche:[9]

The author notes that many dreams of anxiety and persecution began in 1933 at the very beginning of the Third Reich, so that the dreamer seems to anticipate what was going to happen long before it occurred.

Charlotte Beradt recognizes that dreams go directly to our emotional core, no matter what elaborate disguises are introduced, and in these dreams people recognized deep down what the regime was all about, though many fought long and hard to deny the reality. The book is a fascinating study of the way in which people were terrorized into accepting inhumanity, and rarely rejecting Nazism. But there is a message for us in it. She asked then, as we might:

> If all of us abhorred the Third Reich, why did it exist? Must there not have been feelings, unknown in our conscious mind, that condoned it, accepted it, willed it? Even among those who lived in fear and trembling of the Nazis, might there not have been in them somewhere, deep down, a layer of soul closely kin to that regime of terrible domination? To understand ourselves, and the possibility of Nazi terror, we must study the dreams it evoked so that we shall truly know the 'stuff as dreams are made on'.

Bruno Bettelheim, a concentration camp survivor and psycho-analyst, tried as a prisoner to find someone who had dreamt of the ordeal of transportation to the camp and could find no one. He expected his own dreams to repeat the trauma, but they did not. Probably, the unconscious was too busy processing current worries to introduce self-destructive repetition at that point. However, Bettelheim wrote of the ways in which control was maintained, and his remarks have pertinence for us as women and as members of our society. There is much we can learn from *The Informed Heart*, his book which chronicles the attempted annihilation of a minority group:

> The Gestapo relied mainly on three other methods of destroying personal autonomy. The first . . . that of forcing prisoners to adopt childlike behaviour. The second was that of forcing them to give up individuality and merge themselves into an amorphous mass. The third consisted of destroying all capacity for self-determination, all ability to predict the future and thus prepare for it.

Do leaders maintain power over a mass of individuals or do we delegate tasks to leaders so that 'power becomes mainly a problem of group masochism instead of one of force', as psycho-historian Lloyd Demause argues?[10] Do we project onto 'them', the evil ones, all our bad feelings, so that we don't have to acknowledge our own unaccepttable attributes? How much more comfortable it is to say 'He is the evil one' than to admit that we may play a part in that evil?

The answer is hard to fathom but, if we return to Jung, we do see hope. He prophesied that the only chance our civilization has for avoiding nuclear hell is if enough individuals can stand the tension of opposites in themselves.[11] If we can own responsibility for our thoughts, dreams and inner life, we have hope. If we all take personal responsibility, we don't give our power away to others who abuse it in fulfilling their own sadistic fantasies.

Larry Sargeant, a therapist and 'dream educator' working in New Mexico, pursues the issue of personal awareness in his article 'Dreams in a Nuclear Age.'[12] He says:

> The tension of opposites to which Jung refers is our ability to recognize and accept our own darkness, evil, inferiority and woundedness . . . Jung has said that in the projections of our shadows upon the world, we turn the world into replicas of our unseen faces.

Traditionally we have done this with other races, cultures and countries. By disowning (projecting), we cannot come to heal the disturbed, 'bad' part within. Yet it is only by becoming conscious of our shadow selves that we can heal ourselves and our world. We can learn about our own shadow and the collective shadow that we develop nationally. The Nazis projected their shadow, their dark part, onto the Jews, blaming them for all possible ills. Similarly, the Americans project their collective shadow onto Communists, wherever they appear – Vietnam, Nicaragua, or Grenada, it really doesn't matter. By acknowledging this fact, we move towards changing it.

Randy Morris, a social psychologist, collected dreams of nuclear nightmares of Hiroshima residents. What he has to tell us provides a fitting conclusion for this section:[13]

> Some dream theorists posit a part of human mind common to all human beings. I believe that nuclear nightmares represent an impulse on the part of this collective psyche to confront directly the horror of nuclear war, literally 'to imagine the unimaginable', and by so doing to take the

first step toward healing this festering rupture in the family of man. These dreams, as expressions of pure emotion, have the power to motivate people to work in new ways for the peace movement.

Sex differences in dreams

Cultural factors, age and sex influence our dreams to a marked degree. This pertains to aggression (O'Neill, 1977); to content in dreams (R. Williamson; R. L. Van der Castle); and to so many other factors that Carolyn Winget and Milton Kramer conclude:[14]

> The exploration of dreams content has repeatedly demonstrated that the dreams of men and women can be differentiated along a number of parameters. It may be safe to say that at all ages the male-female difference in dream content is one of the firmly established facts that non-laboratory study of dreams has clearly demonstrated . . . the sex of the dreamer may be one of the most salient features in determining certain types of content.

Women's dreams are built around intimacy, whereas men's dreams are more concerned with issues of separateness, extending their share of influence, and power. Calvin Hall, famous for his studies of dream content, argued that men's dreams contain more male characters, physical aggression, sexuality, physical activity, tools and weapons and outdoor settings. Women's dreams contain more female characters, known characters, verbal activities and indoor settings. The conclusion reached about this 'ubiquitous sex difference in dreams' was that men's unresolved problems as revealed in dreams centre more on their relationships with men than with women, while women focus on their relationships with either sex about equally.[15]

Women tend to have a greater incidence of unpleasant emotion in dreams and refer more frequently than men to everyday problems. Earlier chapters have shown just how widespread anxiety is in our dreams, and the research by De Martino bears this out.[16] When equal groups of men and women were tested, he found that more women reported dreams with colour, with themes of falling; more had dreams of frustration and being unable to move; and more had premonition themes.

My early experience that women talked more readily about their dreams, and recalled them with greater ease, is backed up by clinical research.[17] Women had significantly more dream recall than did men, but in contrast women who repressed emotions again found dreams hard to recall. Research by Cary Cooper just reported tells us that women who don't express feelings of stress, or don't find ways of alleviating emotional distress but keep it bottled up, are more likely to develop breast cancer. Pay attention to your dreams; they'll tell you when you are becoming over-stressed, then you can take remedial action.

George Domino examined the differences in attitude towards dreams displayed by men and women. In his study of 102 men and 94 women, he found that the attitudes of women were more in tune with results from recent laboratory research:[18]

> Thus, more females agree that everyone dreams every night, that dreams occur in colour, that some conscious control of dreams is possible and that dreams parallel to some degree one's waking personal style.

Helena's dreams were very much a reflection of her 'personal style'. Unable to let go of an unsuccessful love affair, she dreamt about the man every night for two years after she had ended their relationship. She added, 'I talk about my dreams a lot. Men think that's strange because they don't seem to remember theirs. I think dreams are very significant.'

Norah was familiar with this difference in content:

'I am interested in my husband's dream life as, although he often has dreams reflecting anxiety, he also has enjoyable, adventurous dreams which are like going to a good film; they give him entertainment and refreshment. I would guess this latter feature is more common in men because of the difference in upbringing between boys and girls.'

An oft-repeated question is 'Do people dream in colour?' Judith certainly does:

'My dreams are pervaded by one overwhelming colour or, rather, sense of colour, either red and yellow, which means warmth and contentment, or dark and grey, which I associate with loss and pain.'

Like many women who have an art training, her colours play a significant role in her dreams. As an aside, her dreams are often accompanied by smells and very vivid tactile sensations. But, like most women, she dreams in colour. Sunin found that more women than men, about 85 per cent of us, regularly dream in colour.[19]

Carrington, writing in Hall's *Clinical Use of Dreams*, notes how mentally ill patients' dreams differ from the norm. Schizophrenic women, for instance, have more dreams of hostility and threatening situations as well as more bizarre dreams, including mutilation and loss of control. A typical issue for women is the expression of anger and control. We prefer to turn anger on ourselves instead of expressing it for fear of rejection or refusal, or simply because no one ever said it was OK to get angry, that anger was a normal human emotion.

Women often talk about guilt and some of us even feel guilty about what we dream. Such feelings are fostered by people around us as a means of manipulation and control. 'If you don't do it, no one else will'; 'You're the only one who really understands me so won't you love me/care for me/stay with me/look after me'; and 'If you were a proper wife/mother you would do all the housework/stay at home/put our interests before your own.' Getting hooked on guilt enables others to control you. It decreases your personal power to make choices for yourself. The more you understand your emotional make-up, your strengths and weaknesses, the more power you discover to promote emotional good health. It's to this subject that we now turn.

Empowerment

Empowerment means learning to harness your own power – not power over others but power over your own life. We can learn to tune into our own abilities by responding to inner directions contained in dreams. On a very simple level this can relate to concrete situations such as job interviews. Maggie's dream came a couple of days before an interview for her first nursery appointment:

'I was escorted into an important interview place. It was full of differing levels and opportunities which overawed me and I seemed to be getting privileged treatment.

'Then I am sitting facing an interview panel. I look pretty and my normally unruly hair is styled to absolute perfection. I look relaxed and answer the questions in a particularly confident and informed manner.'

Looking back, she realized that she was confident deep down, but on a conscious level she was a bag of nerves, dreading the ordeal. However, her dream feelings triumphed. She got the job and the head told her, more than once, that she had never known anyone interview so well! Maggie added:

'The feelings from that dream have continued, strong and enduring, and return at interview times. Thank goodness I had this dream and, moreover, that it was in favour of myself since it isn't like me to treat myself so positively in waking life.' Her confidence in her own capabilities improved enormously through this one dream.

Despite consciousness-raising groups, assertiveness training and therapeutic workshops, the vital work of self-discovery is to a large extent neglected within the feminist movement itself. It is pushed into some compartment called 'psychology' or self-indulgence and largely dismissed. This is a real pity since, as you've seen, self-knowledge frees us to be ourselves and direct our lives. The starting point can be a startling dream. Anaïs Nin drew attention to this in *A Woman Speaks*:

> Our culture put a taboo on dreaming, said it was a waste of time, it was an escape, didn't have much meaning . . . our culture placed a taboo on introspection, on seeking to find the meaning of it all . . .
> That's also why, I think, we have the much more dangerous explosion of drugs. That was the mechanical way to unseal the tremendous taboo that had been put on dreaming, imagery and sensation. That was a very tragic way to reach the inner world.

As Phyllis Chesler shows in *Women, Money and Power*, in our western society power accrues to those whose access to making money is the norm and to those who understand financial matters, namely men. As she says:

> Not to earn money directly in a money culture is equivalent to non-existence or at least worthless existence.

So, while money brings power, women are told that being a homemaker and mother is of far more significance. Ironic, isn't it, that these same homemaking activities are defined as unproductive labour and are not rewarded economically. Also, there is a hidden message that women who handle money well are unfeminine and a threat.

As women, when we unify all the fragmented parts of ourselves, then we can become truly powerful. When we are whole we can meet others, unite and use that power effectively, positively to change our world which still operates to restrict women economically. When we are in control of change, that's when we will see change.

We are skilled at hiding behind masks, presenting a persona which conceals those parts of ourselves we wish to hide from the world. However, too often for comfort, dreams present the 'real' you, as Linda verified:

'My dreams often portray me as a weak, ineffectual person yet most people see me as confident and determined. The dreams show my true self.'

Dreams chronicle progression in empowerment. Sarah provided a simple example:

'My dreams of collecting baggage used to be very anxious. I couldn't start the journey without every piece of luggage. Now, in dreams, I sometimes decide not to bother with it at all.'

She has moved from being dependent on having everything 'right', from needing to have all her symbolic security items around her. Now she can be herself without any 'baggage' and she definitely feels a lot freer! Trudy gave another simple dream to demonstrate her increased assertiveness and belief in herself. She used to dream that 'the police always got the better of me, but now I get the better of them!' Authority figures don't intimidate her any more.

Flying dreams, which we've already looked at, are useful pointers to where you are in your own self-development. Veronica's flying dream series plot her gradual growth towards personal autonomy, as you can see:

'As a child of eight, I started having nightmares where people were chasing me. I was on a pogo stick trying to jump away but could never jump quite high enough. Crowds of people pursued me. Later this dream changed to me trying to fly from the crowds. Sometimes I could not take off; other times I flew so low they could get me, or I suddenly lost power in flight. But, last time I had this dream, I flew by my own volition. I didn't do it to escape. People shouted to the sky and exclaimed in admiration, "A woman is flying!"'

Clearly, her confidence has been increasing in leaps and bounds. Marilee Zdenek, a pioneer in the field of creativity and right-brain techniques, has developed a programme which includes dreams as a major force.[21] As she says, 'The power is within; the decision whether to communicate with that power is up to you.'

Developing the right brain, which specializes in holistic, visual and spatial perception, feeling and senses, as opposed to the left-brain verbal, logical, linear thinking emphasized in our western educational tradition, enables us to get to the heart of our own creativity. The desire and boldness to nurture that side increases our creative power:

> You have the power to use memories of the past to enrich the present, to use the happy times to nurture you, and to use the hard times as a catalyst for growth.

That power belongs to you.

It has been demonstrated that the brain retains memories not available to the conscious mind but that these surface during dreams. Thus we gain access to that which is often hidden:[22]

> I was a war baby and my earliest memories are of skies filled with aircraft, barrage balloons or searchlights. These appear in my dreams either as straightforward memories, allegories or surrealistic nightmares; always in colour and always accompanied by a powerful atmosphere.'

Emma Goldman, that early feminist fighter for female emancipation, wrote of this:[23]

> It is necessary that woman learn that lesson, that she realize that her freedom will reach as far as her power to achieve her freedom reaches. It is therefore far more important for her to begin with her inner regeneration, to cut loose from the weight of prejudices, traditions and customs. Away with the ridiculous notion that to be loved, to be sweetheart and mother, is synonymous with being a slave or subordinate. It will have to do away with the absurd notion of the dualism of the sexes and that man and woman represent two antagonistic worlds.

Julie, who wrote from Reading, considered differing attitudes:

'I think dreams are a very feminine thing. Maybe we women are less frightened of this part of our nature than men. It's like letting yourself drift in a sea of feeling . . . I think men are afraid of us because of this dark side they sense to be in themselves. When, one day, they come to terms with it, it will be much better for us and for them.'

The process of individuation, discovering yourself as a unique person, is part and parcel of learning who you are. In dreams we confront ourselves, and the purpose of dreams is to reveal, not conceal. When we live in harmony with our dreams we do find wholeness. This means, for many of us, moving towards the position where we seek control over our own lives, have economic choices, gain joy from mutually satisfying relationships, and can be equal, subordinate or dominant, depending on the situation at the time. It is much healthier to find out who you are, as Joyce Jennings Walstedt's research revealed. She concluded:[24]

> A number of women have structured their entire lives around pleasing and serving men because this was the predominant mode they learned as they were growing up. They experienced feelings of being loved, normal, and safe when they did so, of being anxious and unlovable when they did not. The irony, however, is that by following this cultural prescription, some women remain in a powerless, vulnerable position throughout most of their adult lives.

Many of us fear power because we feel it makes us unfeminine. We see powerful people as being inconsiderate so we give our power away, but power is not synonymous with aggression. Power, as we've seen, can liberate us. We give our power away when we say, 'You made me angry,' instead of, 'I feel angry with you.' We do it when we say, 'If it hadn't been for you I could have . . .' Other people can only contribute to our feelings; only in exceptional circumstances can they control them. Political and economic realities obviously play a part – it would be naïve to think otherwise – but on the whole women abdicate responsibilities to their own disadvantage.

Some people have formal power invested in them, in their job for instance, but everyone can have personal power. We enhance such power by recognizing weaknesses. We enhance it by accepting and building on our strengths. The first step to empowerment is increasing self-knowledge, and dreams can be the key. There is no other psychological product that is less controlled or more spontaneous than our dreams.

Your dreams are there every night. All you have to do is give them some room in your waking life. That will turn the key to such a treasure trove that you will wish you had started years ago. Enjoy the bounty; you deserve it!

Notes

1. Selma Hyman, 'Death-In-Life – Life-In-Death: Spontaneous process in a cancer patient', *Spring, An Annual of Archetypal Psychology and Jungian Thought*, Switzerland, 1977.
2. Napthali Lewis, *Dreams and Portents*, Samuel Stevens Hakkert, Toronto, 1976.
3. Paul Bakan, 'The Right Brain is the Dreamer', *Psychology Today*, Vol. 10, Part 6, pages 66-68, 1976.
4. R. C. Smith, 'A Possible Biologic Role of Dreaming', *Psychotherapy and Psychosomantics*, Vol. 41 (4), pages 167-76, July 1984.
5. Maggie Scarfe, 'The Sleep Clinic' in H. Rubenstein, *The Complete Insomniac*, Jonathan Cape, 1974.
6. D. Carroll, S. Lewis and I. Oswald, 'Effects of Barbiturates on Dream Content', *Nature*, Vol. 223, August 1969.
7. T. Tihansky, 'Case Report: Mixed Arthritis', *Medical Hypnoanalysis*, Vol. 3 (3), pages 118-20, July 1982.
8. Sheila Triggs, letter, *The Guardian*, 16 December, 1985.
9. Charlotte Beradt, *The Third Reich of Dreams*, Quadrangle, New York, 1968.
10. Lloyd Demause, *Foundations of Psychohistory*, Psychohistory Press, 1982.
11. B. Hannah, *Encounters with the Soul*, Sigo Press, Santa Monica, California, 1981.
12. L. Sargeant, 'Dreams in a Nuclear Age', *Journal of Humanistic Psychology*, Vol. 24, No. 3, pages 142-56, Summer 1984.
13. R. Morris, 'Nuclear Nightmares', *Dream Network Bulletin* 3 (1-2), page 4, 5, 1984.
14. C. Winget and M. Kramer, *Dimensions of Dreams*, University Presses of Florida, 1979.
15. C. Hall and B. Domhoff, 'A Ubiquitous Sex Difference in Dreams', *Journal of Abnormal and Social Psychology*, Vol. 66, No. 3, pages 278-80, 1963.
16. M. F. De Martino, 'Sex Differences in the Dreams of Southern College Students', *Journal of Clinical Psychology*, 9, pages 199-201, 1953.
17. R. W. Williamson, R. V. Herkel and W. Boblett, 'Reported Frequency of Dream Recall as Related to Repression, Sensitization and Intelligence', *Journal of Clinical Psychology*, Vol. 26 (3), 1970.
18. George Domino, 'Attitudes Towards Dreams, Sex Differences and Creativity', *Journal of Creative Behaviour*, Vol. 16, No. 2, 1982.
19. Mary A. Mattoon, *Applied Dream Analysis: A Jungian Approach*, V. H. Winston and Sons, Washington DC, 1978.
20. Phyllis Chesler and Emily J. Goodman, *Women, Money and Power*, William Morrow, New York, 1976.

21. Marilee Zdenek, *The Right-Brain Experience*, Corgi, 1985.
22. B. Brenneis, 'Male and Female Ego Modalities in Manifest Dream Content', *Journal of Abnormal Psychology*, Vol. 76 (3 pt. 1), December 1970.
23. Emma Goldman, *The Tragedy of Women's Emancipation*.
24. Joyce Jennings Walstedt, 'The Altruistic Other Orientation: An Exploration of Female Powerlessness', *Psychology of Women Quarterly*, Vol. 2 (29), Winter 1977.

Appendix 1

Dream Questionnaire

1. How many times a week do you remember dreaming?

2. Do you keep a record of your dreams?
   If the answer is 'Yes', how long have you been doing so?

3. Do you have recurring dreams?
   Please describe.

4. What are some of the subjects that you frequently dream about?

5. Do you have nightmares or anxiety dreams? Please describe.

6. Have you ever found a nightmare helpful?

7. Can you control your dreams? Please identify methods.

8. Please describe any vivid childhood dreams.

9. Are your dreams more noticeable at any particular time of the month?

10. Have you ever had a dream which anticipated future events?
    Please give details.

11. Do you dream about sex? Please give a dream example.

12. How do you feel about your dreams?

13. Please give details of ways in which your dreams are helpful or important to you.

14. Why do you think we dream?

15. I would be grateful if you could use the remaining space to include any other views, comments, etc.

Many thanks for your help.

Brenda Mallon
Crescent Villa
20 Circular Road
Manchester
M20 9LP

Select Bibliography

There are so many books and articles about dreams that it would take a book in itself to list them all. I have included here only those which have been particularly useful in my research or which I regard as good starting points for further reading.

L. Berger, I. Hunter, and R. W. Lane, *The Effects of Stress on Dreams*, International Universities Press Inc., 1971.

Bruno Bettelheim, *The Informed Heart*, Thames and Hudson, 1960.

Bruno Bettelheim, *The Uses of Enchantment*, Penguin, 1978.

Eric Berne, *Games People Play*, Penguin, 1968.

F. Bonime and W. Bonime, *The Clinical Use of Dreams*, Basic Books, New York, 1962.

Stephen Brook, *The Oxford Book of Dreams*, Oxford University Press, 1983.

L. Caligor and R. May, *Dreams and Symbols*, Basic Books, New York, 1968.

Phyllis Chesler, *Women and Madness*, Avon Books, New York, 1972.

Ronald W. Clark, *Freud: The Man and the Cause*, Granada, 1982.

Sukie Colegrave, *The Spirit of the Valley*, Virago, 1979.

R. Corriere, K. Werner, L. Woldenberg and J. Hart, *Dreaming and Waking: The Functional Approach to Dreams*, Peace Press, USA, 1980.

Raymond de Becker, *The Understanding of Dreams: or the Machinations of the Night*, Allen and Unwin, 1968.

Anne Dickson, *A Woman in Your Own Right*, Quartet, 1982.

Colette Dowling, *The Cinderella Complex*, Fontana, 1982.

J. W. Dunne, *An Experiment With Time*, Faber and Faber, 1958.

J. Downing and R. Marmorstein, (eds.), *A Book of Gestalt Therapy Sessions*, Harper and Row, New York, 1973.

Luise Eichenbaum and Susie Orbach, *Outside In, Inside Out*, Pelican, 1982.

Luise Eichenbaum and Susie Orbach, *What Do Women Want?* Fontana, 1984.

Sheila Ernst and Lucy Goodison, *In Our Own Hands: A Book of Self-Help Therapy*, The Women's Press, 1981.

Christopher Evans, (ed. Peter Evans), *Landscapes of the Night*, Gollancz, 1983.

Ann Faraday, *The Dream Game*, Temple Smith, 1975.

David Ffoulkes, *Children's Dreams: Longitudinal Study*, Wiley Interscience, 1982.

M. L. von Franz, *Problems of the Feminine in Fairytales*, Spring Publications, Zurich, 1970.

S. Freud, *The Interpretation of Dreams*, (standard edition, 1900), Vols. 4 and 5, Hogarth Press, 1953.

Nancy Friday, *My Mother, Myself*, Fontana, 1979.

Patricia Garfield, *Creative Dreaming*, Futura, 1976.

John Grant, *Dreamers*, Ashgrove Press, Bath, 1984.

Celia Green, *Lucid Dreams*, Institute of Psychophysical Research, Oxford, 1968.

J. A. Hadfield, *Dreams and Nightmares*, Penguin, 1974.

C. S. Hall, *The Meaning of Dreams*, McGraw-Hill, New York, 1953.

J. Hall, *Clinical Uses of Dreams: Jungian Interpretations and Enactments*, Grune and Stratton, 1977.

Nor Hall, *The Moon and the Virgin*, The Women's Press, 1980.

Esther Harding, *Woman's Mysteries*, Rider, 1971.

E. H. Hartmann, *The Biology of Dreaming*, Charles C. Thomas, Boston, 1967.

M. D. Hartmann, *The Functions of Sleep*, Yale University Press, 1973.

Hans Holzer, *The Psychic Side of Dreams*, Doubleday, New York, 1976.

A. Janov, *The Primal Scream*, Abacus, 1974.

Kathleen Jenks, *Journey of a Dream Animal: A Human Search for Personal Identity*, The Julian Press, New York, 1975.

C. G. Jung, *Dreams*, Princeton University Press, 1974.

C. G. Jung, *Man and His Symbols*, Aldus Books, 1964.

A. Kinsey, W. Pomeroy, C. Martin and P. Gebhard, *Sexual Behaviour in the Human Female*, W. B. Saunders, 1953.

Joel Kovel, *A Complete Guide to Therapy*, Pelican, 1978.

R. D. Laing, *The Divided Self*, Pelican, 1965.

Gay Gaer Luce and Julius Segal, *Sleep*, Coward, McCann and Geoghegan, New York, 1966.

E. Maccoby, (ed.), *The Development of Sex Differences*, Tavistock, 1967.

Janet Malcolm, *Psychoanalysis: The Impossible Profession*, Picador, 1980.

Ann Mankowitz, *Change of Life: A Psychological Study of Dreams and the Menopause*, Inner City Books, Canada, 1984.

J. M. Masson, *The Assault on Truth: Freud's Suppression of the Seduction Theory*, Faber, 1984.

Mary Ann Mattoon, *Applied Dream Analysis: A Jungian Approach*, V. H. Winston & Sons, 1978.

J. M. Natterson, (eds.), *The Dream in Clinical Practice*, Jason Aronson, New York, 1980.

Anaïs Nin, (ed. Evelyn J. Hinz), *A Woman Speaks*, W. H. Allen, 1978.

Ann Oakley, *Taking It Like A Woman*, Jonathan Cape, 1984.

303

Ann Oakley, Ann McPherson and Helen Roberts, *Miscarriage*, Fontana, 1984.

F. Perls, R. Hefferline and P. Goodman, *Gestalt Therapy*, Redwood Press, 1951.

Plato, *The Republic*, translated by B. Jowett, Random House, New York.

E. L. Rossi, *Dreams and the Growth of Personality*, Pergamon Press, 1972.

Dorothy Rowe, *Depression, The Way Out of Your Prison*, Routledge and Kegan Paul, 1983.

Winifred Rushford, *Something is Happening; Spiritual Awareness and Depth Psychology in the New Age*, Turnstone Press, 1981.

Charles Rycroft, *The Innocence of Dreams*, Oxford University Press, 1981.

Maggie Scarfe, *Unfinished Business: Pressure Points in the Lives of Women*, Fontana, 1981.

Florence Seaman and Anne Lorimer, *Winning at Work: A Book for Women*, Running Press, Pennsylvania, 1979.

Marjorie Shaevitz, *The Superwoman Syndrome*, Fontana, 1985.

Gail Sheehy, *Passages*, Bantam, New York, 1977.

Penelope Shuttle and Peter Redgrove, *The Wise Wound*, Penguin, 1978.

Robin Skynner and John Cleese, *Families and How To Survive Them*, Methuen, 1984.

Dale Spender, *Invisible Women: The Schooling Scandal*, Writers and Readers Publishing Cooperative Society, 1982.

William Stekel, *The Interpretation of Dreams*, Liveright, New York, 1943.

W. O. Stevens, *The Mystery of Dreams*, Allen and Unwin, 1950.

Sundance Community Dream Journal, Vol. 3, No. 2, Summer 1979, ed. Dr Henry Reed, 503 Lake Drive, Virginia Beach, VA 23451, USA.

L. Weatherhead, *Psychology, Religion and Healing*, Hodder and Stoughton, 1951.

M. D. Ullman, S. Krippner and A. Vaughan, *Dream Telepathy*, Turnstone Books, 1973.

M. D. Ullman and Nan Zimmerman, *Working with Dreams*, Dell, New York, 1979.

Wilse B. Webb, *Sleep: The Gentle Giant*, Prentice Hall, New Jersey, 1975.

Benjamin B. Wolman, (ed.), *Handbook of Dreams: Research, Theories and Applications*, Van Nostrand Reinhold, New York, 1979.

R. Wood, *World of Dreams*, Random House, New York, 1977.

Index

Index

abortion 67, 68, 73-6, 214
abuse 19, 29, 31, 33, 95, 132, 193,
    201, 202, 206
accidents 60, 128, 152, 214, 229,
    231, 278, 281
adolescence 12, 14, 45, 82-6
ageing 58, 59, 111
aggression 13, 37, 51, 103, 208,
    219, 221, 251, 292
alcohol 28, 202, 265, 276, 282
anger 37, 44, 60, 96, 103, 104, 107,
    123, 131, 190-1, 208, 215, 219,
    268, 282, 294
anima/animus 23, 160
animals 12, 40, 44, 45, 48, 104,
    141, 146, 149, 157
    cat 119, 141, 157-60, 201, 220
    cow 238
    crocodile 218
    deer 151-2
    dog 35, 44-45, 63, 69, 73-4,
        105-6, 119-20, 152, 157,
        214, 220, 253
    dolphin 56
    dragon 46
    duck 46
    fox 46
    goat 44, 106
    hamster 152, 154
    horse 124, 177
    lamb 44, 140
    lion 141
    mice 152
    ostriches 46
    pig 105, 208
    pony 109
    rats 152-4
    sharks 150
    stork 64
    sheep 45
    snakes 53, 96, 155-6, 174
    tiger 48
    wolves 45, 105-6
    worms 46, 53, 155
anorexia nervosa 41, 284
anxiety 29, 40, 46, 51, 64, 67, 69,
    72, 94, 106, 112, 116-18, 120,
    128, 130, 135, 136, 146-99, 215,
    224, 254, 256, 260-1, 265, 289,
    292
approval 35, 106, 128, 208, 215
archetypes 23, 105, 162
assertiveness 20, 22, 34, 48-9, 101,
    122, 126, 128, 130, 137, 144, 157,
    165, 176, 214, 219, 221, 295
astral projection 24, 241-5
authority 27, 29, 33, 48, 111, 188,
    267
autonomy 32, 41, 106, 133, 155,
    212, 262, 290, 296
axe 31, 163, 217

baby/babies 12, 24, 34, 37, 38, 57,
    63-70, 72-4, 86, 104, 110, 111,
    116, 119, 127, 141, 146, 169-70,
    202, 232, 250, 269

birth 56, 58, 64-6, 68-70, 72, 74, 86, 120, 127, 183, 232, 264

blood 14, 35, 50, 52, 66, 68, 73, 76, 148, 157, 165, 200, 217, 225, 229, 231-2, 236, 259, 279

boat 115, 173

books 40, 41, 131

brothers 33, 36-7, 57, 92, 112, 114, 153, 156, 210, 216-7, 220, 224, 257, 270

bus 157-8, 167-8, 192, 254, 264, 273

career 76, 96, 212, 251

carers 32, 59, 122, 145, 161, 220, 240, 263

cars 18, 98, 116, 124-5, 147, 152, 159, 187-90, 205, 226-7, 265-8, 278

caverns 28, 153

cellar 124-5, 255

chased See *pursuit*

childhood 11-12, 19, 20, 25-49, 81, 89, 91, 94, 128, 153, 155, 165, 175-6, 191, 197, 204, 208, 212, 215, 238, 254, 257, 270, 279, 280

child/children 15, 19, 20, 25-49, 54, 57-9, 64, 68, 72, 76, 89, 100, 109-11, 115-6, 118-24, 127, 130, 168-9, 181, 202-3, 222, 289, 296

church 34, 218, 224, 232

clothes 52, 67, 81, 100, 109, 119, 131, 146, 191-3, 218, 265

coffin 35, 76-7, 233

colours 52, 56, 63, 66, 98, 105, 108, 138, 177, 224, 228, 232-3, 240, 261, 277, 287, 292-3, 297

communication 30, 48, 77, 111-13, 117, 131, 142, 178, 194, 214, 223-4, 234-5, 237, 251, 268, 297

computer theory 21, 111, 142

conception 57, 64-5, 127

conflict 33, 93, 96, 102, 106, 109, 134, 158, 159, 165, 182, 210-11, 216, 218, 266, 269, 278, 284

conformity 47, 106, 108

contraception 54

control 15, 31-2, 41-2, 49, 71, 80, 93, 111, 134, 136, 154-5, 157, 159, 168, 175, 178, 186-7, 219, 245, 256, 258, 269, 274, 285-6, 290, 294

counselling 13, 16, 17, 115, 130, 134, 166, 264

creativity 24, 44, 50, 111, 138, 260

crying 14, 31, 39, 95, 111, 121, 126, 156-7, 160, 162, 164, 175, 190, 261

danger 19-20, 43, 66, 74, 125, 137, 152-3, 161, 174, 178, 208

daughters 15, 18, 30-1, 34, 59, 63, 67, 75, 90, 98, 108, 116, 120-2, 151, 165, 188, 211, 232

death 11, 15, 29, 30, 38-9, 58, 64, 72, 75-7, 102, 109-14, 151-2, 157-8, 160, 164-5, 177, 202, 209, 212, 214, 216-7, 220, 224, 226, 231, 233, 246, 269, 284, 299

demon/devils 105, 146, 163, 220, 225

dependency 18, 29, 36, 41, 48, 72, 110, 124, 137, 158, 167, 171, 188, 208, 221, 265

depression 14, 42, 51, 58, 67, 112, 118, 153, 177, 185, 191, 209, 233, 256, 258, 261-4, 275

despair 28, 67, 98, 108, 131, 176, 177, 190, 202, 216, 225, 251, 289

directions 18, 29, 95, 96, 106, 161, 167

disaster 88, 207, 237-9

divorce 115, 119, 149, 174, 186

doctors 45-6, 51, 66, 73, 78, 112-13, 225, 258
dolls 67, 104, 111, 254
doors 36, 66, 83, 88, 93, 105, 110, 116, 122, 135, 147, 156, 159, 160, 174-5, 178-9, 183, 225, 239, 272
dream
   analysis 13, 52
   association 21-2
   diagnosis by; 17, 22
   diary 21, 56, 105
   dictionary 22, 160, 253-4
   drawing 21, 126, 201, 255
   erotic 54-5, 80, 92, 94, 97-9, 274
   famous people 85, 102-3, 140, 162
   groups 141, 256, 258-9, 278
   humorous 116, 119, 140
   incubation 23, 279
   interpretation 17, 20, 22-3, 88, 252
   lucid 23, 285-6
   patterns 17, 22, 50, 54, 56
   recall 11, 21, 52, 58, 62, 70, 139, 247, 281, 292
   recording of; 16, 22, 50, 57, 61, 138, 167, 223, 247, 259, 265
   recurring 11, 26, 28, 37-8, 41, 45, 52, 87, 89, 95-6, 115, 134-5, 149, 161, 163, 166, 169, 176, 180, 203, 209, 212, 257, 260, 266, 275, 278
   rehearsals 43, 65, 106, 109, 163
   series 23, 153, 196, 219, 255
   setting 58, 67, 147, 157, 174, 176, 218, 266, 271, 276, 292
   sex differences in; 292-4
   warning 22, 24, 60, 75, 101, 166, 224-8, 231, 247, 277, 279

working on; 16, 63, 143, 168, 252
workshops 20, 166, 246
wish-fulfilment 38, 64, 70, 83, 100, 102-3, 173, 241
drowning 30, 149, 212, 231, 238
drugs 218, 265, 282, 295

education 26, 47, 107, 133
eggs 56, 57, 65
empowerment 49, 60, 254, 264, 277, 294-9
empty-nest syndrome 58, 262
escape 41, 43-4, 53, 118, 122, 125, 137, 152, 157-8, 161-4, 182, 189, 227, 262, 288
evil 31, 33, 35, 81, 102, 105, 158, 162, 164, 208, 261, 291
examinations 41, 107, 135, 146, 171-2
eyes 63, 98, 105, 144, 170, 196

failure 88, 101
fairy tales 45-6, 106, 172, 217, 253, 259
falling 41, 44, 52, 71, 119, 121, 126, 146, 149, 160, 181, 182, 190-1, 292
family 11, 15, 26, 28, 33, 42, 69, 90-1, 107-29, 134, 138, 145-6, 156, 170, 194, 202, 213, 217-8, 231, 234, 238, 246, 260, 267-75
fantasy 24, 41, 43, 46, 80, 93-4, 181, 202, 285
father 11-16, 19, 28, 32-5, 42, 76, 89, 90, 108-14, 151, 202, 209, 215, 233, 236, 246
fear 11, 25, 28, 33, 40-1, 44-6, 66-8, 71-2, 77, 84, 89, 94-5, 106, 116, 121, 125, 131-2, 135, 147, 152-3, 156, 161, 163, 171, 194, 204, 221, 237, 243,

256, 260, 286-9
fertility 58, 60, 64
fire 19, 40, 75, 176, 214, 227, 237, 239-40, 244, 261, 269
fish 56-7, 127, 143-4, 250-1
flying 25, 41, 43, 122-3, 241, 243-4, 296
food 139-40, 143-4
forgetfulness 72, 95, 120, 142, 166
freedom 32, 96, 159-60, 164, 183, 242, 267, 297
friends 33, 48, 52, 74, 83, 90, 98-9, 105, 107-29, 135, 154, 161, 196, 235, 240
frustration 121, 123, 130-3, 136-7, 155, 179, 196, 292

games 30, 42, 53, 100, 209, 210, 222
garden 39, 63, 78, 112, 169, 181, 232, 236
gestalt therapy 22-3, 264-5, 276
ghosts 40, 113
glass 56, 63, 236
grandfather 39, 42, 109, 114, 155
grandmother 28, 38, 68, 106, 114, 228, 233, 238, 279
grief 28, 31-2, 39, 44, 98, 111-12, 151, 175, 216, 234, 288
guilt 20, 31, 34, 67, 81-2, 91-4, 96-9, 108, 114-15, 134, 155, 157, 160, 168, 170, 173, 187-8, 209, 262, 270, 294

hair 38, 66, 100
healing 23, 75, 280-1, 284, 291
helplessness 31, 41-2, 63, 106, 112, 130, 201, 216, 272
hormones 54, 58, 72, 261
hospital 14, 66, 69, 72-4, 95, 121, 130, 135, 148, 212-13, 230, 234, 257, 277

hotels 57, 96, 104, 140, 196
house 39, 40, 42, 45, 63, 68-9, 84, 105, 112, 123-5, 128, 146-7, 152, 173-9, 202, 205, 213, 217, 236, 253-5
husbands 18, 68-9, 78, 88-9, 92-4, 98, 112, 115-17, 123-6, 143, 147, 151, 174, 186, 205, 231, 234, 293

identity 30, 45, 161, 168, 221, 282
illness 17, 41, 110, 114, 224, 277-85
incest 32, 59, 89-92, 138, 216
independence 34, 48, 60, 84, 91, 125, 163, 167, 171, 219
insects 157
    butterflies 43
    spiders 156-7
    scarab 56
intercourse 46, 53, 55, 81, 87, 92, 95, 100-1, 103-5, 168
isolation 14, 37, 108-9, 112, 159, 167, 180

jealousy 38, 119, 127, 209
jewellery 56
journeys 56-7, 60, 106, 126, 181, 256, 265, 296

keys 124-5, 150, 178, 189, 213
killing 150, 162, 164-5, 186, 201, 207-10, 217
kissing 35, 80, 83, 87, 98-9, 273
knives 51, 66, 75-6, 163, 202-3, 206, 208, 213

labour in pregnancy 66, 69-71, 77, 79
lateness 88, 173
lesbian 40, 88, 94, 97-9, 103, 271-5
letter 15, 114, 151-2
lifts 134, 146, 180-3
light 78, 84, 110, 122, 124-7, 135,

175, 177, 189, 263, 286

loss 72, 74, 77, 98, 108-9, 112, 118, 146, 166-70, 293

lost 71, 98, 108, 118, 146, 161, 166-70, 254, 287

love 17, 20, 38-9, 62, 83-4, 91, 98, 102, 104, 107-8, 118-9, 128, 138, 189, 212, 219, 268

luggage 126, 296

lunar cycle 50, 59-60

marriage 15, 18, 30, 58, 93, 115-22, 124, 128, 149, 155, 174, 185, 217

martyr role 51, 92

masturbation 98, 101

Meher Baba 69

memories 17, 39, 93, 123, 128, 240, 252, 268, 292

men 16, 34-5, 53, 55, 81-2, 85, 94-5, 101, 107, 117, 122, 129, 169, 174, 189, 192, 203, 209, 215, 217, 251, 269, 292-3

menopause 58-9

menstruation 35, 50-62, 90, 100, 245

mirrors 96, 170

miscarriage 64-5, 73-6, 78

money 270, 295

moon 50, 59-62, 90, 260

mother 12, 15, 18-19, 26, 28, 30, 34-5, 42, 47, 54, 57, 67, 71, 85, 89, 90, 94, 98, 107-15, 120, 122, 124, 129, 158, 161, 164, 168, 203, 209-14, 227, 235, 254, 267-75

murder 29, 41, 147, 163, 207, 237

myths 52-3, 60-1, 80, 102, 163, 217, 272

naked 40, 81, 95, 98, 191-2

neighbours 11, 33-4, 121, 151, 203, 237

newspapers 17, 41, 47, 97, 214, 288

nightmares 14, 28, 49, 66, 97, 135, 155, 164, 177, 208, 210, 226, 133, 249, 260, 263, 276, 279, 283, 285, 291, 296-7

nuclear war 277, 286-92

nurses 59, 67, 70, 82, 113, 115, 131, 135, 169, 212, 278

oppression 179, 243, 245

orgasm 18, 81, 86-9, 92, 100-1

ovulation 50, 54, 55-9

pain 12, 14, 27, 31-2, 46, 50-1, 59, 73, 95-7, 109, 120, 175, 200, 213, 218, 232, 240, 258, 269, 279

panic 98-9, 119, 142, 161, 187, 194, 260, 265, 270, 287-8

paralysis 71, 154-5, 281, 283

passivity 22, 44, 47, 99, 104, 137, 154, 168, 186, 201, 206, 208, 220, 252, 262, 271, 272

paths 43-4, 46, 187, 274

penis 40, 46, 88, 96, 99, 103-4, 155, 273

periods See *menstruation*

permission 45, 51, 81, 123, 186

police 148, 163, 187, 203, 233, 238, 272, 296

power 11, 16, 20, 29, 32, 34, 41, 43, 45, 48, 53, 56, 59-61, 65, 82-3, 87, 102-6, 108-9, 144, 152, 154-5, 158, 163, 170, 179, 186, 190, 203, 210, 216, 219-21, 237, 245, 258, 262-3, 271, 290, 292, 294-8

powerlessness 20, 26-7, 30-1, 34, 41-2, 46-7, 67, 98, 133, 153, 162, 179, 186, 205, 218, 221, 228, 269, 294-8, 300

precongnition 24, 60, 70, 77, 223-4, 226, 228-34, 248

pregnancy 12, 20, 35, 53, 56-8,

63-79, 127, 146, 194, 245, 279

pre-menstrual tension 50-4, 62

prison 153, 160, 185, 235, 243-4, 267

problem solving 110, 118, 127, 139, 141-4, 241, 252, 254, 292

psyche 43, 53, 57, 58, 74, 162, 174, 192, 200, 276, 289, 291

psychic phemomena (See also *telephathy, warning dreams*, etc) 223-49, 289, 292

pursuit 44, 46, 54, 119, 135, 156, 160-6, 182, 203, 215

Queen 162, 197

questionnaire 17, 20, 149, 248, 301

radio 17, 47, 59, 151

rape 53, 81-2, 95, 97, 147, 164, 214-5, 272

regression 59

rejection 15, 36, 60, 170, 198, 211, 213, 269

REM sleep 21, 24, 51, 261, 275, 280, 282-3

repression 22, 91, 99, 115, 147

rescue 19, 28, 29, 36, 48, 118, 153, 187, 209, 216, 251

responsibility 30-4, 37, 55, 71-2, 87, 135, 153, 165, 169, 186, 243, 260, 288

right-brain 24, 110-11, 129, 142, 160, 182, 286, 296-7, 299

ring 121, 255

rites of passage 58, 67, 171

roads 19, 60, 116, 126, 189, 191, 226-7, 229, 277

rooms 26, 28, 44, 58, 75, 96, 105, 110, 122, 132, 149, 174-5, 179-81, 254-5, 280

running 41, 96, 98, 157, 161, 167, 238

school 13-14, 19, 25, 35-6, 40, 47, 65, 67, 86, 95, 99, 100, 107, 119, 131, 133, 146, 157, 169, 171, 191, 261

schizophrenia 255, 261, 280, 294

screaming 28, 31, 38, 41, 68, 75, 77, 98, 111, 116, 119, 130-1, 135, 164, 202, 218, 234, 237, 261, 286

sea 30, 64, 115, 239

searching 71, 121, 161, 195, 213

secretaries 132-3, 136, 145, 277

self-awareness 16, 22, 60, 89, 206, 256, 259, 291

self-confidence 12, 49, 52, 84-6, 108, 165, 171, 187, 262, 281, 295

Senoi tribe 23, 48, 52, 153, 262, 285

separation 27-9, 39, 43, 71-2, 84, 91, 115, 126, 159, 193, 208, 268

sexuality 12, 34-5, 45-6, 50-2, 54-5, 62, 67, 80-106, 155-6, 162, 214-17, 222, 267-75, 292

  sex differences in dreams; 277, 293-4

shadow 23, 29, 75

shamans 17

siblings 15, 36-7, 127, 156-7, 216

sisters 12, 29, 31, 35, 37-8, 42, 68, 89-90, 110, 113-14, 156-7, 164, 188, 203, 210-11, 223

skin 45, 152, 159, 191

sky 11, 43, 238, 289

sleepwalking 26

sons 31, 57, 65-6, 71, 76-7, 92, 98, 115-17, 121, 261, 284

soul 26, 113, 165, 200, 242

spirituality 20, 23, 60, 77, 96, 181, 244

stabbing 51, 75, 102, 182, 201, 206-7

stairs 29, 31, 43-4, 124, 146, 149, 174, 180-3, 193

strangers 88, 93, 121, 207, 236, 288
stress 41, 51, 67, 69, 77, 131, 135,
    166, 182, 192, 194, 210-11, 261,
    264, 293
subconscious 43, 72, 75, 81, 99,
    111-12, 115, 135, 141, 165, 169,
    224, 234, 252
suicide 14, 28, 202, 216-17, 233,
    267, 287
sun 11, 20, 43, 69, 181, 279
support 68, 91, 117, 125, 128, 137,
    149, 167, 189, 208, 215, 221, 265
swimming 57, 118, 191-2
symbols/symbolism 12, 20, 22-3,
    29, 35, 42, 45, 56-7, 61, 69, 88,
    92, 102-3, 110-11, 115-16, 121,
    124-5, 150, 162, 164-5, 170,
    175-6, 180, 183-4, 187-8, 198,
    228, 252-6, 259-60, 273

taboo 35, 44, 55, 59, 81, 89, 97,
    196, 295
teachers 40, 47, 98, 131, 157, 191,
    286-7
teeth 193-5, 279
telepathy 24, 223-6, 234-7, 248
telephones 78, 178, 235, 273
television 17, 40, 47, 59, 78, 83-4
therapy 17, 20, 108-9, 129, 142,
    170, 201, 217, 250-76
threat 152-3, 158, 161, 163, 169,
    174, 176, 180, 208, 220
toilets 37, 52, 68, 131, 146, 195-8,
    209
toys 119, 124, 254
trains 56, 173, 238, 270
transition 20, 25, 48, 212
trapped 122, 177, 254
trauma 33, 96-7, 150, 164, 182,
    201-2, 216, 290
tree 22, 78, 123, 181, 243, 287
tunnels 57, 190, 237

umbrella 46
unconscious 11, 22-3, 27, 45, 71,
    103, 111, 122, 138-9, 236, 241,
    252, 255, 260, 266, 277, 285,
    290-1
unfinished business 17, 23, 39,
    112-14, 128, 174, 182, 184-5,
    199, 201, 278

vampire 35
victims 34, 41, 153, 162, 179, 204,
    217, 269, 278
violence 50, 53, 89, 95-6, 114,
    146-9, 176, 198, 200-22
virgin 18, 34-5, 85, 260
vulnerability 26, 40-2, 51, 131,
    158, 162, 192, 273

walls 14, 28, 78, 81, 96, 126, 133,
    135, 174-5, 177, 180, 183-6, 196,
    216, 254, 277, 279
war 165, 177, 277, 286-92
water 57, 60, 63, 115-18, 123, 127,
    140, 146, 153, 184, 188-9, 192-3,
    195, 197, 209, 229, 239, 250, 287
windows 46, 66, 105, 121, 123,
    174, 177, 184, 224, 227, 254,
    287-8
witches 17, 60, 158, 245-6
work 34, 42, 61, 65, 90, 98, 112,
    130-46, 155, 168, 183, 286

Index of authors

Bardwick, Judith 47
Bart, Pauline 58, 62
Benedek, Therese 53, 57, 62
Bernes, Eric 210, 222
Beradt, Charlotte 289-90, 299
Bettelheim, Bruno 45, 290
Boss, Medard 64, 79, 162, 280
Caligor, L. & May, R. 251, 275
Castaneda, Carlos 242, 249
Cartwright, Rosalind 266
Cayce, Edgar 233, 249
Cooper, Cary Prof. 137, 293
Corrierre, R. & Werner, K. 252, 275
Dally, Ann 47, 121, 129
De Martino, M. F. 292, 299
Demause, L. 291, 299
Dement, W. 255, 274, 280
Dickson, Anne 221
Domino, G. 293, 299
Dowling, Colette 199, 273
Dunne, J. W. 248
Eichenbaum, L. & Orbach, S. 31, 211, 222
Eisenbud, Jule 36-7, 247, 249
Eliot, T. S. 106
Elliott, Michele 33-4, 49
Evans, C. 21, 142, 252
Ernst, Sheila & Goodison, Lucy 258
Freud, Sigmund 17, 22-3, 46, 53, 88, 103, 155, 246, 252, 283
Friday, Nancy 31

Garfield, Patricia 49, 54
Green, Celia 286
Hall, Calvin 292, 299
Hall, J. 201, 221, 294
Hall, Nor 61, 250, 260, 275
Hartmann, Ernest 51, 62, 303
Havelock Ellis 55, 62
Hearne, K. 285
Hyman, Selma 278, 299
Jenks, Kathleen 251, 263
Jung, Carl 23, 44, 123, 125, 141, 145, 179, 234, 236, 252-3, 255, 291
Karpman, S. 153, 172
Kiley, D. 122, 129
Kimmins, C. W. 40
Kinsey, A. 80, 86-7, 106
Lawrence, Marilyn 49
Mankowitz, Ann 58
Manley, F. 262, 275
Masson, J. M. 155, 172
McConville, Bridget 225, 249
MacEneaney, Polly 49
Morris, R. 291, 299
Nin, Anaïs 138, 145, 255, 260, 295
Oakley, Ann 74
Parlee, M. B. 62
Perls, F. 22-3, 252, 265, 276
Pliny F 55
Robbins, Tom 61-2
Rossi, E. L. 221-2
Sargeant, L. 291, 299
Sarton, May 121, 129

Scarfe, Maggie 199, 282, 299
Serois-Berliss, M. 51, 62
Schatzman, Morton 142, 145, 285
Shuttle, Penelope & Redgrove,
 Peter 51-2, 62
Skynner, R. & Cleese, J. 222
Staff, V. S. 241
Stevens, W. O. 226, 249

Storr, Anthony 202, 221
Ullman, M. 247, 249, 256, 275
Van der Castle, R. 54, 62
Webb, B. Wilse 80, 106
Winget, C. & Kapp, F. 69, 79
Winget, C. & Kramer, M. 292, 299
Zdenek, Marilee 110, 129, 296, 300

Fontana Paperbacks: Non-fiction

Fontana is a leading paperback publisher of non-fiction. Below are some recent titles.

- ☐ FLYING HIGH: THE WOMAN'S WAY TO THE TOP Liane Jones £3.50
- ☐ A DICTIONARY OF TWENTIETH CENTURY QUOTATIONS
  Nigel Rees £4.95
- ☐ ANOTHER BLOODY TOUR Frances Edmonds £2.50
- ☐ WOMEN DREAMING Brenda Mallon £3.95
- ☐ STALIN Alex de Jongh £5.95
- ☐ EATING PARIS Carl Gardner and Julie Sheppard £2.95
- ☐ EUROPE BY TRAIN 1987 Katie Wood and George McDonald £4.50
- ☐ THE HOLOCAUST Martin Gilbert £6.95
- ☐ THE ENEMIES WITHIN: THE STORY OF THE MINERS' STRIKE
  Ian MacGregor and Rodney Tyler £3.95
- ☐ JUST WILLIAMS Kenneth Williams £2.95
- ☐ LEADERSHIP AND THE ONE MINUTE MANAGER
  Kenneth Blanchard, Patricia Zigarmi and Drea Zigarmi £2.50
- ☐ THE SUZUKI METHOD Jack Fryer £2.50
- ☐ HOLIDAY TURKEY Katie Wood and George McDonald £3.95
- ☐ HOLIDAY YUGOSLAVIA Katie Wood and George McDonald £3.95
- ☐ JEALOUSY Nancy Friday £3.95
- ☐ VERY POSY Posy Simmonds £3.95
- ☐ SLIGHTLY FOXED Angela Fox £2.95
- ☐ THE BOOK OF LITERARY LISTS Nicholas Parsons £3.95
- ☐ THE FIRST SIX MONTHS Penelope Leach £4.95

You can buy Fontana paperbacks at your local bookshop or newsagent. Or you can order them from Fontana Paperbacks, Cash Sales Department, Box 29, Douglas, Isle of Man. Please send a cheque, postal or money order (not currency) worth the purchase price plus 22p per book for postage (maximum postage required is £3).

NAME (Block letters) _____

ADDRESS _____

_____

_____